FIGURATIONS

NEXT WAVE

New Directions in Women's Studies

A series edited by Inderpal Grewal,

Caren Kaplan, and Robyn Wiegman

FIGURATIONS

Child, Bodies, Worlds

Claudia Castañeda

Duke University Press Durham and London 2002

© 2002 Duke University Press

All rights reserved

Printed in the United States of America on acid-free paper ∞

Typeset in Quadraat by Keystone Typesetting, Inc.

Library of Congress Cataloging-in-Publication Data

appear on the last printed page of this book.

CONTENTS

ACKNOWLEDGMENTS

This book has taken shape across a series of geographic and institutional locations, all of which have contributed in various ways to its making. I am fond of saying that I found the History of Consciousness Program at the University of California at Santa Cruz in the back of a book in the dead of a New England winter. On the back of this book was a small, closely cropped photograph of a swimming pool, its perfectly turquoise blue water glinting in the California sun. While I still mourn the loss of that outdoor pool, my writing in this book bears the mark of the students and faculty at Santa Cruz, a mark that has been written over and crossed by subsequent encounters. In her capacity as a graduate supervisor, and then as a colleague and friend, Donna Haraway has challenged and supported my work in the most profound way: in her person and in her work, she helped me to find new ways of seeing and living my worlds. Jim Clifford provided important feedback concerning issues of transnational cultural exchange. Among my intellectual peers from this time, I especially thank Laura Hyun-Yi Kang, Targol Mesbah, and Anjie Rosga for the rare combinations of friendship, integrity, and generous intelligence they continue to bring to the practice of academic work.

From Santa Cruz I moved to the Centre for the History of Science, Technology, and Medicine at Manchester University in England. I am grateful to John Pickstone, Penny Harvey, and Tim Ingold for arranging my stay, and to Roger Cooter and Lyn Schumaker for their support of my interdisciplinary work. Roberta Bivins and Helen Valier provided much needed intellectual companionship during this time and after. Rosa Medina is simply a queen, whose irreverent curiosity always gives me hope.

John Law, Vicky Singleton, and Lucy Suchman have been steadily supportive Science Studies colleagues at Lancaster University. Maureen McNeil provided important mentorship during the period of writing as well. The work of my writing group at Lancaster with Anne Cronin and Imogen Tyler has been an important intellectual touchstone for this work. I am also grateful to Imogen for her company and assistance in proofreading and formatting the manuscript. Hilary Graham, Jane Kilby, and Sarah Franklin read portions of the manuscript at critical points in the writing of this book. Anu Koivunen worked alongside me as I revised chapters, cheerfully keeping me to a strict schedule and providing fragrant cups of strong coffee with hot milk, in addition to offering her thorough scholarship and a keenly critical eye. Jackie Stacey gave me many hours of her time over the final stretch, when I felt as if I could think and write no further. I also owe the introduction to Targol Mesbah's exacting guidance at the eleventh hour. Ken Wissoker at Duke University Press saw the book through its acceptance and review for publication, and Leigh Anne Couch has been a most attentive managing editor through the long process of its production. Finally, I wish to thank my various families for their love and support over many years, without which this book (among many other things) would never have been possible.

Earlier versions of chapters 1, 3, 4, and 5 have appeared elsewhere. Chapter 1 was previously published as "Developmentalism and the Child in Nineteenth-Century Science," 2001, *Science and Culture* 10, no. 3 (September 2001), 375–410. Chapter 3 was previously published as "Child Organ Stealing Stories: Risk, Rumour, and Reproductive Technologies," 2000, in *Positioning Risk: Risks, Technologies, Futures*, edited by Barbara Adam and Joost Van Loon (London: Sage Publications), 136–254. Chapter 4 was previously published as "Incorporating the Trans-national Adoptee," 2001, in *Imagining Adoption*, edited by Marianne Novy (Ann Arbor: University of Michigan Press), 277–300. Chapter 5 was previously published as "The Child as a Feminist Figuration: Toward a Politics of Privilege," 2001, *Feminist Theory* 2, no. 1, 29–53.

FIGURATIONS

Introduction
Figurations: Child, Bodies, Worlds

This book begins with an assumption so apparently self-evident that it seems almost impossible to imagine an alternative: that the child is an adult in the making. What is the child but a human in an incomplete form, which must acquire the necessary traits and skills to live as an adult? What else can one hope for a child but that it will grow physically, intellectually, and emotionally in order to function as an adult in the world? What could be more obvious than the fact that the treatment of a child will have a decisive effect on the adult it will become, or that the children of today are the citizens of tomorrow? I argue that embedded within these assumptions is a conceptualization of the child as a potentiality rather than an actuality, a becoming rather than a being: an entity in the making. However else it may be described, and whatever natural or cultural differences might be seen to distinguish one child from another, the category "child" seems to carry with it an unmistakable and incontrovertible fact: a child is by definition not yet that which it alone has the capacity to become. It is in this unique capacity, in this potential, I suggest, that the child's availability—and so too its value as a cultural resource—lies.

In this book, I consider the child's appearances across a range of cultural sites to suggest that it is repeatedly figured as an entity in the making. I argue that this insistent figuration, in turn, plays a unique and constitutive role in the (adult) making of worlds, particularly the worlds of human nature and human culture. In so doing, I also suggest that the study of the child is important not only with respect to children and their experience of the world, but also with regard to the making of worlds more generally.

Barrie Thorne's observation that "both feminist and traditional knowledge remain deeply and unreflectively centered around the experience of adults" (1987: 86) remains a fairly accurate description of the state of social and cultural theory, both feminist and otherwise, today. This is not to say that there is no critical work on children and childhood from feminist and other critical perspectives. Important work has been done on the inequality between children and adults (Jackson 1982; Lorde 1984) and on the consequent misrepresentation and misuse of childhood in both popular and academic knowledges[1] and on alternative theories of childhood (Henriques et al. 1998; James and Prout 1990; James, Jenks, and Prout 1998). These efforts have certainly highlighted the absence of adequate representations and understandings of childhood and children's experience. But rarely has the question of the child translated into wider theoretical debates.[2] Neither have theorists given sustained attention to the value of the child in the making of adult worlds, and so to the way this value often works against the "best interests" of those whom the category purportedly identifies.

The relative absence of attention to childhood at the center of wider issues is important not only because it fails to locate children at the center of social, political, and cultural concerns. It is also significant, I argue, in that its endurance is precisely bound up with the uses of the child's value in and as a particular form. Consequently, it is critically important to understand and respond both to the ways in which the child (as one among a number of categories of [unequal] difference) comes to accrue significant cultural value, as well as the work that it does along the way. Asking how and why the child as a figure has been made a resource for wider cultural projects brings the child into the foreground of analysis regarding its uses and value for adult discourses, and provides the groundwork for imagining an alternative order of things.

This book investigates ways in which the child's potentiality is made and remade in particular sites. While all categories, including that of the adult, can be deconstructed to expose the instability of their contours or borders,[3] what is specific to the category of the child is the identification between the child and mutability itself. It is not simply that "the child" is a sign, category, or representation that can be read in multiple ways. What is distinctive about the child is that it has the capacity for transformation. In fact, such a transformation is a requirement; it is a necessity for the child, so to speak, "by nature." This implies that the child is also never complete in itself. It is precisely this incompleteness and its accompanying instability that makes the child so apparently available: it is not yet fully formed, and so open to re-formation. The child is not only in the making, but is also malleable—and so can be made.

While the category "child" bears on actual children and their experiences of the world, this book is not about that relation, at least not directly. I do not seek to offer an account of how these assumptions affect real children, although I am convinced that they do. Instead, this book is about the endurance of a particular configuration of the child as an entity in the making, and its prolific and multiple uses across disparate cultural sites. If the child's appearance is more than incidental across the strikingly broad range of sites that I consider, from science to the media, the academic world, and word-of-mouth circuits of rumor, what is the significance of this repeated use? If the child appears not only where actual children's lives and experiences are at stake, but also where they are decidedly not, then how can we account for its pervasive presence across such disparate sites? What is it about contemporary configurations of the child that make it available to such a wide range of constituencies and for such divergent uses? With what qualities or characteristics has the child been endowed to make this availability possible?

Figural Bodies

Figuration is my principle tool for describing the child's appearances in discourses as well as across them. In contrast to literary uses of figuration that would define it in terms of signification or representation, my use of this term turns on a relation between the semiotic and the material: figuration entails simultaneously semiotic *and* material practices.[4]

This concept of figuration makes it possible to describe in detail the process by which a concept or entity is given particular form—how it is figured—in ways that speak to the making of worlds. To use figuration as a descriptive tool is to unpack the domains of practice and significance that are built into each figure. A figure, from this point of view, is the simultaneously material and semiotic effect of specific practices. Understood as figures, furthermore, particular categories of existence can also be considered in terms of their uses—what they "body forth" in turn. Figuration is thus understood here to incorporate a double force: constitutive effect and generative circulation.

In this project, figuration provides a way of accounting for the means through which the child is brought into being *as* a figure, as well as the bodies and worlds that this figure generates through a plurality of forms. Using this approach, I suggest that each figuration of the child not only condenses particular material-semiotic practices, but also brings a particular version of the world into being. In conceptualizing figuration as a dual process, furthermore, my account of the category "child" also insists that even apparently generalized figurations are particular. They are the effect of a specific configuration of knowledges, practices, and power, such that providing an account of the child's figuration entails generating accounts of necessarily powerful and yet still contestable worlds.

To understand the child in terms of figuration locates the child in a wide nexus of linked transformative trajectories that point to the uses of its mutability. Among the most significant of these trajectories is the distinctively human and embodied transformation that goes by the name "development." Through its bodily interactions with the world, including its entry into language, the child is seen to develop into an adult. Contemporary notions of child development rest on the dual assumption that the child has the potential for transformative and progressive change, and that its expression takes a particular bodily form. So, for example, the child is seen to change physiologically over the course of its development, becoming increasingly adept at using its body to negotiate the world. Biology (such as hormones or changes in the brain's structure), social relationships (such as the mother-child bond or friendships), and training (including parenting and schooling) may all play a role in establishing and ensuring these changes. Through this process, the child's ever-changing body is slowly transformed into the comparatively stable, physically mature, and culturally inscribed adult form.

The condition of childhood therefore finds its value in potentiality. At the same time, the form that the child's potentiality takes is consistently framed as a normative one, in relation to which failure is always possible. Just as the child's potential for physical growth must be ensured by specific means, so too the child's socialization and enculturation must be secured. The vast range of psychological theories, government policies, and social welfare programs directed at procuring the child's proper development indicate the pervasiveness of this teleological model of the child across biological, social, and cultural domains. Should a given child either fail to possess or to realize its potential (as in the notion of "stunted growth"), he or she remains a flawed child and an incomplete adult.

And yet within this economy of mutability, childhood can also be a highly valued feature of adulthood. For example, the turn back to one's childhood to repair the adult or to reclaim "the child within" (as in many psychotherapeutic techniques) has become a familiar response to adult problems both within psychotherapeutic regimes and in wider popular discourse.[5] Once the adult's temporal distance from childhood has been secured, the adult draws on the past as a resource for the present. The adult returns to childhood to reappropriate the child he or she once was in order to establish a more stable adult self. Here, the child is primarily valuable insofar as the condition of childhood can be revisited in order to be left behind once again.

Local and Global Worlds

A key argument of this book is that the child accrues power and value across its multiple figurations, and that only by addressing this multiplicity can its cultural force be adequately addressed.[6] A principal challenge for this study is to convey a sense of the power generated in and through the child and its uses, without reproducing the problematically universalizing or global claims that are so frequently made through this very category. Invocations of the child, including the overly generalized description I have offered so far, are historically and culturally specific. While it is possible to make such generalizations in order to suggest the overall argument of this project, the book is framed in terms of the specificity of the child's appearances in time and place. It locates purportedly general claims concerning the child in particular discursive, cultural, and geopolitical contexts. While changing definitions of the child in time and place have been well documented in historical, social, and cultural studies of childhood,[7] my simultaneously located and cumulative approach provides an alternative means of describing and accounting for the particular cultural force of the child (and by extension that of many other such categories). As such, this book is perhaps as much about a theoretical-methodological approach to culture (including forms of nature) as it is about appearances of the child in culture.

To describe figuration in terms of its relation to the material-semiotic nature of worlds is also to locate practices and their associated power not only in specific discursive domains, but also in time and place. There are good reasons for insisting on local differences, as well as claiming global ones, but such differences do not necessarily have to work in terms of an either/or relation. The articulation of global locations is important for my investigations of the child because the child is so often figured in universal or global terms ("we are the world, we are the children"). Throughout this book, I account for the ways in which local figurations of the child are also always imbricated in global processes. Rather than relying on formulations of globalization as a strictly late-capitalist phenomenon, I draw on postcolonial criticisms that suggest that the binding of the national within transnational circuits of exchange has occurred across a historical trajectory that began long before the contemporary period of globalization (see Abu-Lughod 1989; Hall 1991). The corresponding alternative global order of things is characterized by nondependent relations or "disjunctures" between economic, cultural, and political realms (Appadurai 1990). Antiuniversalist notions of the global emerging out of these criticisms attend to shifting organizations of time and space, or what I refer to throughout the book as "circuits of exchange" that work not just across or alongside nation-state boundaries, but instead of them.

Not only is it important to describe the distinct global processes that are implicated in colonial and postcolonial histories, but it is also necessary to consider the potentially multiple kinds of transnational processes that can be at work in one location. With these understandings of the global in mind, I employ the more specific term "local-global" to situate in time and space each of the child-figures I discuss in this book. Itself a rather indeterminate locution, the term local-global works well for thinking about the mix of imagined and concrete materialities through which the child is figured as an adult in the making, and how that figure circulates through transnational spaces. In other words, I use the term local-global to identify transnational circuits of exchange with specific trajectories and histories. From this starting point, the discursive locations of the child-figures I have chosen to address are themselves situated in specific local-globals, whether they make apparently universal claims to the child, or whether they concern the child in more circumscribed transnational domains. As such, I do not see the child-figures I consider in this book as representative of the child or childhood. Instead, they comprise an indicative and limited set of figurations in which the child embodies or is identified with local-global concerns.

The local-global also makes visible the continuities that can be identified across different figurations of the child. Just as the local-global provides specific mappings of transnational circuits of exchange, so too the circuits of exchange I consider have their own collective location. One way of describing this location is to suggest that the book turns on two pivot points. The first is the United States, which is a geographic point of intersection for all of the transnational circuits I consider. This positioning of the book around the United States is partly an effect of my own location in the Euro-American academic world. It also speaks to the United States's distinctly hegemonic economic, cultural, and military global reach. However, I have deliberately avoided centering the project in the United States in order to make evident other global figurations of the child. The global reach of the United States is not everywhere and always the most significant aspect of a given event, experience, or—most pertinently for this book—figuration of the child. Consequently, the United States links the different figurations of the child I discuss in the book, but it is positioned relative to other national or transnational locations depending on the specific figuration at issue.

The English language is the book's second main pivot point. Generated through various kinds of transnational networks located primarily between Europe and the Americas, the predominantly English language resources I have used bear the mark of this linguistic mapping. The specificity of this location can be exemplified by the fact that English uses (apparently) gender-neutral nouns, as compared to other (Indo-European) languages, such as Italian (*il bambino, la bambina*), Spanish (*el niño, la niña*), or Hindi (वच्चा, वच्ची).[8] But like the United States, the space mapped by the English language is a variously centered location. The use of English is differentially located across class, race, and gender hierarchies as well as political and economic ones both nationally and transnationally. So, for example, English is not the principal language spoken in some Latino communities in the United States. It remains hegemonic in a bureaucratic and institutional sense, but not with regard to everyday communication in such locations. Furthermore, in some parts of these communities, men may know more English than women, or children may know more English than their adult counterparts owing to their differential involvement (through school or employment) in the wider English-dominant culture. My claims concerning the child are consequently specific and limited in ways that parallel the "centrality" of the United States or the English language in these examples: they are significant precisely insofar as they are located in local-global time-spaces.

My interest in the child, configured as it is through the concept of figuration, emerges in part out of my engagement with feminist, postcolonial, and science and technology studies. In these (already interdisciplinary and sometimes even anti-disciplinary) fields, scholars theorize the relationship between power, materiality, and inequality as a key feature of the world's making. Together, these three areas of study provide indispensable tools for thinking about how hierarchies are constituted, how they are materialized and lived as the real, and how these hierarchies are (or might be) contested. Indeed, this study would not be thinkable without the work of theorists who have articulated the simultaneous power and contingency of the institutions, facts, technologies, and meanings that make up our bodies and worlds.[9] The present study of the child as a material-semiotic entity both draws on theoretical resources from relevant interdisciplinary work, and brings the child into the center of discussions concerning the making of "facts" about human nature and culture. To address the question of the child in this way, I juxtapose scientific figurations of the child against equally distinct figurations in other cultural domains. This selective juxtaposition emphasizes the power of scientific discourses in everyday understandings and uses of the child, while insisting on the cultural specificity of those scientific claims. At the same time, it insists on the importance of claims to the child's nature in cultural domains other than strictly scientific ones. By placing science alongside other cultural discourses that make claims to the truth of the child's nature in a local-global frame, this book further questions the technocentrism and Eurocentrism that continue to obtain in different ways across this interdisciplinary conjuncture.

Each of the five chapters that make up this book takes as its object a particular figuration of the child in a specific local-global circuit of exchange. But as I have already suggested, this is not a project about the child's appearance in five discrete cultural domains. Neither is it an exhaustive account of the child's discursive construction across such domains. The task in each chapter is to describe in some detail the constellation of practices, materialities, and knowledges through which a particular figuration occurs, and in turn, to identify the significance of that figuration for the making of wider cultural claims. The relationship between the project's broad aims and the specific instances of the child's figuration discussed in each chapter is not straightforwardly additive, but has a more cumulative form. In particular, the book tracks the uses of the child-figure in relation to three crucial elements: the child's status as a natural human body; the processual character of that embodiment; and its imaginative potency. In seeking to explore these dimensions of the child's figuration, I have not looked at the cultural sites where the child's significance might be most readily assumed, such as in education, legislation, or pediatric medicine. Instead, my focus on figuration has led me to less predictable sites, where the child's appearance might not be expected, or where its uses exceed its more conventional representations.

The first two chapters address the child's figuration in scientific domains. Chapter 1 examines the figuration of the child in nineteenth-century science and its practices of collection on a global scale, together with the writing and publication of texts based on the resulting data. I consider figurations of the child in English-language scientific texts situated in a local-global circuit of exchange that extends through Britain, northern Europe, the United States, and the colonized world. Watching the child's often apparently marginal appearances in scientific discourse, I ask how figurations of the child are used to establish hierarchies of race, class, gender, and sexuality as "facts" of the natural human body.

Chapter 2 moves from the nineteenth century to the late-twentieth century, in which scientific disciplines are more clearly separated from one another in theory and practice. Whereas figurations of the child in nineteenth-century discourse draw on "global" evidence collected by "gentleman scientists" who traversed the boundaries of biology, anthropology, and other such emergent disciplines, later twentieth-century scientific discourse draws a different map of knowledge making and practice. This is due in part to the division of scientific knowledge into ever more specialized subdisciplines in the later period. In this chapter, I focus on figurations of the child in developmental cognitive neuroscience, centered in the United States, and linked to Britain and a wider English-language transnational scientific culture. In this scientific local-global, key features of the child's figuration are the developing brain and its associated behaviors as these are materialized through the bodies of laboratory animals as well as actual children's bodies. I ask how the child—specifically the child's brain—is used to figure emergent "facts" about the nature of human cognition and its cultural variation.

Moving away from strictly scientific discourses, chapters 3 and 4 consider figurations of the child in other cultural discursive locations. Chapter 3 is concerned with the child's figuration in the domain of transnational adoption. While transnational adoption is practiced in a number of European countries (including the United Kingdom, Sweden, and Germany) as well as the United States, national histories of adoption are critical to the more recent emergence of transnational adoption. Furthermore, while international human rights legislation on transnational adoption exists, national legislation has had much greater jurisdiction over the practice of transnational adoption until very recently, owing in part to the weakness of international human rights law more generally. This chapter considers the United States as a local-global nation into which children are adopted transnationally, primarily from Latin America and Asia. Race—the child's race as compared to that of the adoptive parents—has been a central issue in U.S. intranational adoption, and emerges as well in the context of U.S. transnational adoption. In this chapter, I ask how refigurations of the child as an adoptee negotiate issues of racial identity raised in the context of transnational adoption.

Another aspect of transnational adoption is that competing and often contradictory figurations of the adoptee may exist simultaneously in different locations. Building on this suggestion, chapter 4 considers the circulation of child-organ stealing rumors in Guatemala, and the reporting on these rumors both within Guatemala and in the international English-language press. More specifically, I examine the ways in which U.S. and Guatemalan media reports figure the child in the production of stories about child-organ stealing. A key issue in the chapter is how the figure of the child becomes central within competing claims to the truth or falsehood of the rumor. This, in turn, suggests that some figurations of the child become hegemonic within a particular discursive domain, whereas others do not.

The final chapter of the book brings my discussion of the child into the more explicitly academic field of post-structuralist and feminist theory. The purpose of this chapter is to show how the local-global circuits in which this book travels are implicated in the making of the child. I track figurations of the child in the work of Michel Foucault, François Lyotard, Teresa de Lauretis, Judith Butler, and others. Having identified problematic uses of the child in these oppositional theories of the subject, I go on to discuss how such appropriations might be rethought.

Jacqueline Rose has previously noted the importance of a knowing ignorance with regard to the child because "if we do not know what a child is, then it becomes impossible to invest in their sweet self-evidence" (1992:

xvii). This book constitutes an attempt to enact the responsibility that "we" adults bear in relation to our child counterparts insofar as we have, can, and indeed must make claims about the child. While currently available ways of making these claims fall into and between the natural and the cultural in what seems a relentlessly hierarchical form, I wish to suggest that worlds could be made otherwise, precisely through some form of un-knowing. My hope is that this book works toward that necessarily unat-tainable end.

1
Developmentalism and the Child
in Nineteenth-Century Science

A short article titled "A Biographical Sketch of an Infant" was printed in the British journal of psychology and philosophy *Mind* in 1877. Written by a father-observer about his son Doddy, the piece included the following passage about a visit to the zoo:

> It is well known how intensely older children suffer from vague and undefined fears, as from the dark, or in passing an obscure corner in a large hall, &c. I may give as an instance that I took the child in question, when 2 1/4 years old, to the Zoological Gardens, and he enjoyed looking at all the animals which were like those he knew, such as deer, antelopes &c, and all the birds, even the ostriches, but was much alarmed at the various larger animals in cages. He often said afterwards that he wished to go again, but not to see "beasts in houses," and we could in no manner account for this fear. (Kessen 1965: 122)

The child's fear of "beasts in houses" appears here as an unknown phenomenon in the midst of a familiar—and family—scene. Wishing to account for this fear, the biography's author, Charles Darwin, turns not to the usual time of a biography, the time of a single life span, but to the "ancient" time of the "savage": "May we not suspect that the vague but very real fears of children, which are quite independent of experience, are the inherited effects of real dangers and abject superstitions during ancient savage times?" (122). The savage whose experience the biography's author saw played out in the body of the child belonged not only to the individual child's biography, but also to the past of human life.

This figuration of the child suggests that the matter at stake in the infant biography was not only that of the individual self (Steedman 1995), but also that of humanity as a whole, across time and space. That is, in the infant biography, the child was figured as an instance of the "human" through which the history of humanity could also be told.

In embodying the long-gone savage through the body of the child he observes, Darwin also invokes a specifically colonial ordering of human history that is achieved by what Fabian (1983) has called "temporal distancing." Temporal distancing is a form of ordering applied to the peoples of the globe. It involves placing chronologically contemporary and spatially distant peoples along a temporal trajectory, such that the record of humanity across the globe is progressively ordered in historical time (see also Gamble 1992). It was by this means that the term "savage" signified not only the European in an ancient time, but even more so the so-called savage living in parts of the world considered remote by the scientists making these claims. Both establishing and relying on what amounted to a raciocultural hierarchy, temporal distancing made it possible to narrate human history by moving from one end to the other of the temporal trajectory along which the world's peoples were arranged.

Fabian's concept of temporal distancing provides an important framework for thinking about how the child, figured as a developing body, has been used in the making of global hierarchies and knowledges. Noting that temporal distancing "inform[ed] colonial practices in every aspect from religious indoctrination to labor laws and the granting of political rights," Fabian asks, "what could be clearer evidence of temporal distancing than placing the Now of the primitive in the Then of the Western adult?" (Fabian 1983: 63).[1] But the writing of human history was accomplished through more than simply temporal means. As the infant biography suggests, the Now of the primitive was not only placed in the time of childhood, but also in the child-body: the child was seen as a bodily theater where human history could be observed to unfold in the compressed timespan of individual development.

That the nineteenth-century child was figured in this way has begun to be discussed in literary and cultural studies concerned with colonial orderings of the world.[2] This emerging literature on childhood and colonialism makes clear that the uses of the child as a figure of a colonial "other" were many and varied. Postcolonial literary theorist Jo-Ann Wallace (1994) has traced the child-figure in British colonial and postcolonial literature. She argues that savage/civilized and primitive/civilized dichotomies formulated in philosophical works informed nineteenth-century representations of the child in this literature. Reading Jean-Jacques Rousseau's *Emile* and John Locke's *Some Thoughts Concerning Education* as key philosophical texts, Wallace notes, "It is as 'primitive' . . . that 'the child' represents to the West our racial as well as our individual past: the child is that 'ancient piece of history,' whose presence has left room . . . for the parent-child logic of imperialist expansion" (1995: 175).

Not only has the child-as-primitive represented both the individual and racial past to the West, for Wallace, but the unequal child-parent relation in Western society has also provided a foundation for the colonial/imperialist order. "Indeed," she argues, "it was an idea of 'the child'—of the not yet fully evolved or consequential subject—which made thinkable a colonial apparatus officially dedicated to, in [British colonial educational administrator] Macauley's words, 'the improvement of colonized peoples'" (Wallace 1994: 176). The point here is not that colonizers treated the colonized in the same way as they treated their own children; on the contrary, by equating the colonized with the category "child," colonial administrators enabled and justified the subjugation of peoples as part of a "specifically colonialist imperialism" (176).

To cite just one more example of how the child's importance for nineteenth-century hierarchies of human difference has begun to be taken up in literary studies, Cora Kaplan has suggested that "protofeminist" writing in nineteenth-century Britain "emphasized the female child's likeness to and/or identifications with racial, hybrid, or deformed others en route to presenting her adult [and no longer child] self as the ethical model of national subjectivity" (Kaplan 1996: 181).[3] That is, in laying claim to normative adult status, the middle-class, white woman writer had to insist upon her difference from the normative adult's others. By establishing the (female) child's identity with those others (racial, hybrid, and deformed), and then distancing herself from childhood, she could establish her difference from the full range of others all at once. In order to achieve adulthood, the woman had to leave childhood behind in her own past, but she also had to leave behind childhood and all that it embodied as a "heterogeneous thing": childlike femininity, raciality, hybridity, and deformity.

In this chapter, I argue that the child was also made a heterogeneous thing through its figuration—its embodiment—in nineteenth-century scientific discourses, where the child-body was used to conjure other kinds of bodies in the time and space of a "global" human history. Darwin's infant biography published in *Mind*, for example, described the child's fear as an effect "quite independent of experience" (Kessen 1965: 123). When the child expressed his fear of "beasts in houses," according to the biography, he was expressing a "savage's" fear that was recorded in his body by experiences occurring in humanity's past. So too, femininity, raciality, hybridity, and deformity—among other attributes—were questions of the body as much as they were attributes of character, and these bodily attributes were constituted to an important extent through a colonial "global" scientific enterprise. The "nature" of the child and the human were not only concepts, then, but also forms of embodiment, which were themselves established through a web of world-making material and semiotic practices.

The "Nature" of Childhood

The literary and cultural analyses cited above provide an important starting point for describing the relation between the category of the child and other embodied categories, such as race, gender, and sexuality, that appeared in the scientific literature of the period. Although my principal interest concerns how the child was figured within this literature, it is important to note that the child-figure I will be describing did not belong only to the sciences. Instead, the sciences both drew on and contributed to a wider cultural domain.

Accordingly, nineteenth-century constructions of the child's nature have been widely discussed in the recent historiography of childhood (Rose 1992; Hendrick 1990; James and Prout 1990; Cunningham 1991; Steedman 1990, 1995; Wallace 1995). Harry Hendrick's account of British childhood since 1800, for example, suggests that with the advent of widespread child factory labor during the industrial revolution, an ideal child nature, previously constructed by and for elite British society, was extended by reformers and philanthropists to the working-class factory child (Hendrick 1990: 40–41). The idea of romantic childhood innocence and the evangelical conviction that childhood required adult investments of "time, concern, thought, and money" were woven together to form the ideological basis for campaigns organized to "reclaim the factory child for civilization" (41). Campaigns undertaken by socialist reformers in the name of rescuing the factory child from exploitative working conditions were also based on a similar conviction about the child's nature (42; see also Steedman 1992).

According to Hendrick, these campaigns did not succeed in changing the lot of working children, but they did "establish the distinctive quality of child labour and, thereby, of children . . . and for the rest of the century, reformers, educationalists and social scientists strove to make real the ideal" (Hendrick 1990: 42). The child's ideal nature subsequently became the foundation for a discourse of universal childhood that brought urban and rural, working-class and middle-class children under the disciplinary surveillance of the school and the law. "The school child" and "the juvenile delinquent" became discursive categories through which children became the objects of institutional efforts to restore the child to its "true nature" (46).

While Hendrick brings scientific discourses into the construction of childhood beginning in the 1880s (when movements for the scientific study of children's development began to use the school as a laboratory [Hendrick 1990: 48]), Carolyn Steedman (1995) has suggested that the life sciences became central to nineteenth-century versions of childhood from a much earlier date. Steedman suggests that the child's nature was figured in physiological terms from the eighteenth century through to the early twentieth century. While Steedman links the child's figuration in scientific discourses to the making of the modern self's interiority, rather than attending to what might be called its exteriority, or embodiment, as I wish to do here, her work on the child and its figuration has been important for my investigation of the child as a bodily figure of the human in global time and space.

The secondary literature on nineteenth-century childhood that I have cited so far generally identifies the child as a figure constituted in and for the West, or for European, Western, or modern culture. While this particular version of the child may indeed have been and continue to be significant in many parts of the Western world, I use the term "global" to refer to a more specific location of the scientific discourse in which the child appears. The primary scientific texts that I cite in this chapter were published in English-language journals, primarily by British scientific societies. As such, they are local to two global domains. One is the set of transnational locations in which they were written and published, together with the transnationally located texts they cited as references. This global is local primarily to Europe and the United States. The second is mapped by the wider scientific and imperial enterprise to which the texts I cite also belong.

The scientific texts I consider in this chapter inscribe the story of human development, which was, as cultural historian Ludmilla Jordanova describes it, "the story that the vast majority of nineteenth century scientists aspired to tell, whether in relation to the earth, organisms, the cosmos or civil society" (Jordanova 1986: 211). The child appears in these texts as a developing body through which stories of human development are narrated. But the making and ordering of scientific "facts," as much recent work in the history of science, feminist science studies, and cultural studies of science has so convincingly argued, is both textual and other than textual.[4] Scientific knowledge making involves an "amalgam of places, bodies, voices, skills, practices, technical devices, theories, social strategies and collective work" (Watson-Verran and Turnbull 1995: 117). Scientific practices, furthermore, use and form things—including bodies—as well as words. While this chapter is primarily based on textual renderings of the child-body, I link at least some of the practices relevant to the child's textual figurations by using the notion of science as collection.[5]

Describing nineteenth-century science in terms of collecting practices brings together the two globals mentioned above, while also signaling the existence of nontextual aspects of the scientific enterprise that were implicated in its textual inscriptions. By mid-century, scientific knowledge making in what can also be called the emerging sciences of (human) "life"[6]— biology, embryology, physiology, anthropology, and others—was to be founded on direct observation of evidence. According to this dominant notion of scientific truth making, life's laws and principles could only be arrived at empirically, from an adequate set of "facts." In order to make a scientific claim about "life," furthermore, the full collection of variations existing on the globe for a given life form, or species, should be obtained. Noting the difficulty of acquiring unusual specimens from different parts of the world, for example, one nineteenth-century zoologist listed all of the "uttermost parts of the Earth" to which fellow practitioners had traveled to carry out their research (Lankester 1885: 665). The data they collected would "clear up doubtful points in the scheme of relationships . . . which [the zoologist] has provisionally constructed" by filling in the missing items from an incomplete and merely local record of life (665).

Among the key questions motivating scientific investigations in the nineteenth century was that of "man's place in nature" (Young 1985). Human history, told as a story of development, was narrated in part through the use of temporal distancing. For example, archaeologists investigating human life history, used "the inhabitants of the uttermost ends of the earth to flesh out the Palaeolithic discoveries of stones and bones" (Gamble 1992: 710).

The use of the colonial world as a "global laboratory" for completing the record of human life history has been described by Gyan Prakash (1992), who details some of the peculiar means by which the stuff of scientific collection was procured in India. The practices he cites run from buying skulls from family members of the deceased, to measuring native visitors in the museum where those same skulls were displayed, to displaying and then photographing persons exhibited as live specimens (158). In many parts of the colonial world, as well as in Europe and the United States, fossils were unearthed, graves were robbed of their skeletal remains, autopsies were carried out on the unfortunate dead, and measurements of every imaginable kind were taken from the living as modern science materialized its "facts" as a global record of life. [7]

Prakash also makes an important distinction with regard to the significance and meanings attached to colonial science that I also wish to maintain—between science as it was practiced and taken up "at home" and science "gone native" (1992: 158). This is less a geographic than an analytic distinction, which attempts to foreground a difference between how science was practiced and used by different constituencies. Nineteenth-century science at home had a global reach; it was local to a wide-ranging colonial enterprise, and so to a globe mapped by colonization. As scientists claimed knowledge of "global" life, furthermore, collection on a global scale became a scientific practice that both relied on and extended the territorial expansion of the colonial project. My own claims about the child's significance in this transnational scientific exchange are nevertheless limited to the specific domain of the elite British scientific societies that published English-language journals. In establishing this limit, I am not assuming that the child I describe had no significance elsewhere, but rather that it may have had quite a different mode of usage and kind of significance in other domains.

In other words, this is a partial story. The significance I am claiming with regard to the child's figuration is located in a specific local-global exchange of scientific knowledge, occurring primarily between Britain, France, Germany, and the United States. While the sciences have been described in terms of their specifically national character, scientific knowledges were also produced through a transnational exchange of information. The memberships of the English societies that published the majority of texts cited in this chapter extended beyond national borders to French, German, and U.S. practitioners in various scientific fields, especially biological and anthropological sciences. With regard to publishing in particular, scientific journals like *Mind* or *The Lancet* regularly published articles in translation from the French or the German, as well as texts written by U.S. authors. In addition, individual articles were often multilingual, since citations from French or German scientists appeared in the original language alongside British or U.S. sources. Many of the authors who published in British scientific journals also wrote versions of their work for more popular scientific magazines, which carried their concerns to a wider reading public, and thereby also expanded the scope of the transnational exchange.

Just as scientific facts were collected and arranged to establish a record of human life history, so too scientific texts recorded the history of life by collecting information from other texts, as well as from the data itself, and narrating it all as a story of development. Information about the child was among the definitive kinds of facts collected; and among the claims made in the texts that recorded that information as scientific knowledge were claims to the ancient time of the savage recorded in the body of the child—a practice Darwin's observations almost casually enact.

The Child: Host of Difference

Remarking on the vision of the savage seen in the child during his visit to the zoo, Darwin wrote: "It is quite comfortable with what we know of the transmission of formerly well-developed characters, that they should appear at an early period of life, and afterwards disappear" (Kessen 1965: 122). This explanation describes human inheritance through time in developmental terms. The characteristics "formerly well-developed" in the adult have been inherited into the present, according to this description, in the form of characteristics that appear earlier in the individual's development and then fade away. That is, they appear in the developing child, but disappear in the adult "we."

Steedman has noted that many scientists translated physiological understandings of the body into popular texts for bourgeois parents in the mid-nineteenth century. Many middle-class parents, especially mothers, kept diaries of their children's development in order to understand human nature better, as the scientists whose child-care manuals they read urged them to do. Darwin's biography can also be read as this kind of parental diary turned back into "science." Contrary to an account of science that would place Darwin and his work at the origin of a nineteenth-century

European scientific revolution (and contrary to a reading of all Darwin's texts in terms of Darwinian theory), his infant biography can be placed among other "baby biographies" of the time, written by father-scientists who used observations of their children to make claims about human nature (Kessen 1965).

Furthermore, while it may seem self-evident that Darwin would write an infant biography with this implicitly evolutionary framework, it is not the Darwinian version of evolution as it is known today that is at work in the biography. The version of evolution that made Darwin's description "comfortable" was not the version of evolution by natural selection that goes by his name, because by the time Darwin was writing the infant biography, he had abandoned that theory in its original form. Darwinian evolution separated evolution from development (Haines 1991). A developmental system of evolution lays out a specific and more predictable trajectory of change over time, while Darwinian evolution, or evolution by natural selection, is "creative" precisely because its trajectory cannot be predicted. Species variation in Darwinian evolution occurs randomly, and only then is it "selected" according to its successful adaptation to a given environment (410).

Those narratives of human life history in "deep" time relied on a non-Darwinian version of evolution (Bowler 1988) for which development, or the "idea of potential growth" (Steedman 1995: 82), was crucial. In developmental evolution, a physiologically generated idea of potential growth was transposed from the individual to humanity as a whole. Once humanity was endowed with the potential for growth, it could also be organized along the developmental trajectory that growth itself performed. This approach could also be put to other uses. As Steedman puts it, "Entire peoples and races might then be seen as part of the childhood of the human race, in need of guidance and protection certainly, but with the potential (however distant in prospect) for achieving the adult state" (82–83). Temporal distancing, in other words, was organized in terms of a specific organic process, with its own progressive form of temporality: development. In turn, development secured an ordering of the world that served organizational, political, and indeed imperial ends, precisely because it became the form of the real. It was the form in which nature was realized.

As many historians of science have suggested, the developmental version of evolution was presented in its most voraciously encompassing form in Herbert Spencer's philosophy of science. Spencer's voluminous writings employed a version of evolution that used individual development as the basis for human evolution, and narrated both as a progressive story (Oppenheimer 1967: 210–12; Haller 1971; Jacob 1974; Hayles 1992; Gould 1977). Alongside others, Valerie Haines (1991) has argued that the mechanism of evolution in Spencer's version was the (neo-Lamarckian) inheritance of acquired characteristics, which Darwin, too, accepted in his later writings. It was arguably more a Spencerian version of evolution than a Darwinian one that prevailed among nineteenth-century scientists in the mid- and late-nineteenth century, and among a wider public.[8] And so it is to Spencer's writings on evolution, rather than Darwin's, that I turn to locate the infant biography and its figuration of the child in a wider scientific discourse.

Among Spencer's voluminous writings were four articles on education originally published in British journals between 1854 and 1859, and republished as a single volume titled *Education: Intellectual, Moral, and Physical* by a U.S. publisher in 1860. Spencer's text was of the first, pedagogical variety. It offered recommendations to the parent, steeped in a biological history of human development. Spencer's narration of human history through the body of the child bears a strong resemblance to Darwin's infant biography in its reference to child observation in the nursery, and to a developmental human history visible in the child. The recording of human history in the developing child-body itself, however, stands out much more clearly in Spencer's text:

> During early years, every civilized man passes through that phase of character exhibited by the barbarous race from which he is descended. As the child's features—flat nose, forward-opening nostrils, large lips, wide-apart eyes, absent frontal sinus, &c.—resemble those of the savage, so, too do his instincts. . . . The popular idea that children are "innocent" while it may be true so far as it refers to evil *knowledge*, is totally false in so far as it refers to evil *impulses*, as half an hour's observation in the nursery will prove to anyone. (Spencer 1963 [1860]: 205–6)

Numerous vectors of difference coincide in this passage, intersecting in a version of development that passes simultaneously from the "savage" of a "barbarous race" to the "civilized man," from instinct to (non-innocent) knowledge, and from (male) childhood to adulthood. Not simply metaphorical, this developmental intersection made itself evident, for Spencer, in the child's instincts, and was materialized even more strikingly in the child's physiognomy—in the shape of the nose, nostrils, lips, eyes, and head.

Spencerian evolutionism's key characteristic, as I have already suggested, was its equation of evolution with morphological progressive development. Embryonic development in particular served as a template for all other kinds of change over time in Spencer's work. For example, in a popular synthesis of his work titled *Illustrations of Universal Progress*, published in 1889, Spencer united embryological development with organic progress in a synecdochic chain that would eventually lead to observations concerning social aspects of human life. Having cited the German embryologists Wolff, Goethe, and Von Baer, Spencer stressed the truth they had established with regard to organisms' individual development:

> In its primary stage, every germ consists of a substance that is uniform throughout, both in texture and chemical composition. The first step is the appearance of a difference between two parts of this substance. Or, as the phenomenon is called in physiological language, a differentiation. Each of these differentiated divisions presently begins itself to exhibit some contrast of parts; and by and by those secondary differentiations become as definite as the original one. This process is continuously repeated—is simultaneously going on in all parts of the growing embryo; and by endless such differentiations there is finally produced that complex combination of tissues and organs constituting the adult animal or plant. (Spencer 1889: 3)

On the basis of this developmental pattern of differentiation, which progressed from the organism in a "primary stage" to its adult state, Spencer proclaimed: "This is the history of all organisms whatever. It is settled beyond dispute that organic progress consists in a change from the homogeneous to the heterogeneous" (Spencer 1889: 3). Spencer subsequently named this pattern of organic development a "law of progress," and applied it to every domain of human life, from biology to psychology, sociology, and ethics (Haley 1978). As a theory of progressive differentiation, biological development became a model for realizing human social, moral, and cultural development as well.

A process of development entailing the appearance and subsequent disappearance of a chain of pre-adult bodies remains implicit in Spencer's description of organic progressive history. The Spencerian formula linking organic and social development became a critically important tool for constructing racial hierarchies, primarily in the United States and Britain

(Haller 1971). In charting how progressive development linked otherwise disparate kinds of change together, nineteenth-century theories of infantile development were often linked to theories of race (Haller 1971: 121–52). The pre-adult bodies that appeared in Spencer's texts were the child-bodies from which ancient fears "afterwards disappear," in Darwin's words; and they are the bodily forms that the "civilized man," in Spencer's term, passed through in his early years, and later left behind.

The way I have described the child's appearance in Darwin's and Spencer's texts up to this point conforms to Steedman's observation that the individual life history of the organism was transposed to the collective in evolutionary theory, and that this relation was figured through the child's figuration as a growing entity. With regard to science, in particular, Steedman has also suggested that physiology was critical to the figuration of the child in terms of growth, or development, and then evolution. The "physiological" body (a term I also used above to name Spencer's description of the child) was based on the notion that function could explain structure, rather than the reverse. Predominant by the 1850s, it was this approach to the body, Steedman notes, that made development a critically important site of scientific investigation (1995: 61, see also Haller 1971). Physiology, in other words, set the body in motion. The physiological body, in turn, became a self-evident basis for a wide range of other claims. No longer explainable in terms of its static, anatomical structure, the body's bones, muscles, tissues, and organs were now understood in terms of their function. And this function became an organizational form that gave shape to understandings of human social arrangements.

Development, accordingly, became newly visible and important as a definitively functional process. Because the question of development, together with "disintegration," was embodied in the child, so too the question of childhood came to be posed in terms of physiology: "By embodying the problem of growth and disintegration in children, children became the problem they represented" (Steedman 1995: 76). For Steedman, the key issue in the posing of children as the problem of growth and its counterpart, disintegration, was "the question of interiority" (76). But the problem posed in Darwin's and Spencer's descriptions of the child, which are physiological precisely in that they embody the problem of human development in the child-body, is not only a question of interiority—of instincts and fears buried in the body by nature over the course of its history, and made visible by the scientific eye. The question of childhood is also posed in their descriptions, I would argue, as a question of normal development. Though the term "normal" itself is not used in their explanations, Spencer and Darwin were describing a child going through normal developmental changes rather than pathological ones, in the familiar space of the nursery or the zoo. That is, they explained what the child-body exhibited to the scientific observer as part of the normal course of individual as well as historical human development. Steedman also describes how interiority, or "personification" was enacted partly through notions of normal and pathological development. From this point of view, the fragility of growth (the possibility that it might be pathological) and the inevitability of death (which made even normal development fragile in the end) gave the self a kind of pathos that was "personified" in the developing child (72–76). The child's figuration as a body undergoing the process of normal-to-pathological development indicates the child's value, within a prevailing nineteenth-century physiological understanding of the body, as a local-global heterogeneous thing.

Developing the Child in Physiology:
The Normal and the Pathological

If there is a historian of "the normal and the pathological" in science, it is Georges Canguilhem, who has defined these terms primarily in relation to the history of physiological concepts and practices. Canguilhem (1991) describes a historical series of transformations by which the normal and the pathological, previously distinguished in qualitative terms, came to be distinguished in quantitative terms instead. Moving from English scientists (Francis Bacon and Thomas Sydenham) in the seventeenth century, to Italian (Giovanni Batista Morgagni), German (Albrecht von Haller), and English (William Harvey) anatomists in the eighteenth century, Canguilhem traces the emergence of the quantitative distinction between the normal and the pathological in concert with the emergence of a specific kind of physiological inquiry:

> Wasn't it said repeatedly after Bacon's time that one governs nature only by obeying it? To govern disease means to become acquainted with its relations with the normal state, which the living man—loving life—wants to regain. Hence, the theoretical need, delayed by an absence of technology, to establish a scientific pathology by linking it to physiology. . . . According to [Thomas] Sydenham [(1624–1689)], there is an order among diseases. . . . Philippe Pinel justified all

these attempts at classification of disease (nosology) by perfecting the genre in his *Nosographie philosophique* (1797). . . . Meanwhile, Giovanni Batista Morgagni's (1682–1771) creation of a system of pathological anatomy made it possible to link the lesions of certain organs to groups of stable symptoms, such that nosographical classification found a substratum in anatomical analysis. But just as the followers of William Harvey and Albrecht von Haller "breathed life" into anatomy by turning it into physiology, so pathology became a natural extension of physiology. (Canguilhem 1991: 324)

Calling this history an "evolutionary process," Canguilhem describes the resulting theory of the normal and the pathological as one "according to which the pathological phenomena found in living organisms are nothing more than quantitative variations, greater or less according to corresponding physiological phenomena. Semantically, the pathological is designated as departing from the normal not so much by *a-* or *dis-* as by *hyper-* or *hypo-*" (Canguilhem 1991: 324). Canguilhem also describes this relation in terms of the normal's priority over the pathological, such that "every conception of pathology must be based on prior knowledge of the corresponding normal state" (329). At the same time, the two are mutually dependent with regard to the scientific establishment of the normal: "Conversely the scientific study of pathological cases becomes an indispensable phase in the overall search for the laws of the normal state" (329). Putting these two descriptions together, the quantitative relation between the normal and the pathological can be described as a continuum, rather than a radical disjuncture.

As a way of describing animal and human life, the normal and the pathological, related in quantitative terms, is not devoid, however, of qualitative valuation. The issue of value is discussed by Canguilhem through the concept of "normativity": "The normal is that which is normative under given conditions" (1991: 370). Normativity, then, is evaluative in the sense that it establishes the "normal" as necessarily contingent on a particular set of conditions. When Canguilhem applies the concept of normativity to knowledge, furthermore (and here I would include biological knowledge), he renders knowledge itself contingent on the conditions of its production. Writing about philosophical normativity, for example, Canguilhem argues that it is always contingent on "the values and institutions of a particular civilization," where "every institution is the codification of a value" (380).

When Steedman suggests that the problem of childhood posed by physiology was answered by evolutionary theory, she turns to the issue, briefly discussed above, of how the individual biography, written as a story of individual development, was used to tell a much wider-ranging story. Steedman's description of how working-class children were incorporated into childhood by way of developmental evolution suggests that a category of normal childhood was at stake. Describing the process by which working-class children were granted a new status as children by way of evolutionary theory, Steedman writes:

> If savages represented the childhood of the human race, or were themselves children, then they were necessarily capable of development and change, for these were the essential potentialities of childhood. By a complicated doubling back of an analogy, the dirty, wild children of the very poor could be assigned to "childhood" by virtue of their savagery. Evolutionary theory used in this way implied loss and disintegration, but it also proffered powerful images of progress and ascent. (1995: 82–3)

This extraordinary passage perfectly describes the paradoxical flexibility inherent in the apparently rigid concept of development. Savages were made developmentally equivalent to children, who were made developmentally equivalent to savages figured as children. Although Steedman describes this flexibility in terms of a series of analogies, I would argue that standards of normal and normative development were also being established in this process.

The relation between the normal developing child and the savage to which it is compared is that the normal child will grow up, if all goes well, to become an adult in its own lifetime, while the savage must wait for aeons to achieve a so-called civilized state, and so effectively remains in a state of development. Because normal development is not guaranteed by the developmental process itself, the outcome of any given developmental process is always in question. Whether or not the "dirty, wild children" newly assigned to the state of childhood would be granted the same potential for normal development assumed for the bourgeois child in the nursery was not given by their status as developing bodies. If urban street children were extended the possibility of normal development, there was always the possibility that they might also be consigned to a state of lost opportunity, of development gone awry. Normal development, ultimately, could only be ascertained once the process had been completed successfully: in the normal adult.

In nineteenth-century physiology, then, development was constituted as a biological normativity. So too, it instituted a system of value organized in terms of the normal and the pathological. Development, understood as a physiologically defined process, assumed that all bodies developed, but they might develop according to either "normal norms" or "pathological norms" (Canguilhem 1991: 379). This model consequently embodied value in the child according to these two norms as well.

That the possibility of both normal and pathological development was actually taken up in this way becomes evident in Spencer's (1876) mission statement for a proposed psychology section of the London Anthropological Institute. Titled "The Comparative Psychology of Man," the mission statement was published in *The Popular Science Monthly* the year before Darwin's biography appeared in *Mind* (1877). Spencer's comparative psychology used the body to entwine evolution and psychology. The resulting physiological psychology involved the study of psychological (or "mental") development in terms of the functional brain and body. The key object of this study, and so too a central figure in the colonial ordering of the world through physiological psychology, was the child. In proposing a methodical study of human mental evolution, Spencer therefore extended the range required of knowledge from the child in the nursery to a colonial assortment of children.

In keeping with psychology's direct association between mental and physical characteristics (Young 1973), Spencer wrote that knowledge of human mental evolution (read development) should be ascertained by examining the "bodily mass and structure," along with the "cerebral mass and structure," and the amount and "complexity" of "mental manifestation" (Spencer 1889: 17). A systematic study of human evolution would also entail examining differences in body mass and structure between the sexes by race, and between the "special mental traits distinguishing different types of men" (259). Race and sex were explicitly identified as bodily traits that would both indicate and correlate with differences in mental evolution. In addition to Haller's observation (mentioned above) that Spencerian evolution linked race to infantile development, this identification suggests that the two were linked to theories of sex and gender as well.

With regard to Spencer's figuration of the normally developing child, physiological psychology is particularly important in that it proposed variable rates of development, which in turn generated pathological, but still developmental, forms of growth. The theory of infantile development

Spencer used, in fact, relied on variable rates of mental development to create embodied racial hierarchies. Rather than arranging racialized groups simply along a developmental and historical trajectory, he pluralized development into the normal and the pathological, and redistributed racialized groups according to this new measure of intellectual attainment. Not only did the resulting hierarchy of child-bodies figure differential processes of child development, but it also figured the racialized and sexualized differences among adult humans that were the necessary outcome of that process. Child-bodies, once again, figured the nature of human differences as a single hierarchy of simultaneously racialized, sexualized, and gendered differences.

The Child Developing "Globally"

While normal development can be figured by a single body that changes over time, a hierarchy of development based on normal and pathological trajectories requires more than one figure. In Spencer's comparative (evolutionary) psychology, the normal child was figured along with a plurality of child-bodies developing at differential rates elsewhere. Variations of normal versus variously pathological development were figured through this "global" group of child-bodies.

His account began with a figuration of the normal child's "juvenile mind" as a starting point of comparison: "How races differ in respect of the more or less involved structures of their minds will best be understood, on recalling that unlikeness between the juvenile mind and the adult mind among ourselves which so well typifies the unlikeness between the minds of savage and civilized" (Spencer 1889: 259). As in Darwin's baby biography, Spencer's ordering of the races according to mental complexity worked by moving from the familiarity of "our" child, to the otherness of the "savage," based on what could be directly observed, what could be seen and recorded. "In the child," Spencer wrote, "we see absorption in special facts. Generalities even of a low order are scarcely recognized; and there is no recognition of high generalities. We see interest in individuals, in personal adventures, in domestic affairs; but no interest in political or social matters. We see vanity about clothes and small achievements; but little sense of justice: witness the forcible appropriation of one another's toys" (259). While the absence of normal adult traits such as justice was a feature of the normally developing child-figure that would be corrected in time, such absences were a more permanent feature of the pathologically developing child-figure.

Like Darwin's biography, Spencer's observations about the child in the domestic space opened out onto a colonial world of human differences. These differences ranged from simple to complex mental capacities, which were seen as the differential outcome of normal and pathological development across humanity. Just as normal children exhibited "simpler mental powers," so too the "lower races" had not "reached that complication of mind which results from the addition of complexity evolved out of those simpler ones" (Spencer 1889: 259). Spencer was interested in establishing a relation between the more evolutionarily advanced "mental complexities" and "mental mass," and further to relate this potential correlation to the relative complexity of the social state (259). In his comparison of the normally developing child with differences among (adult) human races, Spencer used the normally developing and familiar child-body "at home" to figure the "universal and natural" human in hierarchical terms.

At the same time, differential rates of development pluralized the child into a number of pathologically developing bodies in Spencer's text. The difference on which Spencer based his comparison of mental evolution according to race and sex was not only a question of mental complexity, but also, as my previous discussion suggests, of complexity as a function of developmental progress. In a section headed "Rate of Mental Development," Spencer wrote:

> In conformity with biological law, that the higher the organisms the longer they take to evolve, members of the inferior human races may be expected to complete their mental evolution sooner than members of the superior races; and we do have evidence that they do this. Travelers from all regions comment, now on the great precocity of children among savage and semi-civilized peoples, and now on the early arrest of their mental progress. (Spencer 1889: 259)

This passage demonstrates the power of development to constitute hierarchical differences through a normal-pathological continuum. Where mental capacity "developed" from a homogeneous to a heterogeneous form, furthermore, the text traveled from the familiar child observed as the embodiment of normal human development in the nursery to groups of children observed as embodying forms of pathological human development across the colonial globe.

The measure by which these "other" children could be compared to the normative child was not just developmental attainment, but also variable rates of development. Even mental acumen could be devalued by this means, as Spencer's description so explicitly shows: precocity implied accelerated development (growing too fast), and accelerated development ended in premature mental arrest (stopping too soon). Using child-bodies figured in terms of variable developmental rates, Spencerian psychology insistently realized and preserved racialized and sexualized hierarchies of mental development. The multiple child-figures whose unequal mental capacity Spencer "saw" and recorded became the bodily ground of a racialized and sexualized ordering of humans across the globe according to a hierarchy of mental differences, and vice versa.

Unified Developments: Race, Gender, and Sexuality

The means by which sex, race, and intelligence were realized through the figure of the differentially developing and globally located child were not limited to textual practices but also relied on physiological knowledge based in material and semiotic practices that involved bodies themselves more directly. John S. Haller's (1971) account of racial science suggests some of the practices that were involved in materializing physiological bodies with different rates of development, and brings my discussion from Europe to the United States. As I have already suggested, Haller has been unusual for remarking on the importance of physiology and the infant body in the establishment of racialized developmental hierarchies. In his account of U.S. racial science from 1859 to 1900, aptly titled *Outcasts from Evolution*, Haller describes an explosion of anthropometric examinations carried out by physicians on black soldiers during the U.S. Civil War, and then on the newly emancipated black population in the post–Civil War period. According to Haller, this massive collection of data was organized according to a functional and developmental model of the body that drew on physiological understandings and practices imported from Europe.

Physiology, here, included physiological psychology. The data-gathering Haller cites was used to measure mental development as a function of the developing brain. Physiology borrowed a dynamic brain from phrenology, the practice of reading information about an individual from the skull's bony covering. But it also set the skull in motion as a function of the developing brain. Mental development, recorded in terms of the skull's changes, became a new means of materializing the inequalities once assured by phrenology (see also Young 1973).

Haller's account of anthropometry in the U.S. post–Civil War era, which turned from measuring brain size and weight to describing a brain differentiated by cerebral functions and development, relates how mental development was newly ascertained for this physiologically defined brain by incorporating prior methods of evaluation. For medicine and anthropology in particular, brain development, as an index of brain function, was a key means of materializing mental difference: a less-developed brain showed that an individual had failed to reach full intellectual capacity. On the one hand, the configuration of the brain—the relative size of the various lobes, and the degree of definition and complication of the brain's convolutions—indexed brain development. On the other hand, the changing structures of the brain over time indexed increasing function, so that physiognomic characteristics (such as the irrepressible facial angle, for example, and some of those mentioned by Spencer) now measured not brain size, but degree of mental development (Haller 1971: 34–35). Citing U.S., German, and British scientists, Haller describes how a transnational range of scientific knowledges was consolidated in a specific U.S. context, pointing also to wider sociopolitical dimensions of those shifts:

> While Negro and Caucasian children were equal in their infant capacities, no sooner did they reach puberty than the Negro, like the orangutan, became incapable of further progress. With the projection of the jaws and the closure of the cranial sutures, both the Negro and the orang came to the end of their intellectual development. With this as a backdrop, the intermediate Indian, Mongol, and Malay furnished similar arrested or "mummified intelligence." Though European anthropologists provided the foundation for this concept, Americans like John Fiske and Edward Drinker Cope willingly contributed to its greater elaboration. Their interest in cranial suture development, drawn in part from the English studies of Robert Dunn, Frederick W. Farrar and the writings of Herbert Spencer and Filippo Manetta, came at the auspicious hour of America's disillusionment with Reconstruction and the popular appeal for disfranchisement. (Haller 1971: 38)

In this account, Haller describes a shift from using brain size and weight as measures of intelligence to using a more finely differentiated and developing brain for this purpose during the post–Civil War period. With this shift, he further suggests, new and more precise criteria were applied to available measures of intellectual prowess, thereby reinforcing existing racial hierarchies (Haller 1971: 36). When the arrest of mental developmental capacity was attributed to the rate of early development in infant studies as well as in studies of adult brains and physiognomy, time and timing were injected into the racialized body. The races could be compared and arranged against a normative developmental sequence in which the standard of value was the degree of differentiation or complexity, condensed, now, into the individual life span and the physiological body changing through time.

Haller's reading of the European (British and German) literature on which later U.S. versions were based pulls apart a series of quotations cited in the English ethnologist Robert Dunn's "Civilisation and Cerebral Development: Some Observations on the Influence of Civilisation upon the Development of the Brain in the Different Races of Man" (1864) to arrive at the following description:

> More important [for Dunn than the studies of adult, physiologically differentiated brains he cited], however, was the work of anthropologists who, in studying the infant stages of Caucasian, Negro, and anthropoid, saw signs of physiological retrogression. In the infant stage the facial features of all races, including the orang-utan, were very similar. . . . The Negro child, for example, was born without prognathism. His facial angle as well as his coloring was closely similar to the Caucasian child. . . . So, too, with the infant orang, whose facial features showed little resemblance to the adult orang.
> (Haller 1971: 35)

Despite having so carefully described the initial similarity of the Negro child, the infant orang, and (implicitly) the white child, it is on the issue of racialized differentiation through developmental arrest—at the moment of adulthood defined in terms of puberty—that Haller focuses his attention. In so doing, Haller reinscribes the simultaneous invocation and erasure of the child that, as will become apparent, is also evident in Dunn's account. Perhaps because he focuses on racialized difference, the similarity assumed between otherwise radically differentiated entities and the normal child does not enter into his analysis. I retrace Haller's steps through the relevant literature in order to reconsider the child-body that appeared there. Though this body was eventually pluralized by pathological development, as in Spencer's account, it embodied an original unity that preceded differentiation. This child-body's unity constituted a bodily origin, in other words, from which a plurality of racially, gendered, and sexualized bodies then emerged.

I have suggested that nineteenth-century writings on human variation are collections of collections that work in part through the sheer quantity, variety, and global reach of the "facts" that they bring together. Here, figuration works in part to localize and naturalize imperial definitions of humanity as a unity that could nevertheless be ordered through a series of stages. There is hardly a better example of this than Dunn's "Civilisation and Cerebral Development." In this work, Dunn combined craniometric data based on the facial angle and the cephalic index, ethnological data regarding the relative civilization and savagery of Europe and its others, and the latest work on cerebral development in physiological psychology, with descriptions of racialized others. He then wrapped these combined elements into an argument for the future mental development of the races. Insisting on the brain as the material foundation of the mind, the "material substratum, through which all psychical phenomena of whatever kind, and among all the races of mankind, are manifested in this life," Dunn's article moved from the skull to the brain's surface and its various parts, writing a developmental trajectory that inscribed hierarchical differences into every part.

The first site of unity and subsequent differentiation was the skull, which in the developing body did not contain the brain so much as it conformed to the brain's changing features over time. The comparison of skulls did not measure mental capacity per se as it once had, but rather mental capacity as a function of cerebral development, which could be even further divided into the relative development of its three lobes. Since the skull was literally "impressed and stamped" with the "distinctive characters" of the races, according to Dunn's account, the story of development could be told from existing collections of skulls.

The result, not surprisingly given the stunning persistence of racial hierarchies, was a developmental trajectory narrated by Dunn, in which the heads of Saxons, Celts, and Scandinavians of the "European nations" were seen to exhibit "a harmonious development of the whole brain, and a special fulness in the intellectual and moral regions." In contrast, the flatter and shorter foreheads of less well and harmoniously developed brains made for a protruding jaw as the different parts of the skull developed unevenly. A range of racial others, including the "Carib," the "Negro of the Delta of Africa," and the "Australian savage" as well as "the Irish of

Leitrim, Sligo, and Mayo," were seen to exhibit the features of lesser and inharmonious cerebral development (Dunn 1864: 18).

The second and more important site of development in this narrative was the brain itself. Turning to the evidence from physiological psychology, Dunn began again with an initial unity, this time a unity of resemblance. Rather than being a mere mass of tissue, the brain described by Dunn was now differentiated into seemingly self-evident parts. The observer's first impression of different brains, wrote Dunn, was such that "we see the same lobes, the same convolutions, and the three main divisions of the brain, into anterior, middle, and posterior lobes . . . as distinctly and well defined in the one [brain] as in the other" (Dunn 1864: 19). A closer inspection, however, based on the logic of development, would reveal important differences. What the eye could see must not be interpreted according to the visible structural differences, but rather to their function—that is, in physiological terms.

The resulting functional brain consisted of the three previously mentioned lobes now subordinated to their purpose. The anterior lobes were the site of the intellectual faculties, while the middle lobes were for the "personal affections or attributes" as well as the moral and religious "intuitions." The posterior lobes were the site of the "social and affectional activities and propensities," which for Dunn extended to every level of social relationship. He further described the posterior lobes as the site of "those endearing attributes which are the charm of our existence here, binding together in the bonds of affection, the ties of family, of friendship, of country, and of race" (Dunn 1864: 19). There was nothing pertaining to the human races, it seems, for which Dunn could not find a place in the contours of the brain.

This was perhaps especially true for the developmental brain. Through the French anatomist Gratiolet, Dunn further subdivided the brain into three planes of development that brought the human races into the realm of the animal world by way of the mass of zoological data from which these conclusions had partly been drawn. The three planes were the inferior basilar and superciliary, the middle median frontal, and the highest coronal or superior frontal.

The third plane, in contrast to the first two, distinguished man from the animals to which he was compared, and the rest of the article quoted liberally from quite a range of scientists to divide the races according to finer and finer differences. Using the unity of the brain as the original basis of comparison, Dunn differentiated the races—from one another, and in relation to the orangutan and ape—according to a developmental body and its criteria of evaluation. The size and complexity of structure in the convolutions, the shapes of the lobes, the symmetry of the brain and its parts, and microscopic differences in the structure of the gray matter all became evidence for his developmental differentiation of the races. Running literally underneath the resulting developmental trajectory in a series of footnotes that threatened to overwhelm the main text was the body of the developing child in whom all of the differences in brain size, shape, and structure that Dunn associated with race also variously appeared.

Dunn's description of the child-body began with an elaborately obsessive recitation of the German physiologist Carl Vogt's offerings regarding various parts of the brain, and their development in relation to intelligence. This recitation included a list of brains in descending order (medical doctor, woman of twenty-nine, laborer, and idiot), measured according to the length of the frontal lobe. The description continued with Vogt's citation of Dr. Pruner-Bey, the physician to the viceroy of Egypt, and his equally detailed comparison between the white (German) and Negro brains. While Pruner-Bey's comparisons evoked a decided difference between the brains of the two groups, the succession of comparisons he offered also reversed this distancing, until the Negro brain appeared "by the side of the white child":

> In the brain of the Negro the central gyri are like those of a foetus of seven months, the second are still less marked. By its rounded apex and less developed posterior lobe, the Negro brain resembles that of our children, and by the protuberance of the parietal lobes, that of our females. The shape of the brain, the volume of the vermis and of the pineal gland, assign to the Negro brain a place by the side of that of the white child. (Dunn 1864: 22)

This passage recapitulated the overall trajectory of Dunn's argument, from initial material unity to racial differentiation. It first identified a difference or distance between the white (adult male) and "the Negro." This was reconstituted as a proximity or identity, as the (male) Negro brain became the fetal brain, then the female, until its very contours assigned it to a place next to the white child. Whereas the white (male) child was a normally developing body, "the Negro's" path through a series of brain-types traced the normal developmental trajectory in a pathological form.

In the next paragraph, Vogt quoted Huscke as he concluded that "in the Negro brain both the cerebrum and the cerebellum, as well as the spinal cord, present the female and the infantile European, as well as the simious [sic] type" (1864: 23). As the sites of cerebral differentiation proliferated, four kinds of entities—animal as well as human—were collected into a single "Negro" cerebral/bodily form. But with the appearance of the "Negro" child, this chaos of bodies was subsequently ordered along a developmental trajectory—again in a quote from Pruner-Bey:

> The Negro child . . . is born without prognathism, but with a totality of features, which, though characteristic for the soft parts, are not yet expressed on the skull. The Negro, the Hottentot, the Australian, the New Caledonians, do not, with regard to the osseous system, exhibit the differences which arise subsequently. The young Negro possesses a pleasant physiognomy up to puberty, which commences in girls between the tenth and thirteenth, and in boys between the thirteenth and fifteenth year. (Dunn 1864: 25)

Variable rates of development, in this description, differentiated race and gender at once; the mature body marked by the onset of puberty was a gendered body as well.

According to one account cited by Haller, the developing body also exhibited a Malthusian struggle for existence within itself between intellectual and sexual development. In keeping with a more general hypersexualization of blackness that continues today,[9] this struggle, in the "Negro" child, was won by the sexual (defined in terms of passion as well as reproductive purpose), as the intellect succumbed to its own developmental limit:

> Growing to maturity much faster than white children, Negroes exhibited sexual passion at an earlier age and then, because of mental atrophy, remained through life seemingly enslaved to the sexual impulse. "The conflict for existence between brain growth and reproductive organ growth at puberty," wrote Dr. Eugene S. Talbot, resulted for both full black and mulatto "in the triumph of the reproductive." (Haller 1971: 52)

This confluence of attributes applied to the Negro body in Talbot's single sentence—the racial, the sexual, and the reproductive all linked to inferior mental development—is characteristic of a racial discourse in the later-nineteenth century obsessed with the possible improvement or, more frequently, the degradation and "degeneration" of the races through miscegenation.[10]

The heterosexually reproductive body, as one possible developmental achievement among others, marked the end of the child-body. The child-body, beginning from an original unity and then changing in the process of development, was gradually differentiated through various kinds of development, proceeding at differential rates. The body of the child was imagined as an original unity that gave rise to human difference itself through the play of normal and pathological development. It was at the point of reproductive capacity (puberty) that racial differentiation by this process would unfold according to differential rates of development. Dunn, still quoting Pruner-Bey, offered the following account of this process:

[Puberty] is followed by a rapid transformation in the forms and proportions of the bony skeleton. The transformation proceeds in the cranium and the face; the jaws predominate without an adequate compensation in the cranium. Whilst in the white man the gradual increase of the jaws and the facial bones is not only equalled, but exceeded, by the development, or rather enlargement of the brain, and especially of the anterior lobes; the reverse is the case in the Negro. (Dunn 1864: 25)

Not only were the races constituted through different overall rates of development in Dunn's account; they were also constituted through different kinds of development, which also proceeded at different rates. Always rhetorically posited as the normative form of development, the white body and brain developed, here, in concert with one another, while the Negro brain and body fell out of step. As Dunn continued through Pruner-Bey, the developing Negro body became a body closing down on itself: "The central front suture closes in the Negro in early youth, as well as the parietal part prematurely of the coronal suture. With advancing age the central portion of the coronal suture, the sagittal suture, and all of the parietal sutures close, nearly simultaneously. The hambdoidal remains open the longest, especially at the apex. Generally speaking the suture in the Negress closes sooner than in the Negro" (Dunn 1864: 25). If gender was racialized at the moment of puberty, the racialized body was also gendered: the body closed down sooner, according to this description, in black females. The language is telling here: never referred to as boys or girls, black people were granted youth and age, but not adult subjectivity.

The term child, signifying the normally developing child, applied only retroactively as a differentiating category, since there was no initial difference between the Negro and white child. Quoting Vogt, now, Dunn proclaimed:

> It is undeniable . . . that the sudden metamorphosis, which at the time of puberty takes place in the Negro, is intimately connected with psychical development. The Negro child is not, as regards the intellectual capacities, behind the white child. All observers agree that they are as droll in their games, as docile, and as intelligent as white children, where their education is attended to, and where they are not, as in the American Slave States, intentionally brought up like cattle, it is found that the Negro children in the schools, not only equal but even surpass the white children in docility and apprehension. (Dunn 1864: 25)

Despite this seeming sympathy with the plight of the slave, Vogt went on to say, along with Pruner-Bey and others, that this initial equality was only temporary: "No sooner do they reach the fatal period of puberty than, with the closure of the sutures and the projection of the jaws, the same process takes place as in the ape. The intellectual functions remain stationary, and the individual, as well as the race is incapable of further progress" (Dunn 1864: 25). Both at the individual and group level, according to this account, racial, gendered, and sexual difference were materialized together at the moment of puberty in relation to the arrest of mental development, placing the black person, once granted the status of child, outside of humanity itself as its development turned out to follow a different, pathological norm.

Finally, the female child (and the elderly white person) took the place of the male child in its identity with the Negro child, once that black child had grown up: "The grown-up Negro partakes, as regards his intellectual faculties, of the nature of the female child, and the senile white" (Dunn 1864: 25). All but the white male child, then, were betrayed by the promise of normal development made by the initially unified child-body.

It was against this finality, this arrest, that Dunn wrote. Without questioning the biological data on which Vogt and Pruner-Bey based their conclusions, Dunn argued that the application of a different law of development to the "Negro" as opposed to the white man, was wrong. The brain fashions the shape of the skull, he argued, and if treated properly, the black person's brain would develop accordingly, and with it the skull. His grand gesture of noblesse oblige nevertheless continued to promote white man's "civilization" as the measure of all things to which other races might aspire, with faint hope of attaining equality: "By progressive civilization, the cranial capacity of a race may, in the course of centuries, become gradually increased" (Dunn 1864: 33).

Dunn concluded by revisiting U.S. reports of Indian (Native American) schools that refused Negro children education on the basis of their supposedly limited capacity, and the "minor" cases among "us" of those unable to comprehend topics "possessing a certain order of abstruseness." He completed his "Psychological Differences of the Races of Man" with the following claim to truth: "In all these cases . . . the true interpretation is, that cognative [sic] faculties have not reached a complexity of the relations to be perceived" (Dunn 1864: 23–24). For Dunn, this truth applied to intellectual, moral, and emotional capacities. Just as the brain could be divided into different lobes and sulci with specific functions, so too mental capacity should be divided into those three different functions. Accordingly, Dunn divided the races by varying strengths in the areas of intellect, morality, and emotional capacity.

Dunn's writing in this section more than any other epitomizes the scientific text-as-collection in its breadth of references, and exhibits the irrepressible return of discarded concepts of race. In his concluding, twisted defense of emancipation for U.S. slaves, he recited the entire litany of arguments from development, beginning with the German embryologist Ernst Haeckel's theory of recapitulation, otherwise known as "ontogeny recapitulates phylogeny" (i.e., an individual organism's embryonic development recapitulates the species' development through the ages [see Gould 1977]). Arguing against the immutability of mental capacity on the grounds that further development was possible, he suggested that all of the "failures" of the "lower" races with regard to mental capacity were

in strict accordance with, and what, a priori, might be expected to result from, organic differences in the instruments of higher psychical activities; in other words, in the nervous apparatus of the perceptive and intellectual consciousness. . . . It is maintained, indeed, that "the human brain in its development passes through the characters in which it appears in the Negro, Malay, American, and Mongolian nations, and finally becomes Caucasian, partaking of these alterations. And that the leading characters, in short, of the various races of mankind are simply representatives of particular stages in the development of the highest Caucasian type. (Dunn 1864: 24)

In a fashion that should now be numbingly familiar, Dunn inserted the resulting racial hierarchy into the normally developing body of the Caucasian child in the form of pathological—that is, arrested—development. This time, though, Dunn pushed even further back, to the normal child in its embryonic form: "The Negro exhibits permanently the imperfect brain, projecting lower jaw, and slender bent limbs of a Caucasian child some considerable time before the period of its birth. The aboriginal American represents the same child nearer birth. The Mongolian is an arrested infant newly born" (Dunn 1864: 24).

Dunn translated this infantile trajectory into the superior docility of the African over the "Red Indian," and a defense of emancipation for the African at the expense of both. He presented this argument in the words of the Scottish phrenologist George Combe: " 'The native American is free, because he is too dangerous and too worthless a being to be valuable as a slave; the Negro is in bondage, because his native dispositions are essentially amiable.' The infantile trajectory, and the docility it embedded in the Negro body, allayed the 'generally entertained' fears of the freed slaves' wrath, imagined as 'a war of extermination or of supremacy over whites' " (Dunn 1864: 25). According to this developmental economy, emancipation became imaginable in the present, but equality belonged to a safely distant future. Still quoting Combe, Dunn continued: "In both [the Negro and the Indian] the brain is inferior in size, particularly in the moral and intellectual regions, to that of the Anglo-Saxon race, and hence the foundation of natural superiority of the latter over both. And my conviction is . . . that the very qualities that render the Negro in slavery a safe companion to the white, will make him harmless when free" (25). Dunn's own, final words betrayed the self-induced terror of white supremacy: "I have only to add, we shall see; the ordeal—the test—is at hand" (25).

Normative development, as this brief course through a number of nineteenth-century texts has tried to show, was a powerful technology in nineteenth-century science, terrible in its use of the child to embody its myriad forms of inequality, its global hierarchies. Always already made available for use, the child was not a subject category in the science of development, but a fleshy origin for hierarchies emerging in naturalized progression that realized the spatiotemporal order of a colonial "global" world. This outcome was accomplished not only through language, but also through scientifically authorized figuration of that ordering in and through the body of the child.

The British magazine *Punch* published a cartoon in 1855 of a gentleman pedantically instructing a young boy. Held by the hand, the boy's taut bodily posture and open-mouthed expression suggest some mixture of fear and horror. Three huge prehistoric reptiles surround the pair. Only a tiny church steeple in the distance suggests the suburban location of their swampy surroundings. The caption reads: "A VISIT TO THE ANTIDELU-VIAN REPTILES AT SYDENHAM—MASTER TOM STRONGLY OBJECTS TO HAVING HIS MIND IMPROVED" (see Fig. 1). One of many "scenes from deep time" in the suburban arts and science park of Sydenham, England, this cartoon caricatured the specifically middle-class efforts to educate young minds (Rudwick 1992: 149). Perhaps it also registered a complaint against pedagogical excess ("having his mind improved"), or even a more broadly felt resistance to the encroachments of emerging, "modern" forms of subjection. Could it be that Darwin's son Doddy was registering a similar kind of objection in his fear of "beasts in houses," which Darwin himself could only see as a recidivist apprehension?

Tempting as it may be to rescue Doddy from his father's appropriative explanations, the aim of this chapter has been to show that the child-figure of nineteenth-century science appeared as an instrumental, and indeed vital, bodily container for human variation across the globe and through historical time. Progressive development, figured through this child, constituted and ordered a plethora of human differences in hierarchical series, including child-ness itself. The "normal" child, then, was a figure through which the ordering of children across the colonial globe was realized as well. From the "savage" urban poor child, to the child at the "uttermost ends of the earth," to the bourgeois child in the nursery—all were brought under the scientific gaze, where their bodies materialized a continuum of normal and pathological development that simultaneously told a story of human history—and of human mind, desire, and moral justice.

As I have also suggested, the "normal" child was not assured of being normal until the developing body had traversed childhood and become the normative adult. To be a true adult was to have passed out of development—out of the realm of the pathological (savage, female, racialized, hyper- and hypo-sexual, etc.)—and into the realm of the "normal": to be a "civilized" man in present time. The female, the racialized, the insane, the disabled, and the poor were left behind, in childhood, while

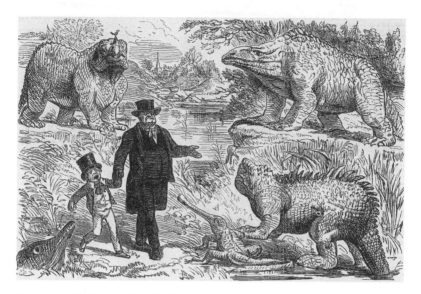

Figure 1: A child's educational visit to the zoo. Cartoon by John Leech for Punch (1855). Reprinted in Rudwick 1992, 149.

adulthood was strictly enforced as a "natural" developmental achievement reserved for the deserving few.

Contemporary scholars, especially sociologists, psychologists, and historians, have commented on the extent to which development continues to establish a normative, universal trajectory for "the human," lodged primarily in the child-body. British sociologists Alison James and Alan Prout have suggested that while some attempts had been made to locate particular social constructions of the child in time and space, a universal "child" continues to predominate in the social sciences. Linking nineteenth-century versions of the child to those of the twentieth century, they suggest that the twentieth century "can be characterized as [the century of the child] precisely because of the massive corpus of knowledge built up by psychologists and other social scientists through the systematic study of children. If the concept of childhood as a distinct stage in the human life cycle crystallized in nineteenth-century western thought, then the twentieth century has seen that theoretical space elaborated and filled with detailed empirical findings" (James and Prout 1990: 9).

Valerie Walkerdine's (1984) cogent critique of this legacy remains an important one for more recent analyses of developmentalism. Writing about uses of psychology in then-current debates about liberal education,

Walkerdine argued that psychological assumptions about the child used by liberals and conservatives alike were problematic because "the very lynch-pin of developmental psychology, the 'developing child' is an object prem-ised on the location of certain capacities within 'the child' and thereby within the domain of psychology" (1984: 154). As a result, Walkerdine continued, inner capacities have been separated from a "social domain which influence[s] or affect[s] the pattern of development and, conse-quently, the conditions of educability" (154). That is, the child's inner capacities have been constituted as the "natural" domain of psychological research, and they also provide a "natural" ground on which social in-stitutions, such as education, work to ensure—and enforce—normative development.

Along with other writers, Walkerdine and James and Prout (1990) have lodged two main criticisms of developmentalism (see also Gergen 1993; Stainton Rogers and Stainton Rogers 1992; Morss 1990). First, "the devel-oping child" is a historically and culturally specific construction, which is therefore not the only way that children might be understood. James and Prout argue further that "time in childhood—children's daily life experiences—" has been "made secondary to the time of childhood, when children are seen as dependent upon and protected by the adult world" (1990: 219). The child has been theorized in terms of a past from which the child will soon develop into the adult; in terms of the projected time of future adulthood; or in a timeless mythical state of innocence, ignorance, and purity (221–30). By displacing children from the present, James and Prout suggest, the temporal constructions that have been applied to chil-dren in theory and practice have tended to thwart and obscure children's active participation in the world. In place of these constructions, James and Prout advocate theoretical and empirical practices that "can grasp child-hood as a continually experienced and created social phenomenon which has significance for its present, as well as the past and the future" (231).

The second critique of developmentalism is that as a part of the con-struction of childhood it has contributed to children's subjection in spe-cific times and places. For example, Walkerdine argues that children are subjected to age-graded, developmental norms in educational curricula that are often incompatible with children's actual abilities (see also James and Prout 1990; Stainton Rogers and Stainton Rogers 1992). In this sense, the child's figuration as a developing body extends beyond the use of the child as a figure to children's lives more directly.

Some critics have also begun to consider biology as part of the wider discursive construction of childhood in terms of developmentalism (see Stainton Rogers and Stainton Rogers 1992: 47–51). They suggest that biologically based developmental narratives circulate in psychological, educational, anthropological, sociological, medical, and psychiatric theories and practices as well as those of social work. These are generally premised on a biological substratum of "nature" with which "nurture" interacts in any number of ways. Scientific (especially biological) figurations of the developing child therefore continue to operate in a wide variety of domains, such that this figuration is enduringly powerful in the making of the real. And the particular nineteenth-century version of developmentalism that these figurations embody still holds a purchase on the real within these domains.

While both the developing child and the critique of developmentalism I am considering here emerge mostly from Euro-U.S. local-globals, they are also more widely relevant because of what some theorists have begun to call the "globalization of childhood" (Boyden 1990; Stephens 1995a). Exported by international organizations to many different parts of the so-called "developing world," child developmentalism has collided with quite different assumptions about childhood and children's different life experiences, to the ultimate detriment of children and their communities (Boyden 1990). So too, the very notion of the "developing world" rests on an inherently hierarchical version of the real that in its inception was bound up with figurations of the child. A focus on the child's figuration in nineteenth-century sciences and beyond might provide an important additional resource for contesting developmentalism because it addresses the workings of ontological privilege in its making.

Figuring Figurations

My description of the child in nineteenth-century scientific developmentalism amounts to a claim that the child was figured in such a way that it came to embody human differences in the specific form of race, class, gender, and sexuality. In addition, the child was figured as the embodiment of a potentially normative developmental process against which hierarchies of these differences were established.

The child's figuration was also bound up with the making of ontological claims to these hierarchical differentiations, perhaps even more than it was bound up with claims to the child itself. In this sense, the child-figure was also constitutive of the emerging disciplinary knowledges—biology, anthropology, and psychology—and their versions of the human real. In turn, these disciplinary knowledges constituted normative hierarchies by way of the child-figure whose legacies remain to this day. The child's value in and for these discourses lies in its figuration as a body that can precisely figure forth such a wide range of differences.

My discussion of the child's figuration in nineteenth-century scientific discourses establishes an initial starting point against which the particularity of more contemporary figurations of the child and the worlds they realize become apparent. As I have already suggested, figurations are particular, rather than general, even—especially—when they are used to make general claims about human nature and culture. I have also suggested that figuration entails the production of value, and that the value of the child accrues across its multiple figurations. Ultimately, the significance of the child-figure, and so too the value that it lends to the general category "child," or "human," lies in the details of its material-semiotic figuration. The relationship I want to establish between different figurations, then, is cumulative rather than comparative: the child's value for adult discourses is constituted through its accumulated particularity across multiple figurations. Indeed, contemporary scientific discourses make no less use of the child than their earlier counterparts. But just as the field of cognitive neuroscience that I consider in the next chapter did not exist as such in the nineteenth century, so too its child-figure is particular to the local-global worlds of practice and significance to which cognitive neuroscience belongs. Next to the nineteenth-century's developing child, the child of cognitive neuroscience is figured in newly developmental terms that realize the child and the human in new ways.

2

Flexible Child-Bodies

At the turn of the twenty-first century, the child continues to be figured as a human in the making in key scientific discourses. Within this broad range of scientific domains, investigations concerning human consciousness have gained a particular salience. So prominent have these investigations into consciousness been, that the 1990s were hailed as the "decade of the brain."[1] A variety of disciplines concerned with human consciousness have converged in their approaches to the brain and its function. In addition to studying features of mature human consciousness, developmental subdisciplines in biology, psychology, and neurology—a multidisciplinary convergence I refer to here as the developmental neurobehavioral sciences—have focused on the child as the site of the developing brain. How, then, has the child been refigured in the neurobehavioral sciences? What form does the child's figuration take in this domain? What kind of (human) body, and what kind of value, does the resulting child-figure realize?

My account of the child's figuration in the neurobehavioral sciences is primarily based on a review of the field presented in *Human Behavior and the Developing Brain*, a collection of articles edited by Geraldine Dawson and Kurt W. Fischer (1994). This collection reviews research that has contributed to an emerging understanding of links between human behavior and the brain, or brain activity. I use *Human Behavior*, together with relevant additional sources in the neurobehavioral sciences, as an indicative site from which to consider an emergent, collective refiguration of the child across a range of scientific fields. Comprising work by researchers in numerous U.S. states as well as the Netherlands and Canada, this edited volume is located in a transnational network of scientific exchange whose existence as a field is not (yet) stabilized. Given its emergent status, many of the newer claims proffered within this field remain more tentative than if the field were more fully institutionalized and established.

As the book's title suggests, Human Behavior is not primarily concerned with the child itself, but with the relationship between the developing brain and human (read mature, adult) behavior. However, the child's figuration within the relevant research remains central to the making of knowledge about the brain and behavior. As such, the child also remains central to the making of scientific knowledge claims about the human, once again not simply as an idea, but in and through the child's figuration. That is, the child's figuration works to ground apparently self-evident claims about the nature of the human.

Using figuration as a tool to understand adult uses of the child also suggests that while a child-figure is particular to a specific discourse, that figuration's claim on the real exceeds its more narrowly defined scientific use. Furthermore, the child's figuration in "science" is cultural both in the sense that it contributes to wider cultural domains, and in the sense that scientific knowledge making is never separate from culture. In the times and places of those local-global worlds where technoscience has become significant, watching how science figures the child suggests ways in which these worlds are changing as well. Scientific figurations of the child-figure are important both because they make claims to the child at an ontological level, and because they make wider claims regarding the world—particularly what it is to be human—by way of these claims.

What, then, are the particular material and semiotic resources through which the child is figured in newly developmental terms in the neurobehavioral sciences? How, in other words, do the specific materialities and semiotic processes bound up in the practice of these sciences contribute to the child's figuration as the site of authoritative ontological claims? In addition to addressing the child's figuration in this specific location, and in relation to the particular kind of existence that it realizes, I briefly consider how scientific figurations of the child are taken up elsewhere, in the media. A 1996 Newsweek magazine article titled "Your Child's Brain," which reported on recent findings in the developmental neurobehavioral sciences, provides an indicative example of how media reports translate the child-figure from the laboratories and clinics of scientific practice to the domestic activities of the family home.

Nineteenth-century scientific developmentalism figured the child by way of a linear developmental process, which rendered normal versus pathological developmental trajectories that in turn constituted the human in terms of racial, sexual, gendered, and class hierarchies. In contrast, late-twentieth-century neurobehavioral sciences figure the child through a different set of practices, materialities, and forms. In a historical review of brain development in developmental psychology included in *Human Behavior*, historian-psychologist Sidney J. Segalowitz (1994) suggests that many of the theoretical concepts at work in the neurobehavioral science derive, in part, from the work of Swiss psychologist Jean Piaget. Piaget himself was convinced of a necessary relationship between the brain and behavior, according to Segalowitz's account, though Piaget did not research this question directly. Working from observations of children, Piaget constructed a theory of child intellectual development made up of four stages loosely corresponding to the child's cognitive capacity at different ages (Piaget 1966).

Within the contemporary neurocognitive sciences, it is not Piaget's description of cognition at each stage that remains important, but rather its form. Whereas nineteenth-century-based versions of development are linear and continuous, the twentieth-century form of development with which Piaget has come to be associated is discontinuous and increasingly complex. Each stage in Piaget's system is characterized by a transformative shift in cognitive capacity. Attainment at each stage is necessary for passage to the next, but that attainment is also transformed as the child gains new cognitive capacities in the next stage. In the same way that a flight of steps is discontinuous while enabling ascent, Piaget's stages yield a discontinuous but also cumulative, increasingly complex cognitive system.

Piaget established his stage theory by observing children undertaking set tasks. Children were the material, so to speak, that he used as evidence to figure child cognitive development in a discontinuous form. In the contemporary neurocognitive sciences, evidence for discontinuous development is generated in a number of different ways, including but not limited to the observation of children's behavior. Because the field is principally concerned with the relationship between brain and behavior (including cognition), the evidence for development primarily includes the brain matter and brain activity. This evidence is generated in research practice by way of different technologies, such as histology (examination of brain cells), measurement and plotting of brain activity by various means, and brain imaging. These technologies materialize the stuff of the brain from which knowledge about the child's brain and behavior is made. Brain matter and brain function can also be associated with behavior by various comparative and inferential means that realize this relationship in numerical or logical terms. Observable behavior here includes everything from involuntary reflexes such as blinking to emotion and cognitive capacities such as mathematical reasoning.

The neurobehavioral sciences figure the child in terms of brain matter and function as these are linked to behavior, but the actual stuff at issue is not always the human child and its brain or brain function. Because development is understood as a property of a wider range of organisms, the human developing body shares key characteristics with other species. Consequently, human development can be studied through the stuff of other, nonhuman bodies. Indeed, the neurobehavioral sciences make claims about the human brain and behavior on the basis of research on both animal and human bodies.

This interchangeability of human and animal bodies does not, however, erase the child's figuration in the making of human behavior in the neurobehavioral sciences. Instead, the stuff of animal bodies provides the material evidence for claims about the nature of human behavior. And these claims are made in part through claims to the child, where evidence from animal studies is translated into knowledge about human development. This translation is especially germane with regard to the child's figuration because of ethical and practical restrictions on research using children's bodies. Animal bodies are used for research that cannot be done on children. The translation from animal bodies to the child means that the materiality of the developing brain claimed through the child's figuration is actually the stuff of kittens, monkeys, and rats. The child's figuration, in other words, has to be effected partly through the materiality of other species.

Indeed, the child can at times seem entirely immaterial to the concerns of neurobehavioral science. In addition to its materialization through other bodies, the child often appears indirectly, in the form of the more generic notion of "human development." The child-figure in neurobehavioral developmentalism therefore often embodies human development implicitly, and in this sense does not necessarily exist as a body in and for itself. And yet, both in cases where the child-figure seems to be absent, and where the child's figuration is more obviously central, claims to human development in the neurobehavioral sciences presuppose the existence of a developing child-body from which the adult human is made.

New Disciplines

According to Dawson and Fischer, their book "ushers in a new era of developmental theory and research," made possible in part by new opportunities for interdisciplinary work (Dawson and Fischer 1994: xiii). The editors go on to suggest that interdisciplinary work is linked to a "growing recognition that the complexities of human nature can be understood best by examining interfaces among systems at several levels, including the neurophysiological, behavioral, and social-contextual levels" (xiii). For them, *Human Behavior* represents a new synthesis of biological and psychological approaches to the developing brain, through which this brain also becomes newly central for understanding human behavior. A review of the field's more general views concerning human behavior and the brain provides a way of apprehending how the child is newly figured in the neurobehavioral sciences, and how this child's figuration contributes to the making of the emerging field and its realizations of human nature.

Novel Knowledges

While the articles in *Human Behavior* diverge in some of their underlying assumptions and approaches, they share a commitment to integrating understandings of the brain with understandings of behavior. As Segalowitz puts it, if brain is the underlying substrate for behavior, then "any mental differences must be reflected in some way by variation in brain structure and activity" (Segalowitz 1994: 132). However, the brain's apparent centrality in this schema does not supercede behavior. Behavior cannot exist without biology, according to this account, nor can it be reduced to biology alone; the two work in a nonredundant relation to one another. According to Segalowitz, researchers who rejected biological determinism because of its conservative political implications explicitly advanced a non-deterministic relation between "nature" (biology) and "nurture" (behavior in the world) in the 1960s. In the process, they theorized the child "at the centre of its own construction," such that experience and environment played as critical a role in child development as did biology (Segalowitz

1994). At the center of the nature versus nurture debate, in which biological determinism sided with nature, was the figure of the child. Theorizing the child in nondeterminist terms became part of the project of rejecting biological determinism.

The new neurobehavioral sciences maintain this figuration of the child, and the nondeterministic version of the human that it figures in turn. Within this framework, Human Behavior focuses on changes in understandings of the relationship between brain and behavior in the history of relevant research. One research team explicitly identifies a shift from understandings of the brain as a computer to understandings of the brain as part of a human organism. Looking back over a twenty-year period, Dutch psychologists Maurits van der Molen and Peter C. M. Molenaar (1994) suggest that understandings of human cognition have been grounded in a notion of information processing that depends on an analogy between mind and computer. As the authors note, the child has been central to this understanding, in the sense that this way of understanding the mind was seen in the child: "The child [has been] viewed as a limited-capacity manipulator of symbols," such that "with age, children become more efficient problem solvers because of the growth in their elementary processes, strategies, metacognition, and knowledge base" (456). In proposing a shift to a more organic understanding of mind, the authors again make claims to the child in order to emphasize the centrality of the brain in cognition: "The child is an intelligent organism . . . not a learning machine, and intelligent organisms are endowed with brains to exercise their cognitive power" (456). In turn, the stuff of the developing brain becomes fundamental to the nature of the child as a figuration of human cognition in process. By figuring the child as an organism rather than a computer, the authors lay claim to the importance of the brain's materiality as a material and functional organ that must be studied in its own right.

The brain, as a functioning part of the human organism involved in behavior and cognition, must also be understood as central to the processes of the child's developing behavior and cognition themselves. That is, cognitive development, as it can be seen and studied in the child, must be studied in terms that are "consistent with brain function" (van der Molen and Molenaar 1994: 456). The stuff of the developing brain is fundamental for understanding cognitive development, and so too the developing brain is a key site of the child's figuration in this field.

As I have already suggested, the general outline of the child-figure that emerges from Human Behavior is constituted in and through a body that includes the brain and interacts with its wider surroundings. The stuff of the developing brain is therefore only one component of the child's figuration. Its significance derives from its relationship with the body and the wider world. And it is the child that comes to figure this relation. How the developing child-brain, the child-body, and the wider world interrelate therefore becomes fundamental for apprehending the specific qualities and value of the neurobehavioral child-figure.

Plastic Brains, Flexible Bodies

What I am attempting to argue here is that the "facts" of neurobehavioral development precede the child's figuration, such that the child-figure takes on these processes and qualities. But at the same time, the child-body is figured as that site in which these processes and qualities can be observed and known. In the following discussion, I suggest that this child is figured as a singularly flexible body. This flexibility is a feature of the discontinuous (steplike) developmental form employed in the neurobehavioral sciences, which precedes the child as a form, but is also lodged in the child through its figuration, as a property that belongs to the child in its very embodiment. In describing this double movement, I refer to the child's figuration when the child is itself being figured in a particular way, and to the child-figure when the child is used as the embodied ground of a particular claim about the developing body and brain.

The term flexible (or flexibility) that I use here condenses a series of spatiotemporal qualities that are attributed to the brain and to wider bodily functions linked to the brain, such as sensation and perception. Three interrelated terms used in the neurobehavioral sciences to figure the child's developmental form come together in this notion of flexibility: plasticity, modularity, and the critical or "sensitive" period. Briefly, plasticity refers to the brain's capacity to change during development. Modularity refers to the way in which specific parts or regions of the brain are dedicated to particular functions, such as vision or speech, and more precisely to the way a particular function can switch from one region of the brain to another during development. The critical period, finally, refers to the discrete time periods during which the developing brain is more plastic, and after which brain connections can no longer be so easily established or altered.

Plasticity and modularity are materialized qualities of the child's developing brain that are contained within the temporal limits of the critical period. It is the critical period, in other words, that establishes the boundary between the child as a uniquely flexible body in contrast to the more inflexible (if not completely stabilized) fully adult body. The child-figure is therefore both spatially flexible (regions of the brain associated with a specific function can shift) and temporally flexible (because the changes are time-limited) in its embodiment.

The child-figure takes on its discontinuous developmental form through the materialization of this flexibility, in the developing brain's cells and their connections. According to the neurobehavioral sciences, the brain is made up of specific cells, called neurons. Neurons are different from other cells in that they are comprised of both a cell body and axons and dendrites. Axons are extensions that make physical connections between one cell and another. In addition to connecting neurons to one another, axons extend themselves over long distances to establish connections between the brain and other parts of the body, such as the eye, ear, and limbs. Neurobehavioral science commonly uses the language of electrical circuitry to describe the system of connections within the brain and to other parts of the body. Axons, for example, are said to be like electrical wiring; they conduct electrical charges through their circuits. Axons make the connection between one point and another, like the cord that connects a television to the wall socket. Synapses are the junction points, or gaps, between axons and cells through which electric impulses are transmitted. As in electrical circuitry, cellular charges travel across synapses. Function, such as vision, physical movement, hearing, and emotion, is materially constituted by the flow of electrical impulses through cellular circuitry composed of axons, dendrites, and synapses (Greenfield 1997).

From this point of view, human consciousness can be materialized almost entirely. Claims about human behavior can be made by seeing how the matter of the brain links up with function (and then behavior), from basic reflexes to complex processes such as memory. To study the developing brain, in particular, is to study the development of human behavior in a fundamentally material form, where consciousness cannot be thought of separately from embodiment and embodiment does not refer to the brain alone. Brain development is itself also very much a bodily matter.

According to the account of development contained in *Human Behavior*, plasticity is a feature of the developing brain in a number of ways. First, synaptic patterns of connection in the brain change through the process of development. This change is discontinuous in the sense that the number of synaptic connections first increases gradually, then accelerates, and then decreases. Huttenlocher, a contributor to the volume, describes this discontinuous trajectory in terms of newly discovered "fine structural changes" occurring from infancy through childhood. This naming indicates the qualitative, as well as simply quantitative change entailed in this process:

> At birth, the volume of the infant's cerebral cortex is only about one-third that of the adult. The subsequent increase in size results largely from the growth of neurons [brain cells] and of their connections. . . . This growth occurs largely during the first year of life. Until recently, it was generally believed that the anatomical development of the human brain is complete or nearly so by age 2 or 3 years. . . . However it is now clear that major fine structural changes continue throughout childhood. (Huttenlocher 1994: 137)

Huttenlocher's comparison between prior and newly emerging versions of brain development suggest that the child is being newly differentiated from the adult by comparing childhood versus adulthood neuronal structure, as opposed to volume. Whereas simple volume establishes no difference between adult and child by age two or three, changes in neuronal structure do establish significant differences between the adult and child brain throughout the period of childhood.

Put another way, from a neuroscientific point of view the child-brain previously became the adult-brain at two or three years; the "nature" of child- and adult-brains was the same, even if the child's intellectual, emotional, and motor "nurture" was not yet complete. In the new framework, the child exists as a discrete entity separate from the adult throughout childhood not simply in terms of behavior (as before), but in terms of the very stuff of the brain.

Huttenlocher further describes this difference in terms of synaptogenesis (the making of synaptic connections) and synapse elimination. The "fine structural changes" in brain development consist in part of both the making and "pruning" of synaptic connections. Reviewing research on synaptogenesis, Huttenlocher notes that early findings included the observation, made from examining cells through increasingly sophisticated microscopes, that synaptogenesis goes through a "chaotic process" in development, whereby connections are made randomly between neurons and other cells. This stage is followed by a process of "withdrawal," such that in the fully developed state, each cell has a specific set of connections that is anything but random. As Huttenlocher notes, this process has been studied in detail for muscle cells (myocytes) as the axons of motoneurons in the spinal column make connections to them.

A key finding in this area of research is that increased use of the relevant muscles during development augments synapse elimination ("withdrawal"), while decreased activity limits it. This finding is consistent with a theory advanced by French neurobiologist J. P. Changeux, Huttenlocher notes, which suggests that early synaptic connections are made randomly, and are excessive to the number needed for mature functioning. Only some of these connections are used, or integrated, in developing neural systems, such that the mature system is characterized by a more selective synaptic pattern than its more random developmental predecessor. The evidence from histology suggests to Huttenlocher that this theory is correct. That is, an excess of synaptic connections is found during early development, followed by a reduction of synapses as the organism matures. A critical part of this selection process is the use of the body (eyes, nose, muscles, etc.). From the cellular point of view, synaptogenesis can be articulated in terms of the establishment or "stabilization" of "functional units." Some synapses are therefore incorporated into some functional units through use, and so become stabilized. Others are not incorporated, and so they are withdrawn. They become inactive and are "resorbed" by the system.

Huttenlocher cites extensive data on animals as evidence for this pattern of developmental synaptogenesis, together with similar evidence for humans from studies of postmortem tissues from adults and children. Using electron microscopy to examine brain tissue, Huttenlocher and his colleagues have established a specific pattern of synaptogenesis from birth to adulthood that supports Changeux's theory. Huttenlocher and his colleagues note that the number of synapses at birth is one-sixth that of the adult. Between two and four months, and up to six months, the number of synapses increases by a factor of ten, such that there are more synapses at this age than in adulthood. This accounting of synaptic connections across the tissues of different human bodies at different ages provides evidence, according to Huttenlocher, for an excess of synaptic connections generated during human development that corresponds to findings in other systems (Huttenlocher cites relevant research on kittens and monkeys showing a similar pattern).

Further evidence is provided by histochemical studies of human brain tissue—studies of chemical processes in cells. Here, chemical "markers" for particular kinds of synapses become the evidence for synaptic activity or absence. So, for example, one group of researchers cited by Huttenlocher measured the amount of glutamate decarboxylase in postmortem brain tissue. The more active the marker, the more synapses there should be. Various studies of such markers have established a similarly discontinuous pattern of synaptic growth for early human infancy, followed by excessive growth, followed by pruning to the "mature" or "adult" pattern (Huttenlocher 1994: 145–46).

The histological research cited by Huttenlocher also establishes a pattern of increased precision in development. This precision is achieved through a discontinuous process, in which the wider body in interaction with the environment (smelling, seeing, grasping, and so on) plays a critical role. In his conclusion, Huttenlocher figures the child in relation to plasticity and this discontinuous process:

> Observations in recent years related to synaptogenesis in humans indicate that the cerebral cortex is a dynamic structure throughout infancy and childhood. . . . During a limited period in childhood . . . the total number of synapses in the cerebral cortex exceeds that in young adulthood. The period during which there is an excess number of synapses appears to coincide with the period during which the brain exhibits increased functional plasticity, raising the question of whether the availability of a large group of synaptic connections that are as yet unspecified as to function may underlie plasticity. (Huttenlocher 1994: 148)

The child—identified here as the human beyond the point of infancy—is figured as a more dynamic body than its adult counterpart. It is a body whose very materiality, both the synapses and the bodily functions (vision, touch, etc.) they underlie, is uniquely generated through the interaction between body and world precisely because this body is so plastic. The developmental process involves "sculpting" synaptic connections into a more precise form that underlies a more precise functional body.

Huttenlocher uses the term "functional plasticity" to refer to the ways in which the selection of synaptic connections occurs not simply through elimination, but also because of the child-body's plasticity, or its ability to respond to changing functional demands, and to the changing use of the brain. Functional demands can be defined as forms of use that are specific to the organism's current bodily state. For example, when a child begins to see, the demands that are made on the brain are particular to the functional capacities of the eye at that time, to the way the child moves its head, and so on. The child looks, and in the process, the brain stabilizes the synaptic connections that are associated with particular ways of seeing. Prior to being able to focus, and so on, the child will have a more diffuse pattern of synaptic connections. It is only through the process of using the eye that these connections can in fact be stabilized. And as these connections stabilize, so too the child's functional capacity for seeing becomes increasingly complex. Synapse elimination, or "pruning" is thus associated with increased functional complexity.

The child that emerges from this research on human development is figured as a body that changes in a discontinuous pattern that results in increased precision and complexity. The plastic developing body becomes the mature, fully adult body with its particular functional capacities, underpinned by the appropriate synaptic connections between brain cells and the extended body. And the child is figured as the bodily ground of mature, adult functioning through its plasticity, insofar as plasticity uniquely constitutes a form of embodiment that can become more precise and complex in just these ways.

In addition to the stuff of the brain itself, the brain's activity is also used to figure this plastic developing child-body. As I have already mentioned, neurobehavioral scientists view the brain as an electrical system. They also, consequently, produce evidence of brain function by measuring electrical activity using devices that detect electrical impulses and translate them into visual forms (graphs) on a screen. Researchers in the field note that these methods are particularly suitable for research on children, for whom other more invasive techniques are prohibited.

Exposing an organism (a child or an animal proxy) to a particular stimulus generates electrical measurements of the desired kind. So, for example, evoked electrical potentials (EPs) are one kind of response to stimulus that has been measured using child subjects. EPs are recorded from gold, silver, or tin electrodes placed on the scalp with a gel or cream that conducts electricity. It is actually the difference between the activation of electrodes at the time of stimulation that is recorded using this technology. So, for example, the difference between an activated electrode and one that receives no input (one that is placed on a part of the body, such as the ear, that

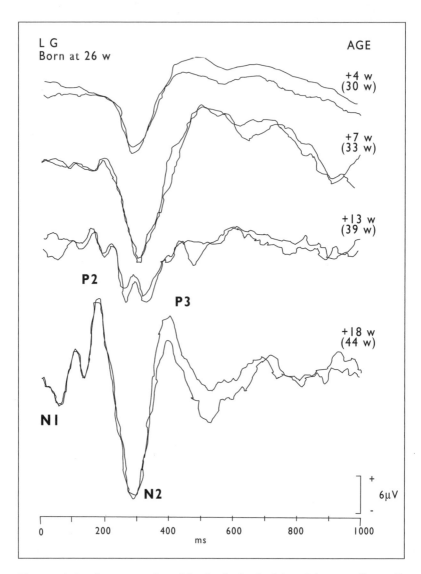

Figure 2: A visual representation of the developing brain's activity—waveforms of evoked electrical potentials (EPS) on a graph.

is known to emit no charge), establishes the activity of the brain at that point. This is called monopolar recording. Bipolar recording, in contrast, registers the difference in activity between two active electrodes.

Psychiatrist David G. Thomas and psychologist C. Donel Crow's article in *Human Behavior*, titled "Evoked Brain Activity in Infancy," reviews research using these kinds of technologies and techniques. Specifically, they

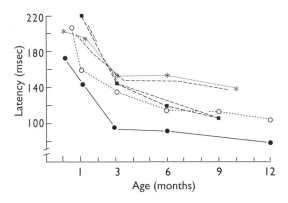

Figure 3: A second translation of EPS, this time depicting brain development through changes in amplitude of waveforms.

report on research measuring auditory and visual evoked potentials (AEPs and VEPs, respectively). These potentials are graphically represented as waveforms (see Fig. 2) or as changes in the amplitude of these waveforms over developmental time (see Fig. 3). Thomas and Crow conclude that despite differences between the studies they review with regard to methods and results, the combined research findings "demonstrate that evoked brain responses in infancy show developmental progressions" (Thomas and Crow 1994: 224). These progressions, once again, show a pattern similar to that suggested by studies of synaptogenesis reviewed by Huttenlocher. That is, they show what the authors describe as an inverted U-shape graph, such that brain activity increases for a period of time during development, expands greatly during a shorter period, then decreases. Thomas and Crow go on to speculate that although at the moment EPs cannot be linked automatically either to actual synaptic connections or to behavior, EPs may eventually provide a bridge between brain and behavior. That is, they might in the future be used to establish a causal, rather than simply correlative, link between the two.

In addition to EPs (a subset of EEGs, which measure electrical activity via electrodes applied to the scalp), research on human brain development has employed newer imaging technologies that, according to practitioners, have opened up important new avenues for research. Writing about these new devices, various authors in *Human Behavior* remark on the importance of technological advances that make it possible to image the brain in action (*in vivo*). Sidney J. Segalowitz suggests, for example, that the new technologies such as positron-emission tomography, or PET, initiated an "important time in the history of developmental psychology" because they "allow us to make neurophysiology-psychology mapping" (Segalowitz 1994: 86). The editors' prefatory remarks also identify the importance of such technological advances, which for them also helped to "set the stage for th[e] new era of interdisciplinary research" (Dawson and Fischer 1994: xiv).[2]

As one among these noninvasive techniques, PET is represented in the book by pediatric neurologist Harry Chugani's (1994) well-known research on infants and children.[3] Positron-emission tomography produces images of brain function by way of a special scanner that detects and records positrons. Positrons are emitted by isotopes injected into the body as they are metabolized. The visual images produced by the PET scanner are brainshapes projected in variegated colors, so that different colors across the spectrum represent different levels of metabolism in different parts of the brain. Positron-emission tomography is considered to be noninvasive in the sense that it requires no cutting of the skin. It works by injecting a radioactive substance into the bloodstream (Chugani 1994). As the editors and Chugani carefully note, the use of PET on infants and children with no known functional problems is considered unethical, because it requires exposing them to radioactive substances only for the purposes of research. For his analysis, Chugani retroactively selected "normal" PET scans from patients who underwent the procedure due to an ultimately unfounded concern.

These PET scans materialize the developing child by way of their colorful and compelling visual representations of the functioning brain. Chugani describes the relationship between metabolism and brain function that justifies his research method as follows: "Since glucose and oxygen are the principal substrates for meeting the energy demands of the brain, measurements of the rates at which these substrates are utilized in various brain regions during development provide a means whereby local functioning energy demands can be related to behavioral maturation" (Chugani 1994: 154). That is, glucose metabolism becomes an indication of energy use. Variations in the developing brain's energy use come to represent variations in brain activity, both between the brain's different regions and over the course of development. Using his "normal" sample of PET scans, Chugani produced a U-shaped pattern in glucose metabolism or energy demand, similar to Huttenlocher's, that Chugani correlates with a similar pattern generated in research on cats (154).

On the basis of this combined evidence, Chugani postulates that there is a direct relationship between glucose metabolism rates and the specific nature of brain plasticity in children. He explains that children who suffer damage to the brain show very little functional impairment as compared to adults with similar damage. He then attributes this difference to the developing brain's special plasticity, which allows it to reorganize its connections when some portion of the brain has been damaged (Chugani 1994: 166).

Using various different kinds of research on brain plasticity together with his own measures of metabolic activity in kittens and impaired children, Chugani points out the repeated similarity of patterns in measures of plasticity as compared to measures of metabolism. Kitten brains act as proxy for the child brain here. Comparing findings on plasticity with those on metabolism, Chugani notes that as plasticity decreases with increased stabilization of synapses, metabolism decreases as well (Chugani 1994: 167).

For Chugani, whose research is linked to his diagnostic practice as a clinician, this correlation is important because it means that plasticity can itself be identified through PET imaging of glucose metabolism. That is, changes in glucose metabolism reflect changes in plasticity. This is significant, he argues, because PET can provide a way of determining more objectively whether surgery on children at different ages should be recommended or avoided for particular conditions. Epileptic children, he notes, are often subjected to surgery for seizure control. Positron-emission tomography as a measure of plasticity could help to suggest the extent to which the child's brain is still plastic at the time of surgery, and so able to reorganize itself effectively afterwards. In addition to such practical considerations, Chugani suggests that PET research can be used to study many different kinds of biochemical processes in the developing brain. Positron-emission tomography therefore comes to provide a picture of the developing child that extends beyond the brain itself to the behavior with which brain activity is associated.

Modular Brains, Able Bodies

Chugani's research also identifies differential glucose metabolism for different parts of the brain, or brain regions. Using PET scans and associated measurements of metabolism as evidence, he suggests that four regions of the brain are prominent in early human development as compared to adult-hood. Up to this point, I have relied on a generalized notion of the brain to consider the material quality of its plasticity. In a sense, though, the brain does not exist as a whole for neurobehavioral scientists. It is divided, instead, into lobes, regions, and hemispheres (right and left). Modularity refers to the way that the brain's differentiation into regions allows for yet another kind of flexibility. The standard understanding of the brain with regard to modularity is that phylogenetically older regions of the brain are differentiated earlier (most during prenatal development) and are associated with automatic bodily functions such as reflexes. Neuroscientists literally see the brain anatomically (autopsied brains of humans and other animals, viewed by the naked eye), as a series of layers, each one associated with increasingly complex functioning (Greenfield 1997). With regard to differences between the "immature" developing child-brain and the mature adult-brain, the cortex (the outermost layer of the brain) is significant for its plastic modularity as compared to other parts of the brain. It is the cortex, rather than the entire brain, that is modular, divided into regions that correspond directly to specific functions, such as vision (the visual cortex), hearing (the auditory cortex), sensation and motion (the sensori-motor cortex). Some regions of the cortex are less clearly defined both in terms of their location and their functioning. These regions are thought to be associated with complex cognitive functions (thinking). Those cortical regions that are associated with specific functions are the physical sites of the brain's modularity. The brain is modular, then, to the extent that different functions, such as vision and hearing, are located in particular, and significantly separate, regions of the brain.

Just as the cortex is divided into regions, so too cortical development is regionally differentiated, such that development itself is also modular. That is, the brain's discontinuous synaptic pattern occurs discontinuously across the cortical regions, each of which has its own "critical period." The "critical period," as I have already mentioned, is a temporal limit within which the brain—now the brain region—remains plastic, and after which its synaptic pattern becomes relatively more fixed. In this sense, the developing brain is not one but many, so that the child-brain's increasing complexity is established through its differentiation into these specific regions at different times. It becomes increasingly differentiated as circuits between neural cells and the body—the eye, the ear, the limbs—are stabilized. In this process, development itself is compartmentalized into material regions as well.

A repeatedly invoked quality of the developing child-body is its ability to compensate for damage either to the brain itself or to particular behavioral capacities because of its modular plasticity. While some of the research in *Human Behavior* utilizes "normal" bodies, normal human development is also constituted through studies of abnormally developing bodies, and indeed through the experimental manipulation of developmental conditions and bodies. Such accounts of brain development continue to be based on the assumption that it is possible to identify patterns of development in terms of the normal (ability) and the abnormal (disability), where the normal is the measure against which all abnormal development is compared. Neurobehavioral science thus establishes a hierarchy of bodies not primarily in terms of race, class, gender, and sexuality—at least not directly—but in terms of ability and disability.

Chugani, like many other of the authors in the book, cites a history of relevant research to suggest ways in which glucose metabolism during development, represented in this case by PET scans, might be related to the brain's modular plasticity as defined (or limited) by the "critical period." Among others, Chugani cites the work of Hubel and Wiesel, which established the critical period as an observable behavioral phenomenon. These researchers manipulated the visual system of kittens by, for example, suturing one eye closed, or exposing the kittens to an environment of only horizontal or vertical stripes. Hubel and Wiesel found what became the critical period by observing the kittens' vision-based behavior after the period of manipulation, when the eye was reopened, or the striped visual environment was removed. In each case, the researchers found that the kittens' visual development was consistent with the type of visual exposure it had experienced. If the eye was sewn shut during a particular period, or if the visual field was limited to vertical input during that same period, the kittens failed to develop mature visual capacity. That is, their visual development was abnormal, because of abnormal visual input during the critical period.

Whereas Hubel and Wiesel relied on behavioral evidence to establish the critical period, subsequent studies linked behavior to the stuff of the brain. In the wake of this research, it became possible to claim that the critical period corresponds to the brain's developmental process. The critical period is that period during which synapses are presumably being stabilized into their more fixed, mature pattern. If there is damage to the brain during or before the critical period, the developing brain's modular plasticity makes it possible for the necessary connections to be remade in another part of the cortex, so that "normal" function is ultimately established. But after a given critical period, this kind of compensation becomes much less possible, and certainly less complete.

This correlation between the critical period as a behavioral phenomenon, and the critical period as a synaptic one has been materialized through comparative postmortem brain tissue studies of kittens, rats, and monkeys who have undergone various kinds of deprivation during and then after a specific critical period. Reviewing this research, Chugani notes that scientists have seen synaptic patterns through the microscope that correspond to the pattern suggested by behavioral studies. When kittens have had one eye sewn shut during the critical period, the synaptic pattern remains excessive and diffuse. For neuroscientific researchers, this pattern signifies that the developing visual cortex has not undergone the normal process of "pruning" that underlies mature visual function. Increased glucose metabolism rates for these organisms as compared to their normally developing counterparts also match this pattern, according to Chugani.

Similarly, Chugani cites research on kittens' somatosensory cortical development under conditions of manipulation. He refers to studies by Spinelli, Jensen, and di Prisco, in which kittens were trained to flex a foreleg in order to avoid a mild electrical shock. The kittens' electrophysiological patterns were then mapped via EEG, and their brains examined. According to these researchers, the resulting EEGs displayed increased activity for these kittens, and their brains showed increased connectivity in the area of the somatosensory cortex corresponding to the foreleg. Testing kittens at various ages, Spinelli, Jensen, and di Prisco found that the critical period for somatosensory development associated with the foreleg was from birth to ten weeks. After ten weeks, alteration in normal development could not be produced by this experiment. Chugani points out, again, that his own PET research on kittens shows a decrease in glucose metabolism rates after ten weeks as well.[4]

Noting the persistent correlation between animal studies of the developing brain together with PET, Chugani goes on to consider glucose metabolism rates in human children as an index of modular plasticity. Using his data from normal children's PET scans, he notes that the pattern of change corresponds to Huttenlocher's study of the overall patterns of increased density followed by pruning in human development. Both locate the end of these developmental changes at eight to ten years. Chugani notes that children tend to recover function at a greatly decreased level after this age as well, and that behavioral studies of the critical period for language development in children also suggest a ten-year limit.

Chugani goes on to cite similar results in the human visual system. Here again, he finds that his PET data correspond with human brain studies, suggesting that a decline in glucose metabolism rate coincides with a decline in the visual cortex's plasticity. His examples include clinical evidence of the effects of visual stimulus deprivation in young children, either due to the use of an eye patch, cataract, or other eye disease. As Chugani puts it, a critical period of eight to ten years from birth "is one of plasticity, since proper stimulation of the eye, commonly combined with an occluding patch over the other eye, can markedly reduce or eliminate" the original loss of input and subsequent lack of pruning. Clinical surveys, Chugani notes, have also established eight to ten years of age as the critical period for visual cortical development, after which plasticity greatly decreases (Chugani 1994: 168).

Emphasizing once again the novelty of findings and approaches presented in *Human Behavior*, Chugani concludes his chapter by stating, "Like the human brain, the kitten brain goes through a protracted period of metabolic maturation, including a phase when [glucose metabolism] exceeds values for the adult cat. Furthermore, the ascending portion of the [glucose metabolism] maturational curve for kitten visual cortex, seen between 3 weeks and 3 months, corresponds to the 'critical period' for this structure in the cat" (Chugani 1994: 170). Having established the consistent correlation between glucose metabolism patterns and those of synaptogenesis, Chugani goes on to suggest that correlating animal studies with human PET studies can yield further important information regarding the process of human development, both normal and abnormal. He writes that "expanding PET technology, when applied with complementary studies in appropriate animal models, provides a new approach to the study of human brain maturation, neuronal plasticity, developmental disorders, and brain reorganization following injury" (170).

Chugani's final list conveniently summarizes the concerns of neurobehavioral science as presented in *Human Behavior*: the study of changes in the human developing brain as it moves toward maturation, the developing brain's plastic quality, the establishment of normal and pathological (disordered) development, and the brain's greater capacity to reorganize itself in response to injury during the critical period. The child's figuration in the neurobehavioral sciences, which takes place through a multitude of practices and technologies, works to establish these qualities and processes as ontologically certain properties of the child-body itself, and to figure this child-body as the embodiment of the human adult in the making.

Multiple Bodies

Critical periods are constitutive of the developing brain's modularity in that they are plural, occurring for different periods and at different times for each region of the brain. From this perspective, the developing child-body is not one, but many; each of the developing brain's cortical regions reaches "maturity" at a different time. The function associated with each range also changes in a corresponding, increasingly complex, way.

A second form of modularity particular to the developing brain is related to how different aspects of cognition, emotion, perception, and sensation are integrated to form a complex, functioning system. This modularity is a feature of the developmental process, and takes a discontinuous form, but a cyclical one (Thatcher 1994; Fischer and Rose 1994). Like various dimensions of plasticity, and other forms of modularity, this cyclical process both constitutes the child-figure in neurobehavioral science and is generated through the child's figuration as a body in which the developmental process can be observed.

In a chapter titled "Cyclical Cortical Reorganization: Origins of Human Cognitive Development," neurologist Robert W. Thatcher offers an account of this cyclical discontinuity through a review of EEG-based research on human subjects from six months to sixteen years of age, which relies on measurements of EEG coherence. Electroencephalogram coherence refers to the continuities in electrical activity across two different regions of the brain. This measurement is made by recording the electrical activity generated by one electrode placed on the scalp and comparing it to the recording of electrical activity in a second electrode, placed in a different location on the scalp. Used as evidence of the brain's activity at a particular location, the two graphs representing electrical activity generated by the EEG at different brain locations can be compared. Electroencephalogram coherence obtains when the graphs are similar; that is, when there is coherence between the electrical activity measured at different points on the scalp.

Thatcher uses EEG coherence as evidence of the density of connections between cortical regions and as a measure of these connections' synaptic strength. Using mathematical equations, he translates EEG results into coherence values, which he calculates as a function of density and strength in the connections between two neural systems (values of density and strength are multiplied together to generate a numeric value). With this method, Thatcher identifies changes in the combined activity of different neural (or cortical) systems as evidence of developmental shifts, which describe a pattern characterized by growth "spurts"—that is, discontinuous rates of growth. Because coherence is constituted as a measure of the combined number and strength of synaptic connections, these growth spurts indicate a "rapid and significant" increase in this number and strength. The pattern of growth is represented in the form of graphs, with accompanying top-down drawings of a schematic head, in which the brain regions tested on the EEG are indicated (see Fig. 4).

Using these graphs as visual data, Thatcher suggests that human cognitive development is composed of both continuous and discontinuous processes. More specifically, different functions do not simply develop independently, nor do they "jump" from one stage to the next. Instead, within each stage, functions are connected with one another such that as one develops, others do as well. The coordinated changes take a cyclical form in the sense that the system of connections is continually disorganized and reorganized. As Thatcher puts it, "It would appear that a specific cognitive function . . . does not simply develop at a specific age and then cease in its development. Rather, cyclical reorganization and reintegration seem to operate at each cycle or subcycle of development" (Thatcher 1994: 251). Thatcher's visual representation of this process suggests how this cyclical form of development can be simultaneously continuous and discontinuous. Here, three major cycles are each comprised of three sub-cycles, which are in turn composed of multiple micro-cycles. At the end of each cycle, a "phase transition"—one at six years and one at ten years—marks a more dramatic shift in cognitive capacity.

The cyclical nature of human development offered by Thatcher constitutes yet another form of discontinuous development through which the child is figured. In this case, the stuff of its figuration is the EEG, and even more so the graphic representations of changes in cortical function across time, together with Thatcher's written analysis of their meanings. Through this materialization of a more abstract cyclical form of development, the child is figured as a cyclically developmental body that is repeatedly "sculpted" into its final adult form. In summarizing his findings, Thatcher succinctly describes this process. He begins by speculating that the patterns

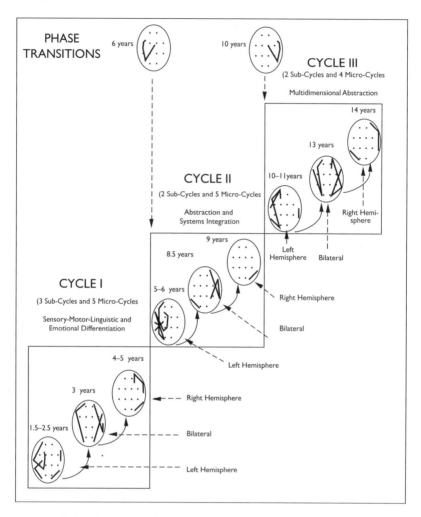

Figure 4: A visual representation of a simultaneously continuous and discontinuous cyclical form of cognitive development.

terns of EEG convergence he has calculated—the repeated growth spurts— "reflect a convergence pattern that narrows the disparity between structure and function by slowly sculpting and shaping the brain's microanatomy to meet the eventual demands and requirements of the adult world" (Thatcher 1994: 257). Development, from this point of view, is a process through which, once again, the child-body becomes increasingly complex and refined in its functional capacities: "According to this notion . . . the postnatal iterative sculpting process is used to fine-tune anatomical structure to meet the needs of diverse and unpredictable environments. The sculpting process unlocks or tailors the functional potential of the stable gross anatomy according to the individual needs and environmental demands" (257). The basic anatomical structure of the brain, laid down prenatally, becomes the subject of a refining process through postnatal development. The child is thus figured as a body being sculpted and re-sculpted into an increasingly refined functioning entity, on its way to becoming a fully functional adult.

This figuration of the child is further reinforced when Thatcher uses Piaget's notion of child development as a "spiral staircase" to describe the spatiotemporal shape of his own model. In this model, "the postnatal cyclical sculpting [presumably] reflects a dialectical process that iteratively and sequentially reorganizes intracortical connection systems" (Thatcher 1994: 257). Quoting Piaget, Thatcher goes on to suggest that the child's development "is 'a sort of spiral staircase in which [intracortical connection systems] are [reorganized] each time the spiral sweeps around, forming successively higher levels of integration'" (257). This intertextual production of the child-body's cyclical spatiotemporal form of development is more than rhetorical. It reflects the developmental neurobehavioral sciences' sustained attention to the relations between the developing brain and behavior.

At the end of the chapter, Thatcher reintroduces the quote from Piaget, but without substituting his own neuroscientific terms. For Piaget each developmental stage involves " 'integration with previous stages, a sort of spiral staircase in which contextual abstractions are reexamined each time the spiral sweeps around, forming successively higher levels of integration.'" (Thatcher 1994: 259). Thatcher's description of the developing brain matches Piaget's model of developing cognition (behavior), claiming that intracortical connection systems correspond to contextual abstractions, and reorganization of the neural system corresponds to the reexamination of contextual abstractions.

Thatcher extends this parallel further by comparing his own findings to Piaget's notion that the child undergoes a process of accommodation and assimilation in gaining mastery of cognitive capacities at each stage of development. Accommodation and assimilation are central, in particular, to the "spiral staircase" model of development because they are the mechanisms of iteration and reexamination. That is, these concepts describe how the developmental process revisits and reorganizes the "same" forms of cognition. Thatcher notes that accommodation and assimilation are central to Piaget's model of intellectual development; they "were so fundamental that Piaget defined adaptation [the shift to a new stage of development] as an 'equilibrium between assimilation and accommodation.' . . . Thus, experience is assimilated and simultaneously modified through the process of accommodation" (Thatcher 1994: 259). For Thatcher, there are suggestive links to be made between the continuous dimensions of the brain's cyclical cortical reorganization, and Piaget's claim that processes of assimilation and accommodation occur within each stage. Neither the brain nor its corresponding behavior, according to this view, proceeds through a simply discontinuous process. Instead, the process of "sculpting" the child into the adult takes an even more complex, spiral form, that is both discontinuous and continuous.

Evolving Bodies?

So far, I have described the plurality of ways in which the neurobehavioral sciences represented in *Human Behavior* figure the developing child-body's flexibility. Central to this figuration is a discontinuous developmental trajectory and form. A spiral model of cyclical reorganization that is continuous within its discontinuity makes the child-figure even more complex. All of the examples I have cited have been concerned with ontogeny—that is, they have been generic, universal accounts of human development at the level of the organism itself. However, some neurobehavioral scientific claims included in *Human Behavior* concern phylogenetic development, or the evolutionary development of the species. I briefly review Francis Benes's (1994) findings on the ontogenetic and phylogenetic development of the corticolimbic system (interconnected regions of the cortex that are seen to integrate thought and emotion) to indicate one way in which phylogeny has been constituted through the child-body's figuration in this field.

Citing a wide range of research on development across the species, Benes suggests that "there is some tendency for the ontogenesis of the . . . cortex in [the] mammalian brain to reflect its phylogenetic development" (Benes 1994: 187). This means that the developing child-brain recapitulates the human brain's evolution in some ways. By studying the developing child-brain as the site of human ontogeny, together with the brains of animals that represent earlier evolutionary organisms, it becomes possible to speculate about the nature of the human brain's evolution at the level of the species. As Benes puts it, studies of the developing (child) brain can "tell us how . . . a complex system [such as] a harmonious collaboration between the limbic system and the neocortex . . . has been achieved. . . . It is useful to examine how such a complex system has been assembled" (178). Furthermore, this assembly must be seen "as a result of both phylogenetic and ontogenetic development of the brain" (178). In keeping with a neurobehavioral scientific division of bodies into normal and pathological, Benes notes that the value of such an approach lies in the information it can yield about normal as well as pathological development. It can "potentially help us to understand not only how the brain has attained its characteristic functions, but also how these functions can be disturbed by perturbations of normal ontogeny" (178).

From Benes's phylogenetic point of view, reptiles are the evolutionary predecessors of mammals (including humans). Following the recapitulation model, and echoing nineteenth-century figurations of the child, this means that the developing human child-brain contains in itself reptile-like brain components. But the human child's evolutionary process has also made it a more complex organ, according to this account. Specifically, the mammalian cortex is made up of six layers, rather than only three as in the reptilian brain. Together with this anatomical difference come variations in the synaptic density, organization, and concomitant function of the mammalian versus the reptilian brain. These variations are generated through the developmental process. One of the developmental processes that differentiates the mammalian brain from its evolutionary predecessors is the making of connections that establish the corticolimbic system.

Benes argues that the connections that make up the corticolimbic system have developed phylogenetically as the three-layer reptilian brain transformed into the six-layer mammalian brain. The human brain's phylogeny has included a "progressive integration" of "phylogenetically older and newer information" (Benes 1994: 198). This phylogenetically progressive process "is now reflected in the six-layered structure of mammalian cortex." It is difficult to separate cognitive function from visceral reactions in the "normal" human adult, Benes concludes, because of the "inextricable relationship between its limbic and cortical components" that is characteristic of this mammalian brain (198). The developmental process follows the phylogenetic pattern in that it entails the making of increasingly tighter connections between the two components. According to this model, the child becomes figured as a developing body whose brain and its associated corticolimbic functions are initially poorly integrated at best, but become increasingly more integrated as the body develops into its fully functional adult form.

The flexible child-body's time-limited plasticity and modularity are joined, here, by yet another form of its increasingly refined complexity, which "reflects" (but does not directly embody) human evolution. This child-body's multifaceted developmental flexibility is the effect of an evolutionary process that makes the human, as one among other mammals, more flexible and more complex than any other organism. The overall effect of this approach is that the child is constituted as different from the adult, while at the same time this difference works in the service of the adult's making as a more precise and complex form of embodied consciousness. This point has not been lost on Turkowitz et al., who are also contributors to *Human Behavior*. They note that:

> It has been tacitly assumed by most students of normal and aberrant development that differences between adults and infants reflect deficiencies in the infant, and therefore represent handicaps which must be overcome if development is to proceed normally. . . . The widespread use of the term "immature" to describe the infant and child attests to the dominance of the view that structure and function are best understood in terms of what they will become, rather than in terms of what they are. (Turkowitz et al. 1994: 510)

It could be said, in fact, that the trope of development ensures this secondary status of the child as compared to the adult. But my own reading of the child in the neurobehavioral sciences also suggests that the child's figuration as a more flexible body than the adult simultaneously establishes this flexibility as a value. That is, the child is endowed with the quality—and so with the benefit—of flexibility as compared to the adult.

Acculturating the Developing Child

An alternative evolutionary story is told, however, by way of the "ecological niche." As in neuroscientific developmental accounts, this version of evolution theorizes an interactive and interdependent relation between organisms and their environments. A given organism (species) is located in a particular ecological niche, and it is the "fit" between an organism and a particular ecological niche that determines the possibility of the species' survival. Adaptation is also a reciprocal process in this model, such that a species may, in its habitation of a given niche, alter that niche to accommodate its particular requirements. So too, the "fit" between a species in one temporal and spatial niche may be much more adequate than it would be in another.

This theory has been taken up by developmental psychologists interested in developmental neuroscience and concerned with cross-cultural variations in child development. At the turn of the twenty-first century, questions of cultural difference have begun to trouble universalist claims about human development. The critique of developmentalism both within and outside developmental psychology generally questions the validity of any universal, linear theory of development on the grounds that such theories fail to recognize cultural differences, which can be significant features of any child's environment. Development, in this alternative view, entails a process of interaction between the child and its environment. Like their nineteenth-century counterparts, contemporary psychologists, in particular, have looked to the child for evidence of human development, but their questions are about cognition rather than simple intelligence, and their investigations are guided by a different conception of human nature in relation to a culturally inflected environment.

For these psychologists, human development must be understood in terms of its cultural context, because culture is an agent in the developmental process. Human nature is the effect rather than the cause of the human organism's interaction with its environment. And environments are produced in and through culturally specific histories, such that culture "guides" or "channels" human nature (Rogoff, Guavain, and Ellis 1991: 293). The "ecological niche" for child development in this framework includes culture in the form of child-rearing practices, as well as natural disasters and historical events. All of these elements are seen as potentially critical aspects of human development, but neither nature nor culture is an independent variable. Indeed, the latter terms lose their prior significance, and are replaced by an expanded conception of the relationship between an organism and its environment.

One group advocating cross-cultural approaches according to this framework describes development as follows: "Development is not assumed to take a fixed, unidimensional course toward a unique or ideal endpoint; rather, the individual is expected to differentiate to fit the niche or cultural setting" (Rogoff, Guavain, and Ellis 1991: 293). Just as development is differentiated by environmental variations, so too, different cultures provide divergent opportunities, such that children cannot be measured according to a single developmental scale. Instead, children's development must be assessed in terms of the specific opportunities and requirements of their particular cultural environment.

While this turn toward an ecological account of development is primarily offered by psychologists who make no claims about the links between psychological and neurobiological development, their approach figures a culturally distinct child whose cognition (in this case) is differentiated from other children's at many levels, from the individual to the sociocultural. This account of development is offered in large part to counter the normative assumptions that emerge from more universalist notions of development, which presuppose a generic environment. Such models tend to generate hierarchies of developmental attainment that favor so-called Western children, as well as girls, monolingual children, and so on. The ecological niche model (derived from Piaget and the Russian psychologist Vygotsky, as well as evolutionary theory) insists instead that each child's development must be assessed in relation to the possibilities and requirements that his or her particular environment, including culture, holds.

This rebuttal to traditional psychological developmental theory is interesting with regard to the neurobehavioral sciences because of the way it blends culture into evolutionary theory. As a component of the ecological niche, culture gains a place in the environment-organism relation. It plays a constitutive role in the process of human development, as it had not done before either in nonneuroscientific psychology or in developmental neuroscience. Unlike its more universalist counterparts, this version of development insists on a child whose cognitive capacities are specific to a particular cultural/environmental "ecology." This means that culture differentiates the child's cognitive nature.

On the one hand, the cross-cultural child is not one, but many culturally specific groups of children. On the other hand, the concept of development itself, as I have already suggested, assumes the existence of the human as a universal category that can accommodate variation. Because the term cross-cultural refers to the existence of different cultures across the globe, the child figured in cross-cultural psychological development is distributed around the world, and so it is also figured as a flexibly global (rather than simply universal) body. To the flexible child-body of developmental neurobehavioral sciences is added the flexibility of cultural differentiation.

What holds firm in all of the neurobehavioral accounts considered so far is the figuration of the child as the embodiment of the human in the making, whose value lies in its flexibility. While many researchers in the field refrain from drawing any direct conclusions from their work with regard to enhancing actual children's development, some (e.g., neurologists, who do research in the context of clinical medicine) are more oriented toward suggesting how their findings can or should be translated into other kinds of practice. In any case, it is generally accepted that, as one neuroscientist puts it, "children must be stimulated—through touch, speech and images—to develop fully" (Shatz 1992: 61). So the issue, from this point of view, is not whether such stimulation is necessary, but what types of environmental stimuli might guarantee normal development.

The idea that children require some kind of input in order to develop fully can be found in the nineteenth-century scientific texts, as well as in the writings of nineteenth- and early-twentieth-century reformers and educators. Indeed, the need to ensure children's "normal" development through some means may be one of the most persistent features of childhood since the "normal" and "normal development" became intelligible measures of "the human" (Canguilhem 1978). What is specific to neurobiology's developmentalism is precisely the direct link it shows (conceptually and visually) between the very matter of the brain and the body's functions. Because this link is itself literally materialized through "use," the environment becomes a crucial actor.

Practicing Development in the Media

The notion that the neurobehavioral sciences' determinative conception of environmental input might be translated into child-rearing and pedagogic practices has proved a compelling one in a February 1996 *Newsweek* cover story titled "Your Child's Brain" by science writer Sharon Begley. Consider, for example, the following excerpt:

You hold your newborn so his sky-blue eyes are just inches from the brightly patterned wallpaper. ZZZt: a neuron from his retina makes an electrical connection with one in his brain's visual cortex. You gently touch his palm with a clothespin; he grasps it, drops it, and you return it to him with soft words and a smile. *Crackle:* neurons from his hand strengthen their connection to those in his sensory-motor cortex. He cries in the night; you feed him, holding his gaze because nature has seen to it that the distance from a parent's crooked elbow to his eyes exactly matches the distance at which a baby focuses. *Zap*: neurons in the brain's amygdala send pulses of electricity through the circuits that control emotion. You hold him on your lap and talk . . . and neurons from his ears start hard-wiring connections to the auditory cortex. And you thought you were just playing with your kid. (Begley 1996: 55)

The notion of the child as a project belongs to a middle-class and Anglo (U.S.) system of values and practices that has been oriented toward the child's physiological, psychological, and moral development, and enforced by child-rearing experts of various kinds, including doctors, psychologists, psychiatrists, and social workers (Steedman 1986). While earlier child-rearing practices were certainly linked to physiological development, the immediacy of that link was never as palpable as the sounds of an electrical current running through just-wired circuits. In Begley's translation of neurobehavioral sciences' recent findings, "we," the parents, become observers of developmental biological processes in the (middle-class, wall-papered) nursery, and we are also now responsible for them in a new way: "our" input literally materializes the child-brain's neural connections. That this notion of the child as a parental project is decidedly middle-class (and represented, here, as white) is suggested by a two-page illustration of a freckle-faced, pink-skinned boy dressed in a beanie hat, overalls, and a striped shirt. The opening caption reads "A baby's brain is a work in progress, trillions of neurons waiting to be wired into a mind." A geometric Tom Sawyer, the boy's head has been sliced in two, exposing the brain. As the boy holds onto one end of an elongated single-lobed brain, his "parents"—represented by two hands, one attached to a white shirt cuff and black suit-sleeve, the other with a bracelet of red circles around the wrist, and a textured brown sleeve—reach out for the other (see Fig. 5).

The circuitry described in this article is a combination of genetic and environmental inputs, which together form an interactive computer-like system, and the relationship between the genes and the "organism" is quite explicitly not determining. There are not enough genes, according to this description, to account for the brain's "incomparable" complexity. Citing Harry Chugani and Carla Shatz, the author describes the child-brain in minute detail. Genes prewire neural connections for autonomic functions like breathing and heartbeat in the embryo. "Trillions and trillions" of other such connections, however, are "like the Pentium chips in a com-

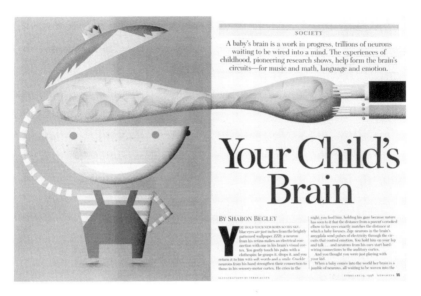

Your Child's Brain

BY SHARON BEGLEY

Figure 5: *Newsweek*'s image of the child as a brain and body being "developed" through input from its environment.

puter before the factory preloads the software. They are pure and of almost infinite potential, unprogrammed circuits that might one day compose rap songs and do calculus, erupt in fury and melt in ecstasy" (Begley 1996: 56).[5] In what Begley calls an "emerging paradigm," neural connections occur in two main sets, differentiated by the importance of experience. Thus, the first stage proceeds as development always has, more or less autonomously. But the second stage requires experience. This formulation is based on experiments, Begley continues, that established a time-limited developmental pattern signified by the phrase "critical periods," or temporal "windows of opportunity that nature flings open, starting before birth, and then slams shut, one by one" and year by year. Endless possibilities are lodged in the child-brain as the center of bodily function. Development does not meet a single limit, but is spread out according to specific functions, each of which "matures" at a different time (56–57).

In this neurologically defined world of the human, the child becomes the site of human potential as well as its possible failure, and in the process parents (not just mothers) and the educational system are assigned a new burden of responsibility for how children "turn out." Everything from Head Start's failures to the fear of a drunken father can be explained in terms of neural connections made or missed. A large number of fundamentally "human" characteristics—emotions, language, mathematical reasoning, and musical ability—depend on experiential factors in which the parents (assumed to be the principle providers of "experience" and education) play a fundamental role. An inset grid depicting "The Windows of Opportunity" graphically represents the main scientific and didactic message: "Circuits in different regions of the brain mature at different times. As a result, different circuits are most sensitive to life's experiences at different ages. Give your children the stimulation they need when they need it, and anything's possible. Stumble, and all bets are off" (Begley 1996: 58). No longer self-generating, development does not proceed along a given trajectory that is sometimes "arrested"; it is a potential that does not even get started without the proper external stimulus.

Additional insets spell these relationships out quite explicitly, and further specify neurologically defined terms of difference. Titled "The Logical Brain" (Begley 1996: 56), "The Language Brain" (57), and "The Musical Brain" (68), respectively, the three rectangular boxes each appear centered on the page, and depict a stylized cartoon image of a child. Made up almost entirely of geometric shapes, with a huge oval head and a tiny triangular body, these images invoke racial and gender differences through shape, color, and iconography. Still universally "global" because "natural," the brain and its function are coded primarily in terms of neural differences. The variations in "skin" color, "hair" style, and gendered dress (a rounded collar for a pink-faced girl with yellow pigtails, a beanie for a brown-faced boy) do not correlate with the more fundamental difference constituted by the maturing brain. Just as the large oval head overwhelms the tiny body, so too the brain overwhelms, or at least challenges, the salience of other "bodily" differences.

Each inset differentiates the different types of brains according to a didactic set of categories: "Skill," "Learning Window," "What We Know," and "What We Can Do about It." "The Language Brain," for example, lists its skill as "language," and its learning window as "birth to 10 years." "What We Know" offers the following description: "Circuits in the auditory cortex, representing the sounds that form words, are wired by the age of 1. The more words a child hears by 2, the larger her vocabulary will grow." The computer metaphor with its electronic circuitry and "hard-wiring" here signifies necessity, contingency, and possibility all at the same time. Without the proper input, the necessary "wiring" will not occur. With the proper input, the "wiring" will not only be permanent ("hard-wired"), but will also ensure continued potential (more words heard equals a larger vocabulary) (Begley 1996: 57).

The "language brain's" proper maturation also depends on adequate physiological functioning, since "hearing problems can impair the ability to match sounds to letters." Accordingly, "What We Can Do about It" includes suggestions on how to ensure the proper hard-wiring as well as proper hearing: "Talk to your child—a lot. If you want her to master a second language, introduce it by the age of 10. Protect hearing by treating ear infections promptly." Such prescriptions are backed up by examples of other parents' successes and failures. Begley cites a study by psychiatrist Janellen Huttenlocher of the University of Chicago, which divided mothers into those who speak to their children often, and those who are "more taciturn," or "less involved." Needless to say, the former group produced babies with bigger vocabularies, and a more "built-up" neural circuitry, likened to a "computer file [that] allows the user to fill it up with prose." With the building of neural circuitry comes not only the realization of potential, but also its possible expansion. Two languages heard at an early age are better than one, and three are so much the better (Begley, 1996: 57).

There are many reasons for suggesting that children learn more than one language, and for advocating some forms of child-rearing over others. My concern here is with the fact that this maturational rematerialization of the child severely locates the potential for change of every kind only in the child, and even to a restricted period of time in the child's life. I do not mean to suggest that this figuration of the child as the sole site of potential change is either entirely positive or entirely negative. LynNell Hancock's article on schools in relation to new biologically based understandings of learning (which appears as an inset within Begley's piece) suggests that education might well become more interesting, interactive, and emotionally oriented than at present. New value might be placed on music and physical education programs, cut in recent years by a conservative government's short-sighted money-saving measures (Begley 1996: 61). But it is not clear that the measures of achievement in the areas of musical ability and so on are any less biased than before.

One of the studies cited in Begley's report, for example, concerns the 1972 Abecedarian project, which divided children from 120 poor families— children who would otherwise have been enrolled in Head Start programs at two, three, and four years old—into four groups, each one enrolled in day-care with a specific educational program geared at developing neural connections. The groups of children enrolled in the day-care special programs as preschoolers attained higher IQ and reading and math scores than their Head Start counterparts (Begley 1996: 61). What goes unquestioned, here, is the much-contested measure—IQ—by which these comparative scores are obtained, not to mention the selection of poor children as the site of possible developmental damage or delay.

This maturational materialization of the child and the child-brain locates the greatest potential for change in the child. At best, this could potentially help to focus attention on children neglected by the public education system, and to promote wide-ranging educational programs that support a more expansive understanding of children's abilities and interests. At the same time, however, its tendency toward determinism lodges potential in the child and locks it in. It can give scientific support to a tendency already evident in the public school system to give up on children earlier, now as a result of parental "failure" to provide their children with the neural connections on which intellectual capacity depends.

More generally, figurations of the child as a potentiality include a mechanism by which this possibility might be either realized or squandered. The risk of failure is therefore inherent in the child's potentiality. So too, the child's value as a potentiality lies partly in the opportunities it affords— indeed requires—for external control and direction. The child is figured as a potentiality in need of control for the realization of that very potential— for while development is full of potential, its outcome is also never simply guaranteed.

Nineteenth-century scientific figurations of the child made use of the child-body as a spatiotemporal form to generate racial, gendered, sexualized, and classed hierarchies on a global scale. Neurobehavioral scientific versions of the child materialize the child-body as a site of human potential and transformation, thereby also assigning the child a potent cultural value as a quintessentially "flexible body" (Martin 1994). Always primed for change because already in process, this child is figured in distinct semiotic-material terms that are fundamentally different from those of the nineteenth-century child-figure. This neurobehavioral child-figure takes on a modular, flexible form of embodiment that generates a specific version of the human, and establishes a discontinuous difference between the child and the adult that did not exist before, even as the child "becomes" the adult through the developmental process. This becoming also takes place in relation to a newly defined limit. In the neurobehavioral sciences, this limit is the moment when the window of opportunity slams shut forever, such that possibility is lodged in the child-body before that moment for each distinct sensory and intellectual function.

And yet at the same time, the nineteenth-century and late-twentieth-century child-figures I have described are put to similar use: the child's value in these scientific discourses is as a body who *is*, in an ontological sense, the human in the making. As such, the child is both that which must be figured in order to make a claim on the human, and the body from which the "facts" of human nature's makings must be ascertained. Their figuration therefore instantiates the workings of ontological privilege: the power to claim what is; what the child is, and what the adult is that the child will become.

The difference between the two figurations of the child can be associated with broader historical shifts in the relationship between nature and culture. As the *Newsweek* article so vividly suggests, nature can now be constituted by the culture of science and scientifically directed parental and institutional pedagogy. The child "matters" as a flexible body and subject in the making. Its neural synapses comprise a body made uniquely malleable and potentially even perfectible in its time-limited plasticity. To be endowed with such positive value is to become the object of interest, desire, and knowledge. If the child-figure's embodiment is so often utterly material, its materiality is also always the (im)materiality of a sign, with its endless chain of significations. Interest, desire, and knowledge are part of what constitutes—realizes—bodies, and part of what bodies realize in turn.

Not all scientific discourses figure the child, nor do different scientific discourses figure the "same" child. But insofar as the child is figured in neurobehavioral science as it is represented in *Human Behavior*, and in *Newsweek*'s coverage of the field, this figuration suggests that the child is indeed bound up with the figuration of the human. It also suggests that the child's scientific figurations can be taken up and even further elaborated in wider cultural domains, perhaps most notably in the media. In both *Newsweek* and *Human Behavior*, it is through the process of figuration that the child, as well as the human that it figures in turn, gain the force and the value of the real.

One of the questions raised by cross-cultural psychology's figuration of the child in terms of the ecological niche is precisely the relationship between nature and culture as they relate to the ontological real. Historically, "cultural" factors have been secondary to "natural" ones in descriptions of ontology. By definition, nature was that which was given in the world, while culture was created, or constructed from natural building blocks. But just as science and its claims to nature are themselves culturally specific, so too "culture" generates ontological claims regarding the nature of the world outside of scientific discourse. It is to such "cultural" claims, and their figurations of the child, that I now turn.

3
Available Childhood: Race, Culture, and the Transnational Adoptee

Although scientific discourses claim authority concerning the child's biological nature and its relation to culture, many other discourses also figure the child in terms of both natural and cultural traits. Actual children are also sometimes involved in corresponding local-global circuits of exchange, as in the case of refugee, immigrant, exiled, and transnationally adopted children. Just as these children's transnational circulation is enabled or enforced through particular relations of power as well as local-global histories and practices, so too different figurations of the child play a significant role within and across these different circuits of exchange. In this chapter, I consider figurations of the child in U.S. local-global discourses of intercountry adoption and the adoptive child's identity.[1]

Transnational adoption raises a wide range of critical and often highly emotive issues that are partly related to adoption in general, and partly specific to adoption across national lines. These issues include the stigma of adoption as compared to biological kinship; the often appalling physical and emotional conditions of care suffered by orphaned children; the extent to which prospective adoptive parents are scrutinized in the adoption process; and the possible exploitation of birth mothers, adoptive parents, and children through the monetary exchanges and lack of regulation that have accompanied transnational adoptions. In addition, the means by which a child is united with adults through adoption, whether transnational or not, includes not only adoption policy and practice, but also ways of conceiving the tie between the child and its prospective parents. To the extent that a child's belonging is assumed to be the product of biological reproduction and "blood ties" within the United States (and elsewhere), adoption remains a less valued way of generating family ties between children and adults. That is, the tie between a child and its parents is not as easily assumed in cases of adoption as in cases of biological reproduction, where biology provides the ground for this tie.[2] The question of how to establish the tie between a child and its prospective adoptive parents, particularly with regard to their respective identities, has consequently been a matter of considerable debate in both national and transnational adoption contexts.

With regard to transnational adoption in particular, the question of children's identity has been addressed in the 1993 Hague Convention on the Protection of Children and Co-operation in Respect of Intercountry Adoption, which was signed by the United States in 1998. Framed in terms of the fundamental principle of "the best interests of the child" set out in the 1989 United Nations Convention on the Rights of the Child, the Hague Convention links the child's best interests to issues of identity in article 16 (part 1). Noting that the "Central Authority" regulating adoption in each country must first ensure that the child is legally adoptable, article 16 states that the authority should then: "Prepare a short report including information about his or her identity, adoptability, background, social environment, family history, medical history including that of the child's family, and any special needs of the child" and "give due consideration to the child's upbringing and to his or her ethnic, religious, and cultural background." Assuming proper consents to adoption have been obtained, the authority should then "determine, on the basis in particular of the reports relating to the child and the prospective adoptive parents, whether the envisaged placement is in the best interests of the child" (Hague Convention, 1993). The resulting linkage between the child's identity and that of the adoptive parent(s) becomes a crucial point of consideration in transnational adoption as stipulated by the Hague Convention.

However, in the manner of many such international human rights instruments, the generalized language employed leaves the Convention open to interpretation. References to the child's identity and background in part 1a are made somewhat more precise in part 1b, which refers to the child's "upbringing" and "ethnic, religious, and cultural background," but even this leaves open the question of which aspects of the child's identity will be significant in a given case. Partly because transnational adoptions involve transactions between two specific nations, and partly because the relevant international human rights instruments employ such generalized language, the matter of which aspects of the child's identity are at stake and how they are addressed can only be answered in relation to specific local-global circuits of exchange. In the United States, the nation with a total number of intercountry adoptions greater than that of all other countries combined, questions of the transnational adoptee's identity are informed by a long history of debate concerning transracial adoption. While U.S. transnational adoption is differently located as compared to national adoption discourse with regard to the actors, institutions, and issues involved, the issue of racial identity carries through from the national to the transnational domain.

Making Race: Adoption as a Reproductive Technology

I identify adoption as a reproductive technology in this discussion in order to call upon a series of associations between technology, reproduction, and figuration. This approach relies on ongoing feminist work in anthropology, cultural studies, and science studies that has brought nature into cultural analysis by denaturalizing ontological, objective claims concerning the truth of nature (Jordanova 1986; Martin 1987; Haraway 1989, 1991a; Stafford 1991; see also Gilman 1985; Laqueur 1990). No longer the assumed substratum of culture, nature has become a question rather than a grounding assumption in this work (see also Franklin, Lury, and Stacey 2000). From this point of view, the body does not preexist the technologies through which its materiality and significance are made and remade (Butler 1993; Haraway 1991b). So too, reproduction is neither simply a cultural phenomenon nor a natural fact, but instead lies somewhere between the two. And reproductive technologies, including natural childbirth as well as in vitro fertilization, necessarily generate particular kinds of bodies.

Indeed, feminists have given sustained attention to the workings and cultural significance of reproductive technologies, perhaps most notably comparatively "new" reproductive technologies (NRTs) such as in vitro fertilization, artificial insemination, and surrogacy; but they have also examined the associated visual, legal, and textual technologies such as photography, court cases, and metaphors. Together, these technologies are used to generate natural facts about bodies. Feminist science studies has observed not only that "every technology is a reproductive technology" (Sofia 1984), but also that many different kinds of technologies come together to produce different kinds of bodies.[3]

This understanding of reproduction links human reproduction, embodiment, and cultural meaning together in such a way that adoption, too, can be seen as a reproductive technology. Within the United States, reproduction has long been associated with the reproduction of race. The terrible dream of racial purity and the fascinated horror of miscegenation, coupled with fears of "race suicide" are among the most salient aspects of the U.S. history of race linked to reproduction. At the same time, historical analyses of race suggest that its significance and embodiment have changed over time and place. Like all such categories, furthermore, the materiality and significance of race as a feature of embodiment has been continually reconstituted (Fernando 1992; Hall 1992; Morrison 1992; Mohanty 1991; Goldberg 1990; Gilroy 1987; Omi and Winant 1986). Considered as one among other reproductive technologies, adoption can be seen to participate in this history of racial reformulation insofar as it involves racialized figurations of the adoptee.

The translation of racial issues in U.S. adoption discourse from the national to the transnational context is apparent in the work of Elizabeth Bartholet, an adoption advocate and human rights lawyer, who has addressed first national and then transnational adoption issues in her writings. In the following discussion, I consider figurations of the child specifically with regard to race in a U.S. local-global discourse, focusing on Bartholet's writings and responses to her work. I locate this more circumscribed discursive domain in a wider field of significance by considering the extent to which its modes of racialized figuration coincide with those employed in the U.S. media.

The importance of transnational adoption as a site of the child's racialized figuration in U.S. local-globals precedes current intercountry adoption practice. In the wake of World War II, and then the Korean War, various charitable U.S.-based organizations were established to facilitate transnational adoptions of children orphaned in war (Ressler, Boothby, and Steinbeck 1988). As a result, European and later Korean children, followed by Vietnamese children, began to be adopted into largely white, middle- and upper-class U.S. homes (Alstein and Simon 1991). Formal (i.e., legalized) transnational adoption procedures and institutions that began at this time expanded in subsequent years, so that the number of U.S. transnational adoptions rose to 10,097 in the 1980s, then leveled off in the 1990s to values in the 9,000s (National Committee for Adoption 1992), rising again to its highest level after 1990.[4]

Current figurations of the adoptee appear in a local-global United States that is different from that of the 1980s and earlier, partly because the adoptees' countries of origin have changed since then. As some countries temporarily or permanently shut down their transnational adoption systems owing to charges of corruption, baby selling, and even baby farming, other countries have legalized the practice. Currently, the largest number of adoptees come from Russia, followed by China, South Korea, and Guatemala.[5] In addition, the signing of the Hague Convention by the United States as mentioned above, and the U.S. government's decision to grant automatic citizenship to transnational adoptees (in 2000) have wrought further changes.[6]

My inquiry into figurations of the transnational adoptee begins among the pages of *Reconstruction*, a U.S.-based journal. Described by its editors as "particularly concerned with providing a forum for uninhibited commentary on African-American politics, society, and culture," *Reconstruction* issued a special report in 1992 on the long-debated politics of transracial adoption within the United States. The report includes a lead article by Elizabeth Bartholet titled "Where Do Black Children Belong? The Politics of Race Matching in Adoption." This article is followed by a series of responses by key figures in the adoption world. Contributors to the special report include Anita Allen, Georgetown University Law Center professor and author of *Uneasy Access: Privacy for Women in a Free Society* (1988); Ezra E. Griffith, professor at Yale University in the Medical School and the Department of Afro-American Studies; Joan Heifetz Hollinger, principal author of *Adoption Law and Practice* (1988), a reporter for the proposed Uniform Adoption Act of the Commission on Uniform State Laws, and professor at the University of Detroit Law School; Lillian B. Lansberry, vice president of the Adoption Exchange Association and president of the Black Adoption Recruitment Network; William L. Pierce, president of the National Committee for Adoption, and coauthor with Christine Adamec of *The Encyclopedia of Adoption* (1991); and Rita J. Simon, professor at American University, and author of many books on transracial adoption (1977, 1987, 1994). By no means representative of the national discourse as a whole, *Reconstruction*'s report is a staged debate on transracial adoption in which specific modes of racialization are variously employed. To the extent that the contributors to *Reconstruction* are also important actors in the adoption world, the modes of racialization they use in formulating their positions may have implications for future adoption policy and practice. However, their significance for my purposes concerns their figuration of the child with regard to race, the role of race in relatedness (or family), and in particular the kinds of raciality that the authors variously use, as well as those they refuse.

A version of Elizabeth Bartholet's article in *Reconstruction* appeared in her *Family Bonds: Adoption and the Politics of Parenting* (1993). In both her scholarly and more popular work, Bartholet situates the national debate on transracial adoption in a broad framework of reproductive choices that includes IVF and transnational adoption. For reasons that will become apparent, Bartholet projects a future in which adoption will take place primarily on a transnational and therefore transracial basis. This brings the domestic debate on transracial adoption into a transnational domain not addressed directly by *Reconstruction*.

In order to locate Bartholet's figurations of the adoptee's race in a wider local-global framework, I also consider two quite different technologies of racialized reproduction, a *Time* magazine special issue on immigration and a Benetton *Colors* magazine issue on race. While these magazine articles do not address the question of adoption, both have generated visual representations of a racialized and globalized future that resonate with Bartholet's vision. I use these visual representations to mark a shift between prior modes of racialization in adoption and new ones that seem to be emerging not only in Bartholet's writings (which do not necessarily circulate outside the United States), but in particular local-globals as well. In my previous work on this subject, I argued that the incorporation of transnational adoptees into U.S. families depended not only on adoption policies, practices, and institutions, but also on the transformation of the foreign adoptee into a "familiar" family member, a son or daughter (Castañeda 1993). Whereas in the prior period this transformation seemed to be organized in terms of homogenization or assimilation, the current mode, particularly with regard to race, seems to be oriented toward a multiculturalist valorization of racial diversity.

I use *Time* and Benetton's publications here as visualizing tools that help to specify the particular mode of racialization that I find in Bartholet's work. Each of the articles is differently representative of racialized and globalized worlds. Locating Bartholet's work in this wider domain of late-twentieth-century "global" culture makes it possible to indicate in a necessarily preliminary and suggestive fashion a mode of racialization that is also a way of imagining "global" humanity and "global" family relations. Not only does the adoption debate use this mode of racialization, but in so doing it also contributes a particular racialized vision of the child as adoptee.

Among the actors in the U.S. adoption debate, Bartholet is one of the few who can draw on both her legal authority and her experience as an adoptive parent. Bartholet is a former civil rights lawyer now specializing in family law, the adoptive single parent of two boys born in Peru, and one of the many women for whom adoption was a last resort following IVF failure.[7] Her more popular work on adoption, with its well-crafted mix of auto-biographical narrative and legal style of reasoning is arguably among the most widely influential U.S. work on adoption published in the 1990s. Together with *Family Bonds* (1993) and the less autobiographical *Reconstruction* article, Bartholet's work addresses a wide range of audiences and has appeared in diverse publications, from the *Pennsylvania Law Review* (Bartholet 1991) to the California Center for the Future of Children's newsletter (Bartholet 1992a) to *Adoption Law and Practice* (Bartholet 1992b), a sociologically oriented anthology on adoption practice and the law (see Hollinger, above). Since *Family Bonds* is partially excerpted from the *Reconstruction* article, I read them jointly here, bringing together debates about transracial adoption within the United States with debates about race in transnational adoption.

Throughout her writings, Bartholet advocates abolishing all legal measures and adoption agency policies that would require a racial match between a child and its adoptive parents. In "Where Do Black Children Belong?" she argues this position explicitly in relation to a history of race in U.S. adoption. For Bartholet, this history begins with a brief period in which transracial adoption was allowed during the 1960s. While racial matching had been a de facto and largely unquestioned practice in adoption until the mid-twentieth century, the civil rights movement of the 1960s was the most important among the multiple forces that raised public awareness of "minority" children previously neglected by the adoption system. Owing in part to its integrationist principles, the civil rights movement helped to change adoption policy as well as adoptive parents' desires, ushering in a brief but important era of "relative openness" regarding transracial placements. This was followed, according to Bartholet, by the near-total elimination of transracial adoption because of ensuing protests against such adoptions (Bartholet 1993: 94–95).

For Bartholet, the members of the National Association of Black Social Workers (NABSW) were, and continue to be, the strongest proponents of racial matching, and the moving force behind the translation of racial matching as a concept into long-standing and widely instituted state adoption policies. The following quote by the NABSW exemplifies, according to Bartholet, the standard argument against transracial adoption:

Black children should be placed only with Black families whether in foster care or for adoption. Black children belong, physically, psychologically and culturally in Black families in order that they receive the total sense of themselves and develop a sound projection of their future. Human beings are products of their environment and develop their sense of values, attitudes, and self-concept within their family structures. Black children in white homes are cut off from the healthy development of themselves as Black people. (Bartholet 1992c: 28)

For Bartholet, the NABSW's success in translating this position into policy and practice was largely due to the "threat" of "black power" that was "exercised directly or through the workers' professional peers" (28). Since previously unspoken agency rules were only temporarily lifted in favor of transracial adoption in the 1960s and then fully codified in the 1970s, U.S. adoption has been organized around racial matching policies both codified and unspoken. These matching policies continue to be upheld in present adoption practice and law, Bartholet argues, despite the fact that so many children wait to be adopted because of the racial mismatch between available children and prospective parents (Bartholet 1993: 95–99).

Against this historical backdrop, Bartholet argues that in prioritizing the racial match between parents and children, adoption policies promote separatism through families. They constitute a kind of anti-miscegenation tactic that re-roots biological notions of race in the adoptive family. The NABSW's argument that transracial adoption is a form of genocide is the strongest statement among many that "root" children in their community by imagining both race and culture as inhering in the child. Opponents of transracial (and transnational) adoption, argues Bartholet, invoke children as a natural—that is racial—resource that must be protected, while at the same time ignoring the child's actual interests, above all the need for a home (Bartholet 1992c).

In place of racial matching policies, Bartholet offers an invitation to a world in which racial meanings have changed. In *Family Bonds*, she offers a differently racializing view—a refiguration—of the child within the family, which in turn becomes a model of "common humanity" (Bartholet 1993: 143):

We can celebrate a child's racial identity without insisting that anyone who is born with a particular racial makeup must live within a prescribed racial community. We can recognize that individual members of various racial groups choose to define their identities and to define themselves in relationship to racial and other groups in an endless variety of ways. We can believe that people are fully capable of loving those who are not biologically and racially similar but are "other" and that it is important for more people to learn to do so. We can regard the elimination of racial hostilities as more important than the promotion of cultural difference.

From this perspective, which I share, transracial adoptive families constitute an interesting model of how we might better learn to live with one another in this society. These families can work only if their members have an appreciation of racial difference and love that transcends such difference. And the evidence indicates that these families do work. (112)

In this passage, Bartholet figures the transnational adoptee in terms of a very particular form of race, relatedness, and family. Unlike the NABSW's formulation, which attached the child to its community by virtue of its shared raciality and the unequal position of that raciality within the broader society, Bartholet's invocation of the child's inborn "racial makeup" does not in any way provide such a link. Instead, Bartholet figures the child in such a way that these differences do not matter. This child, with its "racial makeup" is entirely mobile, able to travel from one "racial community" to another. When a white family adopts a black child, it imports a child that is racially "other" because the child carries with it a given "racial makeup." This form of racialization realizes a world in which such travel becomes self-evidently unproblematic. This is due in part to the fact that racial makeup, as figured by Bartholet, quite specifically and insistently has no cultural content. Racial difference here cannot, and in fact must not be associated with cultural difference. And so Bartholet figures the adoptee as both a racialized body, and as one whose racialization is culturally insignificant.

This, in turn, constitutes the child as a body with certain kinds of choices. The child is figured as potentially having a "racial identity" in this figuration, but in contrast to racial makeup, this racial identity is entirely individualized. Insofar as the child has racial identity (as opposed to a racial makeup), the child nevertheless exercises a liberal "choice," such that the child is ultimately self-racializing. Once individualized and detached from a community and a shared identity, furthermore, this child can be "loved" as an "other" that is by virtue of this same liberal process of racialization, no longer "racially hostile" or "culturally different." It could be said that in this formulation, the child is figured in terms of a racial difference that is utterly surface, a racial makeup, a color, to which no cultural difference or community belonging is necessarily attached. In Bartholet's figuration of successful adoption, the transnational adoptee must be purely racial and purely individual. In this way, the child becomes "available" for adoption.

In frustration at the tenacity of arguments against transracial adoption that appeal to the child's "rootedness" through race and nation, Bartholet adds another benefit to her vision of the adoptive family as a model of racial harmony: "Maybe it is too threatening to think what might happen if people were not understood to belong to their racial, national, or other groups of origin, if they were free to merge across group lines, if they were free not to reproduce more of the group's 'own'" (Bartholet 1993: 43). What the child and its adoptive parents stand to gain from a revamped adoption system in Bartholet's vision is the freedom to merge, and to reproduce something other than the group's "own." This benefit is offered in part to support Bartholet's central contention that the best interests of black children should be defined above all as the need for a home. Her advocacy of transracial adoption relies on the contention that black children are being used in an "essentially adult agenda of promoting racial separation," rather than being ensured that their interests will be served. Anticipating the concern that black families have not been adequately recruited to adopt black children, Bartholet offers the following assessment:

> It is true that more could be done to find black families. More substantial subsidies could be provided and more resources could be devoted to recruitment. But it is extremely unlikely that our society will anytime soon devote more than lip service and limited resources to putting blacks in a social and economic position where they are capable of providing good homes for all the waiting black children. It will always be far easier to get white society to agree on the goal of placing black children in black homes than to get an allocation of financial resources that will make that goal workable. The danger in using black children to pry the money loose is that white society will not see these lives as warranting much in the way of ransom. (Bartholet 1993: 43)

Bartholet's argument for facilitating transracial adoption suggests both that institutionalized racism will prevent black families from becoming adoptive parents in any significant numbers, and that white families who adopt black children constitute a model of racial harmony that compensates for this structural deficit.

Alongside the explicit assumption that most black families are not capable of providing "good" homes because of their social and economic status, and as part of her argument that black-on-black adoption policies are unworkable and even immoral, Bartholet identifies benefits that accrue to black children if they are given the "freedom to merge." Among the resulting benefits of the adoptee's specific racialization is the possibility (offered by Bartholet as a counter to the claim that black children need skills for living in a racist society that only black parents can transmit) that whites "are in the best position to teach black children how to maneuver in the white worlds of power and privilege" (Bartholet 1993: 36). In addition, black children gain "a range of material advantages associated with having white parents and living in the largely white and relatively privileged world that such parents tend to frequent" (36). What does it mean, given Bartholet's description of current U.S. white society as one that does not value black children's lives, that she argues for the value of placing them in the midst of that very society? As William L. Pierce put it in his otherwise favorable response to Bartholet, this "comes perilously close to recommending, as a sort of utopian policy, trans-racial adoption over same-race adoption" (Pierce 1993: 54).

Bartholet is certainly justified in posing adoption as a potential threat to naturalized racial, ethnic, and national belonging. Refigurations of the adoptee, and associated adoption practices, can deconstruct compulsory reproductive heterosexuality as the basis of relationship by separating biological procreation from nurture. Adoption makes families from persons who are not related through biological procreation (and this includes intra-kin adoptions, like the adoption of children by their aunts and uncles, their grandparents, and so on). It can also deconstruct naturalized versions of national, racial, and cultural belonging because it refuses such naturalized ties as barriers to the placement of children. But the possibility of not reproducing more of the group's own is not guaranteed by the freedom to merge. Where power is involved, as in the relation between children and adults, or between different racial and national groups, merging might mean anything from a kind of mutual mutation to erasure, or assimilation.

I would argue, in fact, that in the absence of some kind of belonging prior to adoption, the adoptee figured as a body capable of uninhibited merging (if such a thing is possible) is precisely a reproduction of the group's "own," a figuration made in an economy of the same.

In Bartholet's vision of future adoption practices free of racial matching, the dissociation of race from biology or destiny, its dislocation from a discursive matrix in which race rooted the body in racial and national communities or groupings, is accompanied by a relocation of race to a discourse of choice, freedom, and movement, offered as an invitation to a seemingly anti-racist future. The value of choice, freedom, and movement are assumed in this invitation, but what is being offered along with the vision of racial harmony is greater freedom of choice for prospective (white) parents as consumers in the adoption market. Included in this choice is the choice of racial difference, which is extended to the child in the form of benefits named above, once that child has been adopted.

While it is certainly true that, as Bartholet points out, the practice of sealing adoption records serves to cut off the prior history of the child, the writing of that child's history either with or without that information is never simply given. Adoption imagined as the "freedom to merge" is a kind of morphing in that it proceeds by a similar process of evacuation, selection, erasure, and reinscription. Morphing is an example of this process, but more importantly, for my purposes here, it can be used as an interpretive tool. That is, it elucidates a mode of re-racializing reproduction that does not obey the rules of historical or biological logic. Given that morphing affords the programmer the possibility of regenerating undesirable images—in this case, offspring—morphing's capacity to evacuate history is joined by its capacity for reproduction by replacement, or reinscription. As a mode of figuration, morphing offers a choice of final outcomes, erasing both distant and much more recent histories, and replacing them by its particular mode of reproduction with an always renewable fund of images.

Time magazine's 1993 special issue on immigration coincided with the publication of Family Bonds, and coincides as well with its particular version of racialization. That is, it suggests a relationship between racialization, choice, and the dream of racial harmony that reads back on Bartholet's figuration of the adoptee. The cover of the Time immigration issue shows a head-and-shoulders shot of a smiling woman set against a background grid made up of smaller versions of the same image. "Take a good look at this woman," the caption beckons. "She was created from a mix of several races. What you see is a remarkable preview of . . . The New Face of America." The subtitle reads: "How Immigrants are Shaping the World's First Multicultural Society" (Time, 1993). The face on Time's cover was created as part of a larger project intended to "dramatize the impact of interethnic marriage" caused, say the editors, by recent U.S. immigration. Yet the key shaping agent for this cover girl, named the "new Eve" by Time, is not immigration, but morphing.

Morphing is the same technology that created Michael Jackson's Black or White video and Terminator II. Time used it for the "cybergenesis" of an immigrant nation, represented as a grid of faces. Along the top row of this grid, seven head-and-shoulder photographs of female models are arranged under seven headings: "Chinese," "African," "Anglo-Saxon," "Middle Eastern," "Italian," "Vietnamese," and "Hispanic." Photographs of seven male models labeled with the same seven headings are arranged along the left-hand column. These two series of images are cross-indexed to generate the offspring that would result from pairing each photograph in the top row with each one in the left-hand column. The remaining forty-nine cells of the grid are filled with computerized images representing these virtual offspring. They were generated by running each pair of photographs through a software program called Morph 2.0.

The seven categories mixed together to generate these images are not immediately recognizable as racial categories. They include what might otherwise be considered national (Vietnamese, Chinese, Italian), regional or continental (Middle Eastern, African), or other geographically specific terms (Anglo-Saxon, Hispanic). But they are, precisely, racialized in a particular way: what is being mixed, or more accurately, morphed, are purely physical and surface characteristics. In order for this racialization to occur, the original categories must be evacuated of the histories and politics of culture, geography, and nation that they might otherwise signify. This evacuation, and its specific form of racialization, are made clear by Time's description of the morphing process, in which specific parts of the face are identified as distinguishing features, and then coded as electronic dots. Among the key features chosen were "head size, skin color, hair color and texture, eyebrows, the contours of the lips, nose and eyes, [and] even laugh lines around the mouth" (66). In the resulting grid, the progeny are naked, pristine and untouched potentialities made by a computer and human. For as Time pointed out, the ratio of inputs from each of the photographs was up to the computer programmer. In one case, the 50–50 ratio of input from the two coupled images used for *Time*'s grid generated "a distinctly female face—sitting atop a muscular neck and hairy chest." Rejecting this particular mutation, the programmer simply remorphed the photographs to fit more conventional expectations. Even morphing produces unexpected, "pathological" results, but the undesirable offspring reproduced by the morphing process were simply remorphed according to taste.

This form of racialization does not consist, then, in the establishment of a hierarchy for domination based on biologized or even culturalized racial difference. Its violence—its racism—consists instead in the evacuation of histories of domination and resistance (and of all those events and ways of living that cannot be captured in those two terms), accomplished through morphing as a specific kind of technological (and heterosexual) reproduction. As Donna Haraway has put it, *Time*'s matrix constitutes a form of race mixing without miscegenation and all of the history that the latter term implies: "All the bloody history caught by the ugly word 'miscegenation' is missing in the sanitized term 'morphing.' Multiculturalism and racial mixing in *Time* magazine are less achievements against the odds of so much pain than a recipe for being innocently raptured out of mundane into redeemed time" (Haraway 1997: 264).

What the evacuation of history by morphing does for the "rebirthing of the nation" as well as the adoptive family and adoptee is to produce a space behind the surface, an empty body, on which to write a story. In both cases, that story is reinscribed as the merging of the global into a local U.S. hybridity that is quite precisely not about maintaining racial purity and sociopolitical segregation. The power of morphed reproduction in Bartholet's figuration of the child in transnational adoption, like *Time*'s rebirthing of the nation is not, paradoxically, the power to reproduce in the traditional sense of passing on characteristics, heritage, or even genes (Haraway 1995). Instead, it is the power to reproduce not only without the constraint of history, but without historical contingency.

While this power is largely symbolic, and therefore not equivalent to actually changing the salience of racialized categories, remaking the nation, or changing adoption policy, it is important to remember that the symbolic has material consequences. Even cybergenesis's virtual reproduction had such consequences, if desire can be considered a material effect: several of *Time*'s staff members are reported to have fallen in unrequited love with their Eve.[8] And while *Time*'s morphing produced desires that could not be fulfilled, transnational adoption directly fulfills the adult desire for a child that is made available for adoption. The practice of renaming adoptive children is one small example of the kind of reinscription through which such availability is accomplished. Bartholet's figuration of the adoptee's race is another. It makes the adoptee "racially" available by evacuating the child-body of a historically significant racialization, and replacing it with a "choice" of racial identity and the "freedom" to merge.

History as a Technology of Racialized Reproduction: Responses to Bartholet

The above discussion focuses on Bartholet's racial figuration of the child as adoptee, and the way this figuration enables and supports transracial and transnational adoption. In responding to Bartholet's call for a total elimination of racial matching policies in the "best interests of the child," contributors to *Reconstruction* working in the field of adoption law and practice both contest and applaud her arguments. In the process, they also offer their own racial figurations of the adoptee.

Many of the respondents adjust Bartholet's proposal for a total elimination of any agency or judicially directed stipulations regarding transracial placement of children. They offer variations of what Professor Anita Allen of the Georgetown University Law Center calls "particularized determinations" with regard to race (1992: 27). Only some of these counterproposals address the adoptee's racialization directly. One respondent, for example, proposes that a test should be used to determine potential parents' "capacity for racial 'sensitivity' " (Hollinger 1992: 50). Another observes that arguments for the deregulation of transracial adoption seem to ignore the "unmet need for healthy newborns among black prospective adoptive parents" (Pierce 1992: 54). Allen also suggests that there are valid reasons for the racial preferences of birth parents, adoption agencies, and adoptive parents, citing parental desires linking "culturally meaningful tasks" to "racial characteristics," such as a black woman's wish to corn row an adoptive daughter's hair and "lotion away her 'ash' " (Allen 1992: 47).

Not all of these responses are equally compelling; and many of them seem to succumb to a fairly narrow, and deterministically naturalized definition of blackness and familial relatedness. Among the responses published in *Reconstruction*, Lillian Lansberry's stands out as an effective alternative historical account of transracial adoption within the United States. In presenting this history, Lansberry reaches a conclusion regarding adoption policy that neither reverts to deterministic figurations of the black child, nor ignores the way that histories of racial inequality are embedded in the history of transracial adoption.

Lansberry begins with a history of adoption practice in the last three or four decades. Before the 1960s, according to Lansberry, the availability of healthy white infants converged with adoption policies, in which a desirable infant was defined as just such a healthy white infant from a "good" family, who could also pass as the biological offspring of the adoptive family. Similarly, adoption services were offered to white, middle-class (and presumably heterosexual) couples who owned their own homes. Proof of inability to conceive a child was frequently required, as was the guarantee that the woman intended to be a full-time homemaker. In an adoption economy dominated by white adults seeking healthy white children, and in the absence of any concerted efforts to recruit nonwhite adults as potentially adoptive parents, adoption policies effectively denied children of color (as well as disabled children, older children, and sibling groups) a place in the pool of adoptable children.

The makeup of this pool shifted in the 1960s because of various factors. Most important among these for Lansberry were the advent of the "pill," the legalization of abortion, greater acceptance of pregnancy and motherhood for unmarried women, and the attention focused on black, poor, and disabled children by the civil rights movement and the war on poverty. This shift was an important one for Lansberry, not so much because transracial adoption became possible, but because "the means by which adoption agencies refocused their services is at the very heart of the trans-racial adoption debate" (Lansberry 1992: 52). According to this account, racial matching policies and practices were overturned both in order to augment the numbers of children available to the same constituency of adoptive parents serviced by agencies in previous decades, and in order to facilitate the adoption of children previously disqualified from adoption.

For Lansberry, this shift translated into transracial adoption for quite specific groups of children and adults. That is, while the pool of "adoptable" children was expanded to include children of color—especially "mixed race" children[9]—the providers of adoption services and the clientele they served remained essentially the same. Though some attempts to recruit families of color were made at this time, the "trans" in "transracial" generally referred to the transfer of children of color into white families only. As Lansberry puts it, adoption agencies "unaccustomed to working with families of color" were "more comfortable trying to fit the existing children into the families of their adoptive applicants than they were in learning how to work with a new group of families" (Lansberry 1992: 52–53).

Lansberry does not support racial matching policies per se. But for her, the history of transracial adoption and its continued use in some private adoption agencies indexes the unwillingness on the part of "traditional" agencies to face the challenges necessary to recruit families of color successfully. Combined with the high fees that bar these disproportionately poorer families from adopting healthy children of color, "transracial" adoption continues to signify a one-way transfer of children of color into white families. Lansberry's criticism of adoption policy with regard to race (as well as disability and other categories traditionally deemed less desirable in a child) is directed at the ways in which adoption policies and practices constitute adoptive families through their selection of "adoptable" children and available, eligible adoptive parents. It is not so much that transracial adoption should be illegal, as that it exists in the absence of concerted efforts to recruit and provide services to families of color who, among other reasons for deserving equal treatment, possess historically devalued and extremely important skills for surviving racial discrimination. In conclusion, Lansberry neither advocates nor deplores transracial adoption. She advocates, instead, the selection of adoptive parents for children of color "who can ensure that their daily lives include a variety of healthy adult role models of their same racial/cultural background" (Lansberry 1992: 52–53).

While Lansberry stresses issues relating to the availability of children and parents for adoption, her account also suggests that desirability (What is a desirable child? What makes an adult desirable as a potential parent?) is so closely tied to availability as to make it nearly impossible to separate the two. Her refiguration of adoption with regard to race does refigure race, but not through the child. That is, she refigures the question of race in adoption as a problem of racism rather than the "match" (as either a positive or negative requirement) between the racialized bodies of adoptees and prospective parents. Instead of offering a vision of the adoptive white parent/black child family as a model of racial harmony, she holds out the possibility of an adoption system that would redress the inequalities by which black families have been denied equal access to children, and ensure the significant presence of black adults in the lives of adopted black children.

In both Bartholet's and Lansberry's accounts, the availability and desirability of children as well as parents in U.S. adoption emerge at the intersection of shifting adoption policies, political agendas, social conditions, and moral values, in which race and racism work alongside other significant factors. At issue in the debate about transracial adoption in the United States is the power to define the "best interests" of children, where children "belong," and what kinds of laws and policies will best achieve these ends. Lansberry's history suggests that these issues can be defined and articulated in different terms, which are not limited to positions for or against racial matching. This shift in terms also suggests a way of rereading arguments for the adoptive child's freedom to merge across racial lines. Lansberry's account suggests that this "freedom" should perhaps be constrained by a clearer historical understanding of who is "free," combined with a sharp attention to whose freedom is assumed to be at stake, who or what is being merged, and to what effect.

The responses in *Reconstruction*, including Lansberry's, are limited to the national U.S. debate about transracial adoption, and to the primarily black-on-white focus of that debate. While *Reconstruction* frames transracial adoption as a nationally relevant issue, adoption practices, choices, and politics have been significantly altered since the 1980s with the advent of transnational adoption. As I have already mentioned, the *Reconstruction* article appears in a slightly altered form in *Family Bonds*, where it is included in Bartholet's overall discussion of transnational adoption. *Family Bonds* situates the national debate addressed by "Where Do Black Children Belong?" in a larger framework of adoption at a transnational level, where notions of racial belonging are joined to national belonging as a critical nexus of contention.

Indeed, for Bartholet in *Family Bonds*, the special salience of transnational adoption lies in the fact that no matter how domestic policies change, the future of adoption lies in transnational rather than intranational adoption. For her, "the world divides into essentially two parts for adoption purposes, one consisting of countries with low birth rates and small numbers of children in need of homes and the other consisting of countries with high birth rates and huge numbers of such children" (Bartholet 1993: 141). This global mapping of children's availability is repeated with regard to potentially adoptive parents, but in inverse proportion. In

Western industrialized countries, there are large numbers of such parents, while in the "poorer countries of the world there are very few prospective adopters, in comparison with the vast numbers of children in need of homes" (141).

This mapping of available parents and children is neatly captured by the legal language of "sending" and "receiving" countries. Bartholet borrows this language to describe the current demographics of transnational adoption, where "sending" countries are those with a surplus of children, and "receiving" countries are those with a surplus of prospective parents (Bartholet 1993: 146). Given the current importance of transnational adoption both as an aspect of an increasingly globalized United States and in Bartholet's work, it is important to consider Bartholet's racialization of the adoptee in global terms as well as in the strictly national terms set out in *Reconstruction*. Furthermore, the assumed values of freedom, movement, and choice offered in Bartholet's vision of transracial adoption are linked, in the transnational domain, to an economy of supply (of "available" children) on the one hand, and demand (on the part of prospective parents), reproduction, and consumption on the other. This economy corresponds to the relation of poorer "sending" and richer "receiving" countries of the world.

Bartholet's racialization of the adoptee, this time in a global frame, is elucidated by another technology of racialized reproduction: Benetton's *Colors* magazine. Like *Time*'s morphing of a hybrid nation, Benetton's *Colors* magazine works here primarily as an interpretive tool, useful for describing a specific mode of (globalized) racialization. Liberalism, racialization, and consumption, all on a transnational scale, converge in *Colors*, whose 1993 spring/summer issue was devoted to race. Like all *Colors* issues, this one employs photography along with a playful use of color, language, and typography to make its point. In the manner of fashion magazines, the copy in *Colors* appears primarily as an adjunct to large and often compelling photographic images. Marked by the liberal use of mixed fonts and letter sizes, bold typefaces, exclamation points, and question marks, it comes in two languages, English and Italian. This bilingualism is just one of the many devices that promote Benetton as a global enterprise capable of representing race in all of its forms.

A particular strategy of racial reproduction runs through this dizzying assortment of visually laden pages: race is evacuated as a signifier of specific histories linked to contemporary social, political, and cultural worlds.

In this issue of the magazine, the photographic images and accompanying text are thematically arranged according to a series of different treatments of race. Reminiscent of nineteenth-century racial typologies in their use of individual head-shots and other isolated body parts to represent different racial types (Rony 1992; Stepan 1982), many sections in the series are devoted to an examination of race as a matter of physical difference registered on the surface of the body. Along with heads, there is a two-page spread of ears, a series of pages of full-length frontal nudes, and one showing different hair types beside two fingers of different skin shades delicately smeared with blood. While every head in the taxonomy of racial epithets is accompanied by a particular "who" (the group to which it belongs), "from" (its national and regional location), and "by" (the group that uses the epithet), the historical and contemporary specificity of ethnic groups and their relation to one another are absent. This contingency is displaced by the juxtaposition of heads from all over the world, such that each specific relation is simultaneously decontextualized and recontextualized in relation to other similarly decontextualized ethnic or racial relations. The use of the word "you," the reader, signifies the leveling of differences by this means, the evacuation of specific histories and significations, since the use of "you" holds a place for anyone and everyone, without the need to know anything about the reader in advance.

A second key factor in the evacuation of race is the reduction of race to color as a medium of difference (Lury 2000). The basis of race in ads featuring models representing a wide range of racial groups is no longer biological, no longer an unchanging essence. Benetton reproduces racialized change and diversity by changing its palette of colors (Lury 2000). Race is represented as color, and color is represented as a matter of choice. This reproduction of race proposes a pan-humanity of mix-and-match races-as-colors, recombinable according to taste. Identity remains racialized in Benetton's advertising campaigns, but the essence of this identity is diversity and change in a form—color—that is, ultimately, arbitrary. The two-page spread depicting a row of ears in different skin shades exemplifies this representation of race-as-color (Colors 1993: 12–13). One of the ears is labeled "orange skin?" Its caption reports that the orange tone is caused by an overdose of orange soda pop or mangoes, both of which contain large amounts of beta-carotene. Race, here, is reconstituted as color—the orange of soda pop or mango transferred to the skin.

If there is a thematic unity in this issue of Colors, it is not simply race, but

Figure 6: An advertisement for Philips makes use of the "global" child.

race as a mutable feature that can be altered by choice. This is also the case for Benetton advertising for children's clothing. The arbitrariness of race-as-color-by-choice is useful for thinking about racializations of the adoptee that suggest a similar shift from race as an essential quality to one that can be chosen. In such versions, race is as mutable as color, a medium of difference easily transferred and transformed by choice—the choice of families to adopt a child transnationally, and the child's choice of racial identity. Race-as-color-by-choice makes the "other" child available for adoption through deracination, in contrast to modes of racialization that would root the child to a particular place and community.

This version of race also grounds visions of transnational adoptive family as a model of racial harmony. The value of harmonious transracial and transnational adoption can be rendered in significant part through bodies made available by the reproduction of race as an individual choice. In particular, the child's race is imagined as a surface quality that can be detached, chosen, and finally rearranged in a different palette of colors. Against arguments that link a child to a given community, the adoptee here is racially mobilized, made "available" for adoption, and for a broader vision of racial harmony. Race-as-color is a medium of change and diversity that, perhaps most significantly, is also a medium of ownership: Benetton attempts to actually *own* diversity through its advertising campaigns (Lury 2000). An even more explicit instance of this racial commodification appears in *Colors* in the form of an advertisement for Philips, the electronics company (see Fig. 6). A two-page spread captioned "The universal language of Philips" shows two children, a white girl and a black boy, projected on a wide-screen television in a face-to-face close-up. Each is wearing a sweater with Benetton's trademark splashes of bright colors, and a woolen scarf. Each is wearing headphones, attached by differently colored wires to a single Philips CD player. The sweaters are identical in pattern, but different in their background color (red for the girl, blue for the boy). Benetton, here, lends Philips its ownership of diversity, while occupying the advertisement's visual space as a kind of price for the loan. At the same time, Philips itself claims its own "universal language." In an advertisement that could be titled "Philips, by Benetton," both companies multiply the use of race-as-color in their use of childhood to further their "innocent" ownership of an already arbitrary form of diversity.

Similarly, claims to the transracial and transnational adoptee as the (white) adoptive family's "own" can be made on the basis of the adoptee's racial mutability. While Benetton is concerned with the reproduction of race alone, adoption intertwines the reproduction of race with the generation of families. In corresponding visions, transnational adoption becomes a new reproductive technology of family relations that is also a new reproductive technology of race. Indeed, the mix-and-match of colors generates new relational ties just as the formation of these ties through transracial, transnational adoption generates a new selection of colors.

Incorporations

Adoption, morphing, and global marketing are not the same kinds of practices, nor do they produce the same material effects. I have used morphing and photography here as visual tools to elucidate the printed text and to describe the constitutive effects of adoption as a racializing technology that reproduces the adoptee. The affinities between these three technologies become more important in attempting to specify how transnational adoption debates are implicated in adoption as a transnational materializing practice. Just as adoption debates project imagined futures, so too Time's hybrid nation and Benetton's color-as-choice can be viewed as projections in time, visions of a re-racialized global future.

I gloss the affinities between these visions as "incorporation." From the Latin incorporare, or "the union in or into one body," the term "incorporation" signifies the process by which bodies are constituted as such (the union in one body). It also signifies the process by which a body is made from two or more separate entities (the union *into* one body).[10] In contemporary terms, this second kind of union includes a more specific process, by which economic enterprises gain a particular legal status. While the corporation is hardly new, in the late twentieth century it took on a particular global form: the multinational corporation. Incorporation, then, signifies three different kinds of processes: embodiment, inclusion, and enterprise. These processes, in turn, are associated here with three kinds of "globalized" bodies: the racialized "human" body; the "local-global" U.S. nation or (trans)national body; and the corporation. The technologies considered here in relation to adoption share with it a mode of racialized embodiment that becomes the basis for inclusion in a larger "global" body (the family, the nation, the world), enabled in part by a transnational economic enterprise (transnational adoption fees; Time, Inc.; Benetton).

The three kinds of "incorporations" considered here—Benetton's pan-humanity, *Time*'s immigrant nation, and the transnational adoptee with its racially harmonious family—all rely on unlimited, individual, and historically unburdened choice. Choice, in what some have called the new enterprise culture, is linked not only to desire, but also to culture's economization. Consumer choice is one of the hallmarks of this commodification. But consumer "choice," as anthropologist Marilyn Strathern (1992b) has argued, is severely constrained. The freedom of free enterprise for the consumer only constitutes choice within a limited range of options. And because procreation, she argues, "can now be thought about as subject to personal preference and choice [and] the child is literally—and in many cases joyfully—the embodiment of the act of choice," procreation, too, becomes subject to the limits of consumerism (34). The liberalization of adoption may be a way of serving the "best interests of the child," but it is also a means of increasing consumer choice in adoption—especially transnational adoption—which is at the moment a highly bureaucratic, confusing, and cumbersome procedure.

The figuration of the child's race-as-choice that is offered as a part of this argument implies that the goal of adoption policy liberalization is to figure the child's *race* as an aspect of the embodiment of the act of choice. In Bartholet's formulation, for example, this choice entails a form of racialization that will "promote the elimination of racial hostilities over the promotion of cultural difference" (Bartholet 1993: 112). I would argue, however, that this is a difference "chosen" to make no difference. The child "freed" for adoption is racialized as a body or space left open for the writing of a history, such that this writing, too, becomes an instance of "free" choice. Incorporation, here, works as a process of denaturalization rather than naturalization with regard to the racialized body. It disallows race as a natural fact, as something that means beneath the skin, but at the same time refuses it any historical or cultural significance. This is a relativizing, liberal mode of racialization, in which "race" is both empty and innocent. According to this multivalent signification, "incorporation" becomes a process of racialization working across the three technologies of adoption, morphing, and global marketing.

Finally, transnational adoption discourse can employ a specific mode of racialization to figure the child that is not unique to it. Other technologies are used to generate a similar mode of racialization in quite different cultural domains. This mode exists alongside virulent reassertions of utterly immutable, racially hierarchical terms. An adequate response to these divergent but equally problematic versions of race requires attention to the multivalent and contradictory ways that race is being generated and mobilized as the basis of various kinds of inequality and injustice. In the concluding section, I consider transnational adoption as a technology of the child in order to consider the particular figurations of the child-adoptee *in* and *as* a racialized body, keeping in mind these broader questions.

The Child as the Embodiment of Racial Harmony

At stake in the debate about transracial and transnational adoption is the power to define the kind of body and person that the child will become. In this child, the potential, the possibility, the hope at the heart of the adoption debate is embodied. I have argued that a specific figuration of the child as a mutably racial body is generated when adoption is imagined as a site not only of family making, but of racial and global harmony as well. What I want to emphasize here is that the child, more than the parents, is re-racialized in order to accomplish this harmony. This racialization renders the child newly available as the possible processual embodiment of parental (adult) desire. Not only does race take on a newly valued flexibility across the three technologies I have named, but in the case of transnational adoption, the child-body in particular is figured as transnationally and transracially flexible. Like *Time*'s hybrid but still adult offspring, the child is figured through the incorporation of global differences and embodies "harmonious" global relatedness: the child *becomes* the global.

The cultural critic bell hooks has argued that desire for relatedness with an Other—for my purposes the desire of U.S. adoptive parents for the foreign child—can "act as a critical intervention challenging and subverting racist domination, inviting and enabling critical resistance," but this remains "an unrealized political possibility" (1992: 22). It will remain unrealized, I would argue, both within transnational adoption and outside of it as long as visions of global relatedness maintain their innocence, continuing to evacuate history from race. These histories are not simply "available" for reappropriation, and children are not simply "available" for refiguration. The ways in which global relatedness is imagined and sustained should be accountable to history or, to be more specific, to histories of racial domination and resistance. When global relatedness is figured through the child, this vision should also be accountable to the child, and to the history of adult uses of the child that I am attempting to describe in this book.

Lillian Lansberry's alternative history of transracial adoption, mentioned above, provides one example of such an alternative. Lansberry addresses the history of racial inequalities by which children of color were made available to mostly white adults for adoption. In addition to Lansberry's alternative history, the recent history of what Kathleen Biddick (1993) has called "distributive maternity" among whites and blacks disturbs the simple mapping of available children and desiring adults. Distributive maternity refers to how reproductive technologies (including sterilization) locate reproductive labor among women disproportionately by race and class—and, I would add, location in transnational circuits of exchange (Mohanty 1991). Poor women of color in the United States and poor women of many ethnic and racialized groups in the Third World have been subjected to forced sterilization, and suffer higher rates of infertility and infant mortality. At the same time, scientific resources and public investment in maternity are distributed in favor of the comparatively fewer middle- and upper-class heterosexual women of the dominant races with infertility problems, especially white women in industrialized countries (Biddick 1993; Williams 1991; Davis 1983). The problems related to maternity among the first group of women are largely ignored, partly owing to the representation of these women as the cause of overpopulation and as unable to care for the children they produce—thus the notion of "sending" countries as sources for a steady supply of children. How would notions of children's availability for adoption change if such issues were taken into account?

So far, I have concentrated on racialization as a focal point in this aspect of the adoption debate, and on the relation between race, histories of racial inequality, and their manifestation in terms of how children are made "available" for transracial and transnational adoption. There are other questions to be asked about adoption and its specific incorporations, however, and these are questions about the child: What kind of Other is a child? An adoptee? A foreign child? What kind of "race"—or gender, or sexuality, or any one of so many other social categories—"belong" to a child? What kind of history "belongs" to a child? And how can we answer these questions in a transnational domain when these questions may be answered differently in different cultural communities? To the problem of imagining forms of global relatedness that work against inequalities as they are being generated now, in global cultural forms, this analysis of transnational adoption adds the problem of the child as a body in process. And this problem is posed not just for adoption policy but for other social practices and for cultural theory as well.

The mutability of the child figured as a body in process makes it eminently appropriable; not yet fully formed, it has no prior being that must be displaced and then re-placed. It only has to become, according to taste. Perhaps this is not the familiar, liberal individualism that it might at first appear to be. Perhaps the new world order poses new forms of inequality that do not work in terms of immutable, "natural" attributes. Perhaps they work, instead, through change, through the power to change an other according to taste, or to become an other by appropriation. If so, perhaps we must imagine a different kind of figuration that resists both naturalization and those forms of denaturalization—or deracination—that refuse relevant histories. Such an alternative figuration would also refuse the simple "availability" of children for adult visions of the future.

This said, I think it is important to emphasize again the fact that racialization is only a small part of how children are made available for transnational adoption. Missing from my own account, in particular, is any mention of the extent to which the practice of transnational adoption itself actually produces available children. One of the fundamental premises of transnational adoption is that the children who are adopted will have been spared an economically and emotionally impoverished existence. But transnational adoption is a form of commodification. Even leaving aside the question of whether children—as opposed to adoption services—are being bought and sold in the process of transnational adoption, the key point is that money and children change hands within closely linked circuits of exchange. Children, in other words, are exchanged for money. It is not too surprising, given this commodification, that there have been documented cases of child stealing for the purposes of transnational adoption. Of what, then, does the child's value consist in a transnational market, and for whom?

This chapter has considered the child's racialization, associated realizations of transnational relatedness, and the value of the transracial and transnational adoptee primarily from a U.S. local-global point of view. The value of a child in the transnational adoption market is clearly also generated in and through the inequalities that constitute a given set of local-global economic, social, and cultural relations. These inequalities make transnational adoption desirable as well as possible. The nature of such inequalities has also been dramatically rendered by rumors circulating through the global media that children are stolen for a transnational trade not just in adoptees, but in organs. The term "rumor" that has been attached to reports of child stealing for organ theft suggests that not only children, but also "facts" are accorded value differentially within transnational circuits of exchange. What, then, is the value of a child in transnational circuits of exchange, and for whom? And what is the value of the child figured in the transnationally circulating rumor of child-organ theft, and for whom?

4
Rumored Realities: Child-Organ Theft

In the spring of 1994, news stories and images about an attack on a U.S. tourist suspected of stealing a child for organ theft in a southwestern Guatemalan town hit newspaper stands and flashed across television screens. Alongside the image distributed by Reuters of June Weinstock, a fifty-two-year-old woman lying comatose in a hospital bed and pierced with tubes connecting her to life-sustaining machines, it is possible to detect the shadowy figure of a child, its body cut open for organ harvesting. This chapter is about the child's figuration in the organ-stealing story, not so much in terms of the process of figuration itself, but more in terms of the multiple truths that the child's figurations realize.[1] Focusing on the Weinstock incident, I consider a range of local-global media reports and accounts of the child-organ stealing rumor in terms of which versions of the "true real" they figure.

My concern with the question of truth mirrors that of media reports on the child-organ stealing story: Are the child-organ stealing stories true, or do they merely speak of otherwise unnamed or displaced anxieties? Is the rumor only an index of other anxieties, as some media reports have claimed, or does the rumor speak of a silenced, unspeakable reality, of stolen children and child-bodies divested of their organs? Already identified as a rumor in media reports, the child-organ stealing story's truth is automatically put into question, and yet not definitively refused. How, then, to assess the rumor's truth, and the status of the child-figure at its center?

The rumor's plural tellings across different local-globals index the existence not only of specific worlds, but also of potentially quite different ontological groundings, and accompanying standards of evidence, legitimacy, and morality. Consequently, the rumor's child-figure and its "truths"—are children really being stolen for organ harvesting, or does this child-figure simply signify other anxieties and concerns?—must be considered in relation to the standards by which the truth of the real is established as such. In this chapter, I address the force and value of the child-organ stealing rumor across its different local-global tellings. At the heart of this discussion is the question of which "real" the child-organ stealing stories really realize. Whose evidence will count as valid in deciding the stories' truth or falsity, and who decides?

One way of thinking about child-organ stealing stories as they are disseminated transnationally through the media is to posit a general category, in relation to which specific tellings of the story are particular versions. The child figured in these stories is consequently both "different" in each telling and "the same" child figured in a variety of ways. Individual accounts of the rumor intersect as this "same," insofar as the child-figure (like the story itself) is intelligible at all across the story's different tellings. In describing the story's child-figure in this way, I draw on Jean Comaroff's (n.d.) analysis of the relation between specific instances and "generic categories." Comaroff suggests that this relation requires a "double vision." I also draw later on Michael Taussig's analysis of how a similarly doubled vision enables one to see power working through indeterminacy. Together, these theoretical formulations provide a way of accounting for the existence of multiple, located versions of the real across different local-global domains.

In her discussion of "the child at risk" in transnational contexts, Comaroff suggests that this "generic" category derives its power from "the tension between the general sign and the particular instance" (n.d.: 9). This relationship between the generic and the particular is paralleled, in Comaroff's discussion, by the relationship between the global and the local. As global effects take local shape, she suggests, stories about children at risk and the anxieties they reproduce also change (25–26). For example, in Nigeria, Cameroon, and South Africa, witches are said to steal children and eat their souls, while in the United States, child sexual and physical abuse has become the quintessential form of risk to the child (13–15, 20–21). So the global category of "the child at risk" takes incommensurate forms in specific locations that are nevertheless intelligible under that general category.

This articulation of the relationship between generic categories and particular instances allows for the possibility that the "child" as it is figured in specific local-global versions of the child-organ stealing rumor may also be figured as "global," where the "global" is generic, and the "local" is particular. Comaroff's account of the relationship between the "general" and the "specific" as mutually dependent kinds of invocations is useful for my purposes in this sense, but it does not locate the "general" in relation to the "global" specifically enough. I suggest that "global" figurations of the child, which may also be "generic," are themselves located in specific local-globals. Generic figurations, in other words, are a particular kind of figuration, which are also located. So the child's figuration as "global" is itself necessarily a located, particular instance of the general category "child" (or, in Comaroff's account, "the child at risk"). By definition, it is not possible for a figuration to be general, which is to say unlocated.

Comaroff also suggests that publicly circulating stories about risks posed to children simultaneously name the actual victimization of children, and condense a multitude of anxieties, thereby "collaps[ing] into one carnal sign, diverse sources of angst about an endangered mode of domestic reproduction; about the breakdown of the nuclear family and the commercialization of bodies, procreation, and childcare; about sharp shifts in a gendered division of labor" (Comaroff n.d.: 25–26).[2] It is this double work of stories that I wish to emphasize here as a feature of the child's multiple figurations in the rumor's distinct local-global locations. A rumor is a particular kind of story, which can metaphorically describe fears and raise moral questions; the same story may also chronicle realities otherwise denied (26; see also Shapiro 1994). The child-organ stealing rumor's "truths," told as it travels by word of mouth and through the global media, may therefore lie in both metaphorically and materially consequential details.

But which details are consequential? Like all comparative work, the comparison of "reals" I undertake in this chapter, does not function without some basis against which different instances are made comparable in the first place. I use my own reading of the child's figuration in the "original" rumor as a point of comparison here, for want of a better alternative. Neither an objective nor a disinterested reading, my account of the child's figuration draws again on Comaroff's location of organ-stealing rumors in a wider context of the economization of bodies linked to modern technologies of extraction and commodification (Comaroff n.d.: 18–19). From this point of view, the child-organ stealing story highlights the shifting value of the child that is generated in relation to specific technological practices, namely organ extraction and transplantation, in a global economy.

It is through its imbrication in this globalized and unequal system of exchange that the story's child is literally globalized, its body parts disseminated transnationally. Figured as a collection of organs distributed unequally in transnational circuits of exchange, this child becomes a set of exchangeable body parts, and so too one among many other "global" commodities. The child figured in the story as the victim of organ theft therefore figures particular workings of global capital (a transnational trade in body parts), and the possibilities generated by modern medical science and technology (the possibility of organ transplantation). Because "rumors" about child-organ stealing have been repeatedly associated with the "fact" of transnational adoption, the story's child also figures the documented value of children in a transnational market (child stealing for transnational adoption).

The rumor's dissemination and the dissemination of body parts that it narrates present at least two categories of children existing within an economized, global domain. The child in pieces conjured by the story's insistent reproduction is also distributed to other bodies in other parts of the globe that receive its missing organs. In some accounts, the organs of a poor Latin American child are bought by wealthy foreigners to harvest organs for their own children. Thus the organs of one child are made available to another body, usually a child, through the practice of harvesting. The two child-bodies figured in the story are first, the child whose organs are removed, valued only as a body in pieces; and second, the child who receives the organs. The second child is valued within this same global economy as a whole body, one who deserves the "gift of life" (see Scheper-Hughes 1990, 1992). Its value is figured not in body parts, but in the form of bodily integrity and continued life, presumably at any cost.

A third child-figure also haunts the child-organ stealing story. The harvested child-body in pieces can be read as the figuration of an absent body as well. In some versions of the story, the harvested child-body itself, or some of its pieces, are never found. In this case, it is not the organ alone that is transferred from one child to another, but life itself. The child-body's figuration in the story works through the resulting absence of the harvested child-body as a whole body through its presence as an absence, and through a kind of indeterminacy that extends as well to all three of the child-bodies figured in the rumor.

One feature of this indeterminacy, along with that of the child-body's status (how many bodies? whose body? whose value?), is the lack of separation between the economic and the cultural that is implied by the harvested child-body's place in a global economy of value. The child is exchanged as a living commodity whose value is rendered through economic means. This economic value on the world market transforms the child-body's cultural value as well. The value of life (in the case of the organs) endows the poor child with value in a global cultural economy that it does not otherwise necessarily have for its own sake.[3]

Using the triple, indeterminate bodily figuration of the child that I read in the child-organ stealing story as a point of departure, I turn now to the question of the story's truth, as this truth is generated in a range of media reports. I read the story's multiple tellings as variations on a story that is simultaneously general and specific. That is, I read figurations of the child across its multiple tellings as contested figurations of the "same" child. The point of the exercise is not to distinguish different figurations of the child from one another, but to identify different realizations of truth and falsehood in relation to the "same" child and the "same" organ-stealing story.

Locating Rumors

A basic premise of my discussion is that a story's value and power change depending on where it is retold as well as heard. Considered in these terms, the child in the organ-stealing rumor accrues value across its plural tellings in multiple, specifically located worlds. However, this value is not necessarily consistent or coherent, but can also be heterogeneous. A rumor and its figurations are not easily pinned down, not so much because its origins cannot be traced but more because its power lies precisely in its capacity to inspire its own replication, its fascinated retelling and embellishment. Given that the global media has been issuing stories on child-organ trafficking since 1987 (Pukas 1995), long before the Weinstock incident took place, any possibility of determining an original site for child-organ stealing rumors gives way to the necessity of locating the rumor in terms of its circulation, and its specific if indeterminate effects.

I began my discussion of child-organ stealing stories with the Weinstock incident, in which the rumor reportedly incited a violent attack on an innocent tourist in San Cristóbal Verapaz. The fascination and panic that swirl around the child-organ stealing rumor can be located in Guatemala, where the incidents took place, but also in the reporting on the incidents, which tell of the rumor and in so doing refigure the child and circulate the rumor once again. Redrawing the contours of the event that took place in San Cristóbal to include the global media's dissemination of reports on the incident reorients the child-organ stealing rumor and its effects to the "global" sites of its dissemination.

The Weinstock story was covered not only by the major Guatemalan newspapers, magazines, and Guatemala City-based Notisiete TV,[4] but also by newspapers, magazines, and magazine-style television programs in the United States and Europe. Disseminated transnationally by Reuters's international news service, the story appeared on the April 5 edition of the *New York Times* International page under the headline "Foreigners Attacked in Guatemala." The lead sentence read: "Fed by rumors that Americans were coming to kidnap children, cut out their vital organs and ship them to the United States for transplantation, an extraordinary wave of panic has swept Guatemala over the last month." In addition, Reuters distributed internationally three-minute excerpts from videotapes of the attack on Weinstock that had been made available to Guatemalan cable television viewers in their full five-hour length (Kadetsky 1994). The British Broadcasting Corporation (BBC) and the U.S. television newsmagazine 20/20 also produced and aired documentaries on the question of child-organ harvesting that featured the Weinstock story.

Although these reports differed in the analysis they offered, they generally repeated the child-organ stealing rumor in some form, as part of the circumstances of the attack on Weinstock. Most accounts reported that a group of approximately seventy-five men stormed the courthouse where Weinstock had been taken by local authorities pending further investigations of the allegations made against her. Armed with a truckload of machetes and metal poles brought by a crew of striking road workers, the crowd torched the courthouse and attacked Weinstock, who remained in a comatose state at the time of the reports. Many international news reports also linked the attack on Weinstock to three other incidents in which local residents in rural Guatemalan towns took violent action against visiting foreigners suspected of stealing children, possibly for organ harvesting ("Foreigners Attacked in Guatemala" 1994; Perera 1994; Morello 1994; Frankel and Orlebar 1994; Orlebar 1994; Gleick 1994; Kadetsky 1994).[5]

International news media accounts of the Weinstock incident tended to concentrate on analyzing how such an evanescent thing as a "wave of panic" could be provoked by the child-organ stealing rumor. How could a mere rumor work so powerfully as to result in the absolutely material fact of June Weinstock's comatose condition? These international reports also tended to locate the rumor's power within Guatemala as a nation, or within its rural regions. But again, the story's newsworthiness as evidenced by its distribution through the global media suggests that this power worked beyond Guatemalan national boundaries. The rumor was not only told, but also resonated across plural imaginaries that cannot be located only within Guatemala or its rural and largely indigenous populations.

The Global Media's Child-Organ Stealing Rumor

Mob attacks in Guatemala on two American women suspected of kidnapping children for organ transplants may have been part of a right-wing strategy to create a climate of instability hostile to human-rights monitors. In the more serious of the two incidents, June D. Weinstock, an environmental writer from Fairbanks, Alaska, was engulfed by an enraged mob in San Cristóbal Verapaz, in the Mayan Highlands, after she was seen caressing a child whose mother reported him missing immediately afterwards.—Victor Perera, Los Angeles Times, 1 May 1994

International media reports on the rumor took the possibility of plural and even locally global worlds into account in the process of establishing a standard of validity for the rumor. According to this standard, the only truth of the rumor was its compelling and powerful effect *as* a rumor; the story told by the rumor, and its figuration of the child as the victim of organ harvesting, was granted no foundation in truth, and no claim on the real. The examples that follow suggest some of the available strategies for establishing this standard: First, the term "rumor" itself—as opposed to a verifiable fact or even an authorized suspicion—was used to signify the absence of any serious threat. Second, these reports created a distance between a rational "us" and an indigenous Guatemalan "other" mired in mythological fantasies. Third, the "other" who acts in response to the rumor was represented as psychically inhabiting a prior historical time (see Fabian 1983, discussed in chapter 1). Together, these strategies undermined the authority of the rumor's account of a possible reality, insisting that the potential danger to children that it claimed (being kidnapped for organ theft) was in fact nonexistent. As a result, the child-figure that appears within these located global imaginaries always ultimately signifies something other than itself; it is a powerful icon, a symbol, a signifier. This child-figure's power lies precisely in its capacity to signify, to embody, and even to incite, realities other than those explicitly claimed by the rumor in which it appears.

It is important to note that these strategies were used in reports sympathetic to democratic and human-rights efforts in Guatemala, as well as those that contributed to the silence about possible human-rights abuses by failing to address these issues at all. The suspicion voiced by Perera in the article cited above was based on the notion that the military had much to gain by orchestrating a violent incident like the beating of June Weinstock. The spring of 1994 marked a watershed in Guatemala's thirty-three-year undeclared civil war in which the military-controlled government, backed by the United States, had waged a genocidal campaign against its largely indigenous and poor population. Naming anyone a guerrilla or subversive justified his or her murder, and by this convenient means the military massacred entire highland communities, as well as individual middle-class ladinos[6] suspected of sympathizing with the opposition to military rule or to the economic exploitation of 87 percent of the Guatemalan population (Manz 1988; Jonas 1991). That spring, peace talks in Mexico between the civilian government and leftists guerrillas of the Guatemalan National Revolutionary Union (URNG) had resulted in an agreement to permit a United Nations truth commission to investigate human-rights abuses on both sides. In Guatemala, the Grupo de Apoyo Mutuo (GAM, or the Mutual Support Group, headed by Nineth Montenegro), offered the following analysis: according to the Global Accord on Human Rights agreed on by the Guatemalan government and the URNG, international observers designated by the United Nations would be present to monitor human rights in the country. Incidents such as the beating of Diane Weinstock could impede that process, and GAM called for the authorities to investigate the causes of that violent attack (White 1994). In the *Los Angeles Times* Opinion section (quoted in the epigraph above), Victor Perera (1994) observed that "the military's displeasure with this agreement is hardly surprising, as foreign observers accuse them of responsibility for as much as 95% of human-rights violations committed by all sides during Guatemala's 33-year war of counterinsurgency." In other words, it was the military that stood to lose by foreign investigations of human-rights abuses, and it was the military that would benefit from a disruption of the plan by making Guatemala seem unsafe for foreigners.

Reports siding with this analysis cited the presence of two known military men in the crowd of Weinstock's attackers; the appearance of a crew of workers who provided the men with sticks, which they used to beat Weinstock; and the late arrival of military assistance as evidence that the military was indeed involved in manipulating fears about child stealing for organ trafficking to their own ends (Frankel and Orlebar 1994; Kadetsky 1994; Orlebar 1994; White 1994). A *Newsweek* report offered evidence of "curious circumstances" surrounding the Weinstock incident, as well as a prior attack: "Reliable sources have told *Newsweek* that two members of Guatemalan military intelligence were spotted inciting the crowds that attacked the Santa Lucia police station while [Melissa] Larson was held inside. And a cameraman taped San Cristóbal police doing nothing while Weinstock was nearly murdered—even though the missing child had already turned up safe" (Frankel and Orlebar 1994). The article provided this evidence as support for the "theory . . . [that] right-wing opponents of President Ramiro de León Carpio are stirring up the anti-American sentiments to embarrass the government and to sabotage any movement toward democratic reforms" (Frankel and Orlebar 1994: 24).[7]

The military may well have harnessed the power of the child-organ stealing rumor for its own explicitly political ends within Guatemala, but the question remains, once such a possibility is entertained, why this particular rumor might have been available and effective as a means of generating such powerful effects. Never questioning the power of the child-organ stealing rumor as a galvanizing force, some accounts explained this power by invoking long-standing, sometimes universal myths or fears. Writing for the *Los Angeles Times*, Edward Orlebar suggested, for example, that the "hysteria . . . builds on [the] local legend of Miculash, a Guatemalan bogeyman who stole children to make soap out of them" (Orlebar 1994: A22). In the *Los Angeles Times* Opinion section one month later, Victor Perera argued that the attacks on foreigners "tap into indigenous fears that are at least 500 years old" (Perera 1994: M1). He then attributed these fears to the fact that "when the Spanish conquistadors invaded the Guatemalan Highlands in the 16th Century, Mayan mothers believed the men with pale complexions and blond beards were anemic, and required the blood of brown-skinned infants to become well." Perera's account further suggested that these "ancient" fears may have "resurfaced" owing to the well-documented increase in child abduction for the purposes of adoption. According to Perera's editorial, the Guatemalan Attorney General "reports 20 kidnapping rings and at least 65 fattening houses operating in Guatemala" (M6). While there were documented risks to Guatemalan children because of child theft for adoption, these reports suggested, the fear of child-organ stealing belonged not to the present, but to a distant, ancient past.

Perera's opinion piece included a version of the rumor in which a child is found dead as a result of organ theft, with U.S. one dollar bills and a thank you note stuffed in its wounded body. A similar version of the rumor was also narrated in a *Village Voice* article by Elizabeth Kadetsky entitled "Guatemala Inflamed." The latter report described San Cristóbal as "a small town wired together with rumors, the cables that wire a collective unconscious" (Kadetsky 1994: 25). By tapping into these cables, the author claimed to have reconstructed the events leading up to Weinstock's beating. Here the power of the rumor to incite violence was attributed, with the help of a linguist from Guatemalan City named Boris Martínez, to the *indígena* Pokonchí language's oral (rather than written) mode of communication.[8] Quoting Martínez, the article described this oral mode as follows: "People tend to hear something and they repeat it. This is an oral society. . . . This is how knowledge is passed on, and often something is added" (25). But the rumor was not authorized here as legitimate knowledge or assessment of risk, precisely because of the oral mode's infidelity, its uncertain reproduction—the "something . . . added." In this account, the workings of oral culture disseminated a fear based not in knowledge, but in myth.

Like the accounts of the Weinstock incident, the *Village Voice*'s version invoked the power of myth in *indígena*, "oral" culture as an explanation for the power of the child-organ stealing story. But perhaps because it was concerned with the "female face" of the rumor as an indicator of the "national fixation on body parts" this account invoked the myth of La Llorona, said to be the lover of the Spanish conquistador Cortés (Kadetsky 1994: 27). "La Llorona," wrote Kadetsky in a storyteller's mode, "so curses the betrayal of the murderous white man and colonizer that she slips off to the nearest river and drowns her new infant, the first offspring of a white and Indian union. Forever after, La Llorona, the wailing woman, slinks along late-night riverbanks as she howls her song of mourning, searching for her lost child and snatching those children unlucky enough to cross her path" (27–28). According to this account, the fear of La Llorona's mournful quest lives on in the bodies of contemporary indígena children: "Throughout Latin America and in Guatemala, where memories of conquest remain central to Mayan culture, children shiver on windy nights in fear of La Llorona's thieving grip" (28).

Orlebar's *Los Angeles Times* account also located the cause of Pokonchí indígena peoples' actions in legend, but in contrast to the *Village Voice*'s reliance on a largely cultural and historical explanation, Orlebar attached the rumor to the Guatemalan military's exploitation of already-existing fears associated with the organ-stealing legend. Similarly, Perera's account represented the indígenas who carried out the attacks as motivated both by ancient forces operating in the present, and as emotional receptacles for military manipulations of the rumor. In Orlebar's account, the rumor's terrors were literally reproduced by the military in indígena residents, who in turn acted upon that fear. In either case, the indígena people were represented as acting only when acted upon, as reacting in response to unfounded rumor, though also expressing reasonable fears.

Kadetsky's *Village Voice* article also offered an alternative assessment of the rumor. This alternative appeared in the words of Elena Ixcot, a Guatemalan leader then living in exile in Vermont, U.S. Countering the possibility that the fears of baby snatching might be considered "part of some Mayan cosmovision," Ixcot offered the following analysis in the published interview:

We Mayans are always talked about as pagans, satanists, savages, tons of names, an underdeveloped culture. What is true is that a system of terror arrived in this country in 1523, and this is deep in our minds. When we were growing up we wouldn't walk around alone because they said the cars would take us away. But this is because we've been violated, invaded first by Spaniards, then by the U.S. in the [military coup] of 1954. There is a system of terror and death that has always been in people's minds. (Kadetsky 1994: 27)

Like Perera's and even Orlebar's versions, this narrative relocated invocations of the "ancient" in a historical legacy of invasions such that indígena people's fears were linked to historical events as well as contemporary conditions. From Ixcot's point of view, repetition of the rumor and the acts to which they gave rise constituted reasonable, if not necessarily always accurate, assessments of risk under an ongoing system of impunity.[9]

In contrast to other versions of the Weinstock incident, Kadetsky's *Village Voice* rendition pointed out that while the events cited took place mostly between foreigners and indigenous Guatemalans in rural areas, the fear of child-organ stealing had spread more widely. Middle-class Guatemalans were also circulating the rumor in various forms, and protecting their children on sight of a foreigner. Noting that "the beating in San Cristóbal should not suggest that gruesome fantasizing about the First World is restricted to rural Indians," Kadetsky then recounted the rumor as told in a middle-class home in the capital, Guatemala City:

> A family visiting Houston to recuperate from the tragic kidnapping[10] of their nephew sees the nephew on the street. The boy has no eyes— they've been gouged out for corneal transplants. The storyteller then tells a version of the one about the busload of eight, or 10, or 16 child corpses, one eviscerated and stuffed with dollar bills. On top sits a note reading in English, "This is for the boy's funeral." This took place in Santa Lucía, or Guatemala City. Or even in Southern Mexico. (Kadetsky 1994: 26)

This account extended "gruesome fantasizing" from the indígena population to the middle class in Guatemala. It also refused the possibility that there might be any validity to the risk of child-organ stealing feared by those who repeat the rumor and act on it as a possible truth. Kadetsky concluded, with Orlebar and Perera, that there was no actual risk of children being stolen for their organs.

These reports seem to make little use of the child-figure; the child disappears from the field of vision as the child-organ stealing story is debunked as rumor. Just as the above reports attributed the child-organ stealing rumor's power to incite a violent attack to various causes, they also denied the rumor's legitimacy as a description of potentially multiple truths. That is, while they duly noted the dangers posed by the Guatemalan military, the legacy of colonialism, and neocolonial forms of oppression, these accounts lent no authority to the potential danger of child-organ stealing named most explicitly in the rumor. Child-organ stealing itself was reproduced as an unfounded rumor, while the rumor of organ theft was posed as a danger to the Guatemalan peace process. It was this latter version of the rumor that was authorized as the more rational and politically valid. For the most part, the child-organ stealing rumor realized these truths, not truths about the child itself. Like many other figurations of the child, this one, as described by and in these media reports, constitutes a use of the child-figure and its attendant value for other ends. The child-figure remains salient in the making of this account, if only insofar as the media reports narrate the child-organ stealing stories as a rumor.

In some reports the child-body figured in the rumor is replaced by another figuration of the child, which realizes an alternative truth. In Kadetsky's account, this alternative child-figure appears in a global economy of value, much like the one I have described in my own description of the story's child-figure. Kadetsky identified an opposition between the "high value placed on babies" and the "terrifying cheapness of life" that "can seem like a form of national dismemberment" (Kadetsky 1994: 28). At the heart of this dismemberment was the figure of a child, "ripped" from its mother's arms, not for organ harvesting, but for adoption. "I say ripping," Kadetsky wrote, "because babies are known to be literally snatched from their mothers as well as lifted from hospital beds, swindled from illiterate women who unknowingly sign the wrong papers, bought for sums ranging from pennies to thousands of dollars, and even commissioned from prostitutes who agree to get pregnant" (28). It is not the child-organ stealing story's figuration of the child that works to realize this global and bodily economy of value, but yet another figure that appears in Kadetsky's alternative account.

Counter-Stories:
The Child-Body in Pieces as Misinformation

In addition to news reports on the child-organ stealing rumor that focused on Guatemala, others represented the rumor in terms of fears dispersed across a "modern" and global terrain. Newspaper reports countered the child-organ stealing stories as a "modern urban legend." The modern urban legend is a category used by folklorists to describe the child-organ stealing rumor as a false, but powerful story (Campion-Vincent 1990; Turner 1992; Brunvand 1993). Here, the missing child-body in pieces embodied fears associated with modernity—with the power of medical technologies in concert with economic inequalities on a global scale. Some reports that identified the rumor in this way insisted that its power was so great that it had confused the United Nations, the European Parliament, and the readers of the global news, as well as the citizens of San Cristóbal Verapaz. This confusion arose not because of ancient myths or even national political conditions, but because of these more generic and universal fears.

The modern urban legend concept was frequently used in reports that explicitly countered the child-organ stealing story, including those issued and promoted by the United States Information Agency (USIA) Program Officer for Countering Misinformation and Disinformation. Charged with responding to false stories seen to be damaging to the United States government or its citizens, Todd Leventhal, the program officer, estimated that he had spent eighty percent of his nine years in office (beginning at the end of the Cold War) countering the child-organ stealing or "baby parts" rumor. In his reports for the USIA, Leventhal often cited folklorist Véronique Campion-Vincent, who suggested that the "baby-parts story shows a mixture of spontaneous creation and sophisticated manipulation that is characteristic of our global village" (Campion-Vincent 1990: 9).[11]

In keeping with this description, Leventhal's own work concerned the child-organ stealing rumor as it had been reported in the world "prestige" press (Leventhal 1994). In fact, rumors in general only posed a significant danger for the United States and its citizens, according to the program officer, when those initially carried by word of mouth came to be reported in the world media (Leventhal 1995a).[12] The dangers posed by the child-organ stealing rumor, then, lay not simply in the fact that it was a false story, but even more in the fact that world media coverage exponentially increased the rumor's own prolific reproduction, its capacity to captivate. Not only had the global media circulated the child-organ stealing rumor more widely, but it had also authorized the story as true. For Leventhal, this was a significant problem.

As his USIA report suggested, early media coverage of child-organ stealing did not report the story as completely false. Indeed, child-organ stealing was first published as a fact, and authorized as such through the testimony of judges and other officials. In the 1980s, both the London *Daily Telegraph* (Mauro 1988) and France's *L'humanité* (Pinero 1987) published reports of child-organ trafficking in Brazil. *L'humanité* also published follow-up reports documenting further cases of child-organ trafficking in 1988 and 1992 (Cordier 1988; Pinero 1992). The United Nations, the European Parliament, and numerous newspapers, as well as a number of television magazine programs and documentary films, also maintained the rumor as a valid allegation according to Leventhal's report. *Le Monde* also documented cases of child-organ stealing as part of a report on the European Parliament's official ban on organ trafficking in 1993 (Scotto 1993). In addition, various United Nations investigations on child-organ trafficking had been undertaken, leaving the special investigator convinced of the existence of such trafficking in spite of inconclusive evidence (United Nations Economic and Social Council 1993, 1994a, 1994b). These conclusions, too, were cited in news reports.

Leventhal's strategy for countering "true" reports of the story was also partially devoted to providing counter-evidence.[13] Later media reports countering the child-organ stealing rumor's claims often cited Leventhal, along with folklorists' descriptions of the rumor as a modern urban legend (Leventhal 1995a). Using Leventhal's report, news counter-stories charged that all of the evidence given to support the story had been recycled from one account to another even when that evidence had been contradicted by counter-testimonies given by families, judges, and other parties (Leventhal 1994; Frankel 1995; Pukas 1995).

Leventhal's own assessment of the rumor's power led him to focus more intently on additional strategies. Among these strategies was the distinction between "disinformation" (false stories deliberately spread by foreign governments and other agents) and "misinformation" (nondeliberate but equally false stories). Leventhal argued that misinformation progresses not because of an identifiable agent (such as a foreign government), but in accordance with its popular appeal. Particularly in the absence of any nameable origin or culprit, this appeal makes rumors prolifically reproductive. Further enhanced by the global media, the reproductive capacity of misinformation becomes almost impossible to stop. Leventhal maintained that the best way to accomplish this task was to counter the child-organ stealing rumor by promoting counter-stories that would not simply denounce the story as false (by providing counter-evidence), but would also work at the level of the rumor's power to captivate the popular imagination (Leventhal 1995a).

He further argued that the folklorists' category of the modern urban legend would achieve precisely this goal, because it classifies stories as generically false. "False stories . . . we've all heard them, we've all believed them, and a lot of people have realized they're not true. . . . You can . . . list . . . dozens of different stories that people believe that are *totally* false" (Leventhal 1995a). Once classified as a modern urban legend, the rumor could no longer claim any validity with regard to truth; any such possibility would be rendered invalid by its similarity with other fantastic stories. (One of Leventhal's favorites is the story about a pet owner who tried to dry a dog in a microwave oven, only to explode the dog. See Leventhal 1995a.) But rather than simply countering stories already heard and believed to be true, Leventhal also hoped to predispose his audience to recognizing such stories as false. As Leventhal put it, the aim was to "pigeonhole it in people's minds. . . . I prefer them to hear about it as a false rumor or as an urban legend first" (Leventhal 1995a). The best strategy, according to this logic, was to preempt versions of the rumor as true by supplying a view of the rumor as false through "rational scrutiny." His aim was to "recontext" the rumor according to a particular system of classification and standard of evidence, in relation to which the rumor must necessarily be seen as a false story. In addition, the story would be seen as itself a danger rather than as a valid identification and assessment of risk (Leventhal 1995a).

Two counter-stories that Leventhal claimed as his successes bore the mark of this strategy: a *Newsweek* magazine article and a London *Sunday Times* piece offered counter-stories that attempted to attack the rumor's credibility as a true account. In both reports, this effort was advanced partly on the grounds that the rumor itself posed risks, this time not related to the Guatemalan peace process, but on a different global scale. These risks were related to the rumor's effectiveness not just in Guatemala, but every-where the rumor had been reported as true, and wherever it resonated with the fears of modern urban existence. The June 1995 *Newsweek* article was headlined "Too Good to be True." Its subtitle read: "Tall Tales: Everyone's heard the heartbreaking stories about Third World kids being killed for their internal organs. Just one problem: they're false" (Frankel 1995; here-after cited as NW). The London *Sunday Times*'s slightly more sensational headline read: "A horrifying story began as local gossip and spread to fool the world. The global lie that cannot be silenced" (Pukas 1995; hereafter cited as LST).

Both reports provided specific "factual" counter-evidence to the child-organ stealing rumor. They offered the suggestion that organ trafficking is impossible because, along with the fact that it is illegal, "the entire U.S. transplant system is highly controlled by the United Network for Organ Sharing (UNOS), which registers and tracks each donated organ" (NW; see also Leventhal 1994, 1995b).[14] Additional counter-facts cited were that organs have a short "shelf life" (a heart lasts four hours before degenerat-ing, and a kidney forty-eight to seventy-two hours) (NW, LST), and that organs must be tissue-matched in order to avoid rejection after transplant (LST). Both counter-stories also quoted a UNOS spokesman, Joel Newman, who remarked, "You can't just turn up with a kidney in a cooler and say to some hospital, 'Hey, are you interested' " (NW, LST). By its casual tone, this quote also worked to dismiss child-organ stealing as an unfounded rumor.

The two reports also included versions of the rumor culled from vari-ous Latin American newspaper reports. In one of them, men and women dressed in costumes were said to have lured children into a van, cut out their vital organs, and sold them to rich foreigners for transplant. As *Newsweek* put it, this initial rumor proliferated into even "wilder" rumors as it was retold (NW). A subsequent version of the rumor reproduced in these reports involved an account of child-organ stealing published in São Paulo's newspapers, which told of Eduardo Feliciano Oliveira Jr.'s death in a local hospital. When the autopsy revealed that his eyes had been removed, his abdominal organs were missing, and his abdominal cavity had been stuffed with sawdust, the infant's parents charged the hospital with removing the infant's organs in order to cover up medical wrongdoing. While the family's lawyer made no charge of organ stealing, the story was, as Anna Pukas of the *Times* put it, "caught up in the myth of Third World children murdered for their internal organs that keeps surfacing around the world" (LST). According to these accounts, each story of organ stealing was simply one instance of a wider global myth.

While some stories reproduced in these reports were simply dismissed as "preposterous, bunk, hokum" (NW), others that had circulated through the world press were granted a more detailed response. These longer standing and more widely circulating versions of the child-stealing rumor were printed together with retractions issued by the original teller in response to publicity, or to investigations undertaken by Leventhal and other authorities that were said to prove the rumor false. For example, both reports displayed half-page photographs of blind boys whose eyes had supposedly been stolen. But, the reports asserted, these boys had in fact lost their eyes to infection. In the *London Sunday Times*'s version of this story, the visual "evidence" (a captioned photograph) was corroborated by Leventhal himself, who was reported to have obtained one of the pictured boy's medical records documenting the infection. Both articles also reported a retraction made by the boy's half brother, in which he admitted to lying about the eye theft, and granted that his eyes, too, had become infected.

In keeping with Leventhal's strategy, these reports provided counter-evidence for the rumor's claims while "recontexting" the rumor as an effective but false story. Moving from the apparent absurdity of the rumors to an alternative mythological logic evidenced by the existence of child-stealing rumors since antiquity and in all parts of the world, these reports noted the power of the rumor as an urban legend, rather than as a potential fact. They classified the rumor as "whispers of allegation . . . transformed into pseudofact" (NW), as "urban myth" (LST), and "legend" (NW). It was this mythological power, they claimed, that explained why, "in spite of the lack of evidence," this story "has been swallowed by the United Nations, the World Health Organization, the European Parliament, and much of the international media" (LST). Not only was the rumor false, furthermore, but its reproduction entailed considerable risks to the supply of organs made available for transplantation by donors.

The rumor's classification as mere legend was also combined with alternative explanations of the rumor's power as required by this strategy. For example, the *Newsweek* article cited Campion-Vincent's analysis of the rumor as follows: "Writing in a 1990 issue of *Western Folklore*, a journal of the California Folklore Society, Campion-Vincent notes that though body snatching is a myth, illegal adoptions by foreigners are a real, albeit small, problem. The body-parts rumor began to spread at the same time that illegal adoption rackets were uncovered in both Honduras and Guatemala; children of unknown origin were discovered in so-called fattening houses, from which they were sold to overseas couples" (NW).

Having posed the "fact" of child stealing and selling for transnational adoption against the "myth" of child stealing for transnational organ selling, *Newsweek* went on to suggest that the child-organ stealing rumor was also generated by cultural differences between the First and Third Worlds: " 'The humanitarian impulse of the First World is totally misunderstood in many countries where these rumors arise,' says Bill Pierce, chairman of the Washington-based National Council for Adoption" (NW). Pierce's explanation of this misunderstanding read as follows: " 'In that culture it can be really impossible to understand why a couple of middle-class Americans would want to adopt such a child. The 'logical' answer is that they must want to profit from the child in some way.' It's sometimes easier to imagine the evil within the human heart than to perceive the real mercy" (NW). Because of an intelligible but ultimately illogical line of thought, this counter-story argued, Latin Americans have failed to appreciate the generosity of U.S. adoptive parents. Like these Latin Americans, the UN investigator of the rumor, journalists all over the world, and documentary filmmakers like Judy Jackson (British director of *The Body Parts Business*, a film on the subject), "swallowed the myth whole," all the while "jettisoning or ignoring facts that get in the way of what is admittedly a compelling fable" (NW). These two counter-stories, then, appealed to the readers' rationality, asking us to accept the "true" facts. While admitting our susceptibility to the rumor, they suggested, we could help to avoid the real risks it posed. These dangers included the risk to continued transnational adoption, to organ donation, and so on.

The London *Sunday Times* story added a new twist to the list of dangers. Its quote from folklorist Paul Smith of the University of Newfoundland, read: "The important thing is why people believe them, the ideas and fears the myths express and the way some myths eventually come true" (LST). With this observation, the risk of rumor came full circle, as the *Times* concluded: "It would be tragic indeed if the legend of the organ-snatchers were to become reality just because it was too horrible to believe" (LST). The risk of the rumor identified here, as elsewhere, lay in its generative power. But that power was not turned to an alternative task such as disturbing a peace process, or explaining a culturally inscrutable gesture of "mercy." It was, rather, a power so great that it might actually bring about the impossible truth that it named.

The problem of belief in the rumor existed in these reports (Leventhal's and those he promoted in the press), not only where the rumor's events were said to have taken place (primarily in Latin America), but at a global level—everywhere the fears of modern medical technology, bodily integrity, and global power relations may exist. The rumor's appeal, according to Leventhal, was that it articulated fears about the pace and power of modern medical technology. It also articulated fears about "basic bodily integrity" and about the power of the North, or sometimes the United States in particular, with regard to the South or even the rest of the world. Both the London *Sunday Times* and *Newsweek* articles quoted Leventhal's description of the child-organ stealing story as "a myth about poor people's fears of wealthy people, and about more fundamental fear of mutilation, death, and advances in medical science that they can neither understand nor control." The fears attached to the child-organ stealing rumor traced a map for Leventhal that included Europe, Latin America, and Asia. He identified a "special responsiveness" in regions from which children were adopted transnationally in significant numbers, namely Latin America, Eastern Europe, and Korea. Western Europe was also singled out as a place where the rumor was believed because of widespread support for children's rights and a disposition to anti-American sentiment (Leventhal 1995a).

Leventhal's project of repositioning via the modern urban legend added an overlay to this global mapping, according to those who believed the rumor to be true, and those who knew the rumor to be false—that is, those who accepted the program officer's standard for the true ("information" or "reality") and the false ("misinformation" or "myth"; Leventhal 1994). On one hand, the rumor spoke to "global" and "modern" fears that could affect almost anyone. In response to my question about the child as a particular feature of organ-stealing rumors, Leventhal suggested that rumors pertaining to children are the most prevalent, perhaps because the child is "the most helpless member of society, everybody loves children, so they're a natural focus of these types of urban legend" (Leventhal 1995a). His solution, accordingly, addressed such fears that operated within the framework of the modern as a global phenomenon. However, while such fears had come to affect the number of organ donations, transnational adoptions, and the reputation of the United States, their power did not have any subjective hold in the United States, according to Leventhal. His explanation therefore located the parameters of the possible real and the impossible unreal in different, rational and irrational, regions of the world. Leventhal's approach, together with that of his reported media successes, attempted to fix the indeterminacy—an uncertain questioning of the truth about child-organ stealing rumors—that the child figured in the organ-stealing rumor might otherwise realize.

While the child-organ stealing rumor itself identified dangers posed to poor children in certain parts of the world by medical technology together with the global market in organs, Leventhal and the media reports he promoted rested their attempts to dispel the rumor on dangers posed by the story. They claimed that the rumor's dissemination had two significantly negative effects. First, organ donations decreased, thereby exacerbating existing organ shortages. Second, the charge of child theft for organ harvesting adversely affected transnational adoption, as countries charged with allowing adoptions for the purpose of organ harvesting were forced to shut down transnational adoption mechanisms either temporarily or permanently, and pressured even to outlaw the practice (Leventhal 1994, NW, LST). Both Leventhal and media counter-stories supported this evidence by citing the fact that organ sales were made illegal with the passage of the *National Organ Transplant Act* (1984: 98–507) in 1984, and that the United Network for Organ Sharing (UNOS) administers a federally mandated network that monitors every organ transplant performed in the country. A pamphlet published by UNOS (1995) in the wake of the Weinstock incident stated that this network is "a tightly controlled system where it is illegal to retrieve or transplant human organs outside of this system," and added that the U.S. Department of Justice, as well as the FBI, had found no evidence to support specific allegations of illegal organ trafficking (UNOS 1995: 10). No one, furthermore, had ever been prosecuted under the *National Organ Transplant Act*, and no evidence had been found of any "clandestine clinic" in the United States that performed illegal transplants. Nor had any patients suffering from what UNOS insisted would necessarily be "suboptimal" results turned up in hospital emergency rooms, where the crime would be discovered when the afflicted patient was forced to seek medical care from a "legitimate medical facility" (UNOS 1995: 10–11).[15]

In a section on the "impossibility of concealing clandestine organ transplants," Leventhal argued that in addition to other technical obstacles (to which I will return), "It would not be possible to assemble a team of highly trained medical professionals who would all be willing to engage in such morally repugnant criminal acts and be willing to take the enormous personal risks that would be involved in performing a transplant operation clandestinely" (Leventhal 1994: 38). Furthermore, the transplant procedure requires "a laboratory designed to test histocompatibility, and requires individuals with specialized laboratory skills to conduct the testing." And in addition to the "extremely delicate procedure" of surgically extracting the organ, the donor organ must be transported, "typically by helicopter or plane," and "special preserving solutions must be infused into it. Proper insulation and temperature controlled packaging including adequate ice or refrigeration must be used to protect the organ during shipment. Absolute sterile conditions must be maintained for the organs to remain viable for transport" (38). For Leventhal, this list of highly technological requirements made the possibility of organ theft logistically impossible. Together with the modern urban legend strategy, this list incontrovertibly and effectively undermined any possibility that the child-organ stealing rumor might be believed and repeated as truth.

Child-Organ Stealing: True or False?

While insisting that the child-organ stealing story is in fact true seems a ludicrous position to take, some skepticism concerning the basis of these counter-arguments might be in order. For example, the arguments used in counter-stories about the rumor's truth relied on a trust in the regulatory mechanisms built into legal and medical systems that not everyone shares.

Furthermore, they failed to address the possibility, however remote, that a foreign organ could be presented by illegal means as "legitimately" procured. In the face of more widely accepted evidence of child kidnapping for transnational adoption, they also insisted on an absolute distinction between such kidnapping and child stealing for organ trafficking. However, the record on illegal transnational adoption suggests, at least, that it is indeed possible to establish an elaborate illegal system of exchange that spans many levels and kinds of institutions and personnel. The purported impossibility of establishing such a network was more directly refused by a report published in the *New York Times* (Schemo 1996), which confirmed the existence of child kidnapping for transnational adoption in Paraguay. The *Times* reported that an extensive network of agents in Paraguay had been processing kidnapped children through official foreign adoption channels. The illicit activity included personnel at every step of the adoption process, from women posing as biological mothers, to nursery operators, psychologists, notaries, lawyers, and judges.[16] This relatively uncontested truth of child stealing for transnational adoption makes child stealing for organ theft and transplant seem more possible than the counter-stories wish to suggest. Claims that child-organ stealing is technically impossible—because the tissue must be matched, because organs (except corneas) deteriorate quickly, because hospital records show no trace of organ removal—are also rendered at least questionable by reports of such an extensive network of illegal activity. The supposed technical impossibilities that extend beyond the existence of willing professionals to carry out organ removal rely on the equally questionable assumption that laboratories set up in poor countries such as Guatemala could not successfully type the organ's tissue and blood (required for correctly matching the organ to a recipient).

While organ transplantation may be technology-intensive, and require materials that are not likely to be readily available to the average person, they are not, in themselves, impossible to meet. Neither does the fact that some of the organs most commonly cited in child-organ stealing rumors—livers and kidneys—must be transplanted within twenty-four and forty-eight hours of removal make a transnational traffic in organs impossible; it takes much less than twenty-four hours to fly direct from Guatemala City to any major city in the United States. The five-hour limit for preserving hearts for organ transplant would, however, make a transnational exchange difficult if not impossible. It also seems unlikely that corneas would be a very lucrative organ on the global market, given Leventhal's claim that "5,042 corneas were exported from the United States for use in transplants" in 1993, and 70 to 90 percent of them were provided free of charge (Leventhal 1994: 39). The most daunting technological requirements cited by Leventhal (and UNOS; see UNOS 1994; Rothman 1997), however, exist not during and after organ removal, but in the transplantation procedure, whereby the recipient acquires a needed organ. As long as the organ and the hospital records could be presented with "legitimate" documentation and information, transnational organ traffic, like transnational child traffic, would be possible.

Leventhal concluded his arguments for the impossibility of child-organ trafficking as follows: "In sum, organ transplantation is such an immensely complicated, highly technical, heavily regulated, extremely time-sensitive procedure, involving so many highly trained professional personnel and so much sophisticated medical equipment, that clandestine organ trafficking is, quite simply, an impossibility from a practical point of view. The charges that children are being kidnapped and murdered for such purposes make the allegations even more dubious" (Leventhal 1994: 39). For Leventhal, the rumor's power consequently could not make any legitimate claim to the "real"—actual trafficking in children's organs—that it named.

But of course it was this very technological and professional expert knowledge, capability, and authority on which counter-claims partly relied that the rumor arguably contested. In its telling, the rumor insisted that what some called impossible was not only possible, but all too real. It claimed an authority to which the rumor's hearers might appeal as an alternative source of knowledge and truth. In the end, unraveling the allegations and counter-allegations that run through the stories either documenting or debunking the child-organ stealing story seems nearly impossible. Both sides recycle information such that the reports themselves become as indeterminate as the rumor they attempt to pin down. How are "we" as readers or consumers of media reports on rumor to evaluate its insistent indeterminacy, and so to describe what the child-figure at the heart of that rumor signifies for us?

The Story in Guatemala: Rumor as Truth?

Any evaluation of a story depends on the criteria by which it is judged. Following Arjun Appadurai's suggestion that the imagined worlds of the mediascape provide the possibility of re-imagining dominant visions (1990), it becomes possible to use the story's indeterminacy to question official claims to truth, such as Leventhal's, without necessarily claiming the rumor itself as true. I have suggested that the child's figuration is indeterminate. The power of the rumor works through this indeterminacy as well, where the indeterminacy concerns the truth of the child-figure as a victim of child-organ theft. It is also possible to argue, then, that the rumor's power works through the child figured as a body in danger, or "at risk."

But the risk to which I refer here is not necessarily the risk of a "modern" or "urban" order of things. Instead, the risk realized by this child-figure is indeterminate, and variable. Power, rumor, indeterminacy, and the child-body can be related to one another through an alternative "global" imaginary. Such an alternative is suggested by Michael Taussig's (1992) concept of the "Nervous System," or NS, which accounts for the power of indeterminacy as it works through the body. Whereas media reporting on the rumor tended to distance fear by locating it elsewhere—in those who will not listen to authoritative reason, in indigenous rural or wealthy urban Guatemalans—Taussig's concept of the NS refuses the distancing of terror elsewhere, locating it instead "here," as the "normal" state of things (11–13). The phrase "Nervous System"—or NS—refers to this ongoing, nervously indeterminate order of things. For Taussig, the "here and now" goes by the name of "terror as usual, the middle class way" (14).

For Taussig, the very possibility of such terror depends, much like the rumors, on its passage "from mouth to mouth across a nation, from page to page, from image to body" (Taussig 1992: 2). Terror's transmutability from one medium to another makes any "talk" about terror potentially complicit in extending its reach, argues Taussig, much as the repetition of rumor, as I have suggested above, continues its course even when it is repeated in an effort to curtail that power. Terror's transmutability from one kind of matter or form to another, its shifting materialization and dissemination as utterance, printed word, image, and bodily experience, furthermore, effectively describes its workings across a nation, as in Taussig's example. It also describes such workings transnationally, given the rapidity with which information can travel through transnational circuits, including the media.

One of the examples Taussig uses to illustrate this form of terror concerns the very material constitution of space and place in an unnamed but renowned U.S. university's history, in which that institution "disappeared" (Taussig's term) its surrounding poor community (Taussig

1992: 14). Buildings burned, financial pressure was applied, and streets were rerouted to discourage entry into the area. In a more transnational frame, Taussig suggests further that power in a postmodern world works through disorder rather than order. He asks: "In the postmodern world, as the state, the market, and the transnational corporations enter into a new configuration of arbitrariness and planning, might not the very concept of the social, itself a relatively modern idea, be outdated in so far as it rests on assumptions of stability and structure? In which case what is all this talk about order about?" (14). Leaving aside the question of the "postmodern," the disorderly kind of power Taussig identifies fits as a description of the child-organ stealing story's effective force. The capacity of medical science to transplant organs from one body to another in a transnational and clandestine network of exchange, and the child-body distributed across that network that the child-organ stealing story figures, easily suggest this disorderly kind of power.

If power works through disorder—or indeterminacy—through a "Nervous System," then what kind of response is appropriate? How do we think and write about this story, when it is so difficult to know what is true, what is false, and what the effects of claiming either one might be? Understanding how power works through these linked phenomena requires a double vision, according to Taussig, one which relies neither on order nor disorder, but instead "requires knowing how to stand in an atmosphere whipping back and forth between clarity and opacity, seeing both ways at once" (Taussig 1992: 17). This dual responsiveness, this "optics of the Nervous System" provides an effective way of thinking about power as it works through indeterminacy, and in particular through the indeterminacies that oscillate in the child-organ trafficking rumor and are realized in its multiple child-figure. The child-organ stealing rumor conjures images of organs and tissues—liver, kidney, cornea, heart—the child-body in pieces, wounded and stuffed with money, the child-body lost, missing, gone from an original place, and redistributed in a global economy of bodies to sustain other lives. This confluence of indeterminacies is condensed in the child-organ stealing story.

In order to function, transplanted parts must, of course, be reattached to the receiving body's nervous system. In contrast to "modern" fears that signify an increasingly technological world, a more complex economy of value is at work here, which cannot be understood effectively in generic or universal terms. This value is both symbolic and material, and it is figured through the child-body. This figuration and its attendant value may not be only metaphorical, and this is perhaps the most important point. Using Taussig's criteria of doubt rather than Leventhal's criteria of truth, together with a double and located perspective on "general categories" and "specific instances" (discussed above), the child-organ stealing rumor becomes a coded story. This story tells a truth other than the one it explicitly offers, while at the same time keeping open the possibility that the story's own version of the "real" may in fact be true.

In choosing these criteria, I am also limiting and possibly altering the mode of reading with which I (or my readers) might peruse a newspaper article, sometimes catching the headline in passing, sometimes reading the first paragraph, sometimes reading the entire article carefully. The pace and direction from which one considers an object fundamentally alters how that object is experienced, and what can be said about it (Morris 1988). Leventhal's strategy was aimed at guiding our reading of the child-organ stealing story through the framework of the modern urban legend, which would in turn make the story possibly intriguing, but quickly dismissible as truth. The London *Sunday Times* represented this approach visually by juxtaposing layered cut-out headlines from newspapers in Spanish and French proclaiming the story as true with a linguistically and graphically sensational headline countering their claims as a "global lie." With the speed of recognition, according to the countering strategies employed to dispel the rumor, we are impelled to register the organ-stealing story wherever it appears as a modern urban legend, and be done with it. But doubt and indeterminacy are not so easily dismissed. Not only do they flash by at an equally rapid speed, but they also linger, insisting as the "Nervous System" does, on sustained, if shifting, attention. Rather than choosing one of these modes of attention, given the oscillating power of indeterminacies, using both of them may more adequately address the power of the child-organ stealing rumor and its figurations of the child in plural local-globals.

As I have already mentioned, almost every media account dealing with the child-organ trafficking rumor links its existence and its material force in the Weinstock incident and related events to the more generally accepted "fact" of child stealing for a transnational adoption trade. The "fact" of the adoption trade and the "rumor" of child-organ stealing render the value of the child in different but related ways. In the rumor, the missing child remains missing or is returned dead. The body has been given the monetary value of the bills stuffed in its wound, and the life of that child-body only has value, from the point of view of the crime, as a means of enhancing or giving life in another body (sometimes an adult, but more often a child), within a global economy of body parts.

In the case of child stealing for adoption the missing child remains missing from where it was taken (a hospital, the streets, its own family), but is "found" elsewhere, in a place where it brings a family into being. The missing-and-adopted child's life has value in this case through its displacement and then re-placement to this other family. Like the rumor's organ exchange, this transaction also takes place in a global economy. The difference between the "rumor" about child stealing for organs and the "fact" of child stealing for adoption is that in the latter the global economy is one of whole bodies and social(izable) entities, in which there is an assumed benefit to the child. In the former, the global economy is one of body parts in which no such benefit can be claimed. Within this difference, however, "fact" and "rumor" share child-bodies invested with value according to a global cultural-economic system of valuation.

As we have seen, it is not difficult to maintain that the rumor names metaphorical risks associated with a globalized world and its economies. In fact, Todd Leventhal's reports, as well as most other news reports, provided descriptions of the rumor as just such a story, a story about globally relevant fears regarding bodily integrity under conditions of modern technological progress, as well as economic inequalities across a North-South divide (Leventhal 1994, 1995b). But even metaphorical stories are both more "local" in their particular negotiation of the global, and more historically relevant, than such generalized interpretations allow. As Comaroff puts it, such stories can "animate an alternative modernism that is also an alternative mode of authorization and a critical moral commentary on the contemporary global condition as it collides with the local social world" (n.d.: 10–15). According to this analysis, seemingly identical stories that circulate globally may be related to quite different material conditions and metaphorical meanings depending on the particular historical, political, social, and cultural conditions through which they are reproduced. But if significations linked to the child-organ stealing rumor in its local-global guises change in the slide of meanings from one to the other, perhaps something is lost—or gained—in the transfer.

Child-Organ Stealing in Guatemala: Rumor as Truth?

I now want to suggest that the rumor's story of child-organ stealing reproduces an account of a potentially legitimate risk, and embodies reasonable fears. In her evaluation of organ-stealing rumors, anthropologist Nancy Scheper-Hughes (2000) considers the possible truth of organ-stealing rumors using evidence from India, Brazil, and South Africa. She notes the existence of a global trade in organs, in which both voluntary donations in the context of global and local economic inequalities and organ thefts from dead and possibly also from living bodies have been undertaken. Scheper-Hughes notes that contemporary organ-theft rumors arose in the late 1980s and early 1990s, during a period of democratization in Argentina, Brazil, and Guatemala that followed "the recent history of military regimes, police states, civil wars, and 'dirty wars' in which abductions, disappearances, mutilations, and deaths in detention and under strange circumstances were commonplace" (203). She also documents testimony from prestigious doctors, organ procurers, donors, and medical journal articles that indicate the existence of a global trade in organs, to suggest that just as organ-stealing rumors may be seen as a metaphorical, "surrogate form of political witnessing," so too "urban legends and rumors, like metaphors, sometimes harden into ethnographic facts" (203).

I make this claim specifically about the rumor as a local-global Guatemalan story, that is, in its circulation through Guatemala, because in that context child-organ theft seems possible in relation to a specific national history. The reign of terror that has operated in Guatemala with almost unimaginable impunity, together with the documented fact of child stealing for transnational adoption; the well-known shortage of transplant organs all over the world; and the fact that neither the United Nations nor the European Parliament have changed their position on child-organ stealing as a legitimate risk make it almost necessary to imagine such a possibility.[17] It is the insecurity of doubt rather than the confidence of certainty that compels this conclusion.

Both the European Parliament and the United Nations Special Rapporteur on the Sale of Children (United Nations Economic and Social Council 1993, 1994a, 1994b) issued reports in the 1990s substantiating the possibility that child-organ stealing may indeed be taking place in Guatemala and elsewhere. The USIA, and the media reports it promoted, insisted that the evidence supplied in these reports had been subsequently retracted or proved erroneous. The European Parliament and the United Nations did not retract their reports in response to Leventhal's counter-charges. With them and Scheper-Hughes, I am compelled to insist that the child-organ stealing story is potentially true. I am not committed to the rumor as true, so much as I wish to remain nervous, to restrict the power of the "normal," or what Taussig called "business as usual" to eclipse the existence of that which is deemed abnormal, indeed impossible, on the basis of insufficient technological sophistication and professional morality.

Since the 1980s, a different set of technological capabilities and professional ethics has been brought to bear on Guatemala's bloody history. Forensic anthropologists have been occupied with exhuming skeletal human remains from clandestine mass graves in Guatemala with the aim of identifying the cause of death. A BBC television documentary about this effort suggested the importance of relying on alternative regimes of evidence and truth to sustain as legitimate a possibility that from reigning standards can only be seen as abnormal and indeed impossible. Titled *Traces of Guilt* (Rosin 1996), the documentary featured a team of Guatemalan and foreign investigators who identified the buried bodies through forensic methods with the help of local residents. Against long-standing official government claims that the military never perpetrated such crimes, the team concluded on the basis of the bullets used and the forms of torture employed that the dead had indeed been killed by military forces.

At one point in the documentary, local residents in a town called Plan de Sánchez were filmed helping to identify the bodies of their murdered friends and relatives. Armed government personnel surrounded the gravesite. A familiar presence, the police stood for some as a reminder that reprisals, including disappearance, torture, and death, might ensure for anyone who collaborated with the exhumation effort. The documentary intermittently cut from the gravesite to an interview with an unnamed local resident, whose words were translated through an English voice-over. Among the comments cut into the grave-digging sequences was the following: "The army keeps harassing us, trying to stop us talking to you. But they have to understand that there is a law for us as well, and this has to stop. We're speaking out to break the cycle of impunity so that we are an example to other nations and this can never happen again."

The cycle of impunity to which this statement refers included the massacre of entire villages, including six others that occurred at the same time as the killings in Plan de Sánchez, according to the documentary. Given its reference to Guatemalan resistance as an example to other nations, the statement also signified the much broader orchestration of disappearance, torture, and death suffered by the largely indigenous and poor citizens of Guatemala (Manz 1988; Jonas 1991). Among the skeletons exhumed from

Plan de Sánchez in the documentary were those of two children, each of whose bodies showed signs of torture and death by shooting. According to Amnesty International, among other observers, children have been the targets of other violent campaigns as well. Amnesty International has documented disappearances, torture, beating, raping, and harassment of street children in Guatemala City by police and other security agents including private security firms and other civilians, all of whose actions have gone unchecked.[18] Some children were forced to swallow glue (children living in the streets are known to sniff glue to stave off hunger and for its hallucinatory effects), or had glue poured on their heads by police (Amnesty International 1990, 1992). Some of these children were further subjected to violence at the hands of police for testifying to child agencies and the courts about the violence perpetrated against them and their companions (Amnesty International 1992: 1–2).

Given the level of impunity under which Guatemalan children as well as adults have lived, combined with the persistent denial of wrongdoing on the part of the government, often with U.S. and media complicity (Manz 1988; Jonas 1991), it seems imperative not to dismiss too easily accounts of unimaginable violence, including child-organ stealing. The level of clandestine organization required to carry out secret organ removal does not seem much greater than that required for state genocide or child kidnapping for transnational adoption. In describing the extensive networks of people and organizations that can be involved in transnational, illegal organ harvesting and transplantation, Scheper-Hughes writes:

> The organs trade is extensive, lucrative, explicitly illegal in most countries, and unethical according to every governing body of medical professional life. It is therefore covert. In some sites the organ trade links the upper strata of biomedical practice to the lowest reaches of the criminal world. The transactions can involve police, mortuary workers, pathologists, civil servants, ambulance drivers, emergency room workers, eye bank and blood managers, and transplant coordinators. (Scheper-Hughes 2000: 192)

She goes on to describe how healthy organs traded in the global market are "transported by commercial airlines in ordinary Styrofoam picnic coolers conveniently stored in overhead luggage compartments." Furthermore, the traffic in illegal organs for transplant seems not to be greatly deterred by quite low survival rates (195). Counter-arguments based on the logistical or moral impossibility, or on the necessary failure of illegal transplants, diminish in the face of this emergent evidence.

Still, if the Guatemalan child-organ stealing story were true in any way, a sustained effort would be required to prove the existence of what is necessarily a covert system. If the story is false, that sustained effort could contribute to further exposing and redressing the cycle of impunity under which so many Guatemalan children have lived, along with adults. It could be used to support their efforts, along with the efforts of many others in Guatemala and abroad, to bring economic, cultural, social, and political justice to the poor and indigenous majority of Guatemalans, in terms responsive to their local and global histories, and to contemporary conditions of globalization and terror, the latter of which continues today in spite of the recent peace accord and associated Truth Commission activities.[19]

Figuring Figuration

Having said this, I harbor no illusions that an argument about child-organ stealing published in an academic book is likely to have any effect whatsoever on Guatemalan citizens, child or adult. My point, in making an argument for the rumor's possible truth, is more directly effective within discussions about questions of fact, evidence, truth, and reality, especially as these questions are bound up with the making of "global" inequalities. My reading of the rumor's multiple figurations of the child—as a harvested body in pieces, both absent and present, and as a whole recipient body—is directed primarily at describing the potentially contested nature of the child's figurations, with regard to the "truth" that these figures realize. Which child-figures, and which realizations they engender are constitutive of the making of these inequalities, but contestations over these issues may also contribute to the making of "global" worlds otherwise.

In the preceding chapters, I have made claims to the significance and value of child-figures as if the figurations themselves were uncontested. In fact, my own description of those figurations itself relied on a fairly unitary, or "given" world of reference, in which the authority of each discourse was constituted precisely by the notion of discourse itself as a bounded entity. While a Foucauldian notion of discourse is effective precisely because it makes a different cut than that assumed by, say, disciplinary knowledge, it does still work by establishing an alternative boundary around some set of practices and knowledges. My own focus on a figure whose value and significance accumulates across plural discourses also constitutes an attempt to think beyond this bounding.

But from another point of view, my discussion before this point has implicitly refused figurations of the child other than the ones I could claim. Describing the child's figuration as a contested matter, as I have done in this chapter, suggests that these claims, too, are necessarily situated in a particular local-global economy of significance and value. This economy relies, in turn, on a particular ontic grounding for truth making and realization. This grounding is condensed in my articulation of figuration and the local-global together. To describe the making of worlds through the notion of material-semiotic figuration is to insist that this making is "situated" and "partial" (Haraway 1991a); figurations are simultaneously located within particular discourses, and in or across specific local-globals. That is, the real exists, but it is neither simply "constructed" nor absolute. Instead, the real is simultaneously contingent on how it is known and lived. In other words, the real is always only that which can be real-ized. And so the limits on the real are constituted in terms of that which is ontically possible, as opposed to impossible. A figuration, then, is the condensed real-ization of situated knowledges and practices.

But at the same time, a general category, such as "the child," can be intelligible across different collections of situated knowledges and practices. This means, in turn, that every situated figuration is also potentially subject to contestation, and with it the ontic grounding to which it gives content as well as form. While not all battles are or should be fought at an ontic level, surely the ontic must be part of any political contestation concerning the "nature" of existence in a newly globalized world, where the nature of the real and its attendant value are so frequently at stake.

5

The Child, in Theory: Post-structuralism, Feminism, and Psychoanalysis

Description is a form of ontological politics; it makes a claim to the real. The detailed descriptions of the child's figurations and their location in time and space that I offer in this book do not in themselves, however, constitute effective interventions in the adult use of ontological privilege with regard to the child. This is not because description—a mode of figuration—is an ineffective form of intervention, but because effective interventions must work through the particular materiality and semiosis of the relevant figuration.

In this final chapter, I turn to the child's figuration in "oppositional" theories of the subject. This brings my discussion to the local-global world of academic discourse and publishing, with its own local-global circuits of exchange.[1] This book is located in this world, where theories are produced, published, and exchanged and English is the dominant language. Given that the power of any description depends partly on the nature and location of its reception, I suggest that it is here, in this particular local-global that this book has the greatest chance of making an effective intervention into the workings of adult privilege. No more or less a world than any other, and no less or more situated in ways that link it up with other worlds, this world is the one in which this book, and I as its author, participate. And so it is within this domain that I attempt not only to describe the child's figuration, but also to think through its refiguration.

Working within this framework, I suggest that an oppositional theory that is accountable to the child must address problems elucidated by the child's figuration in such theories themselves. Even within largely effective attempts to represent children as agentic social actors, the child is simultaneously erased or occupied by the adult author's figuration of the child as a theoretical resource, as a space or form through which the (adult) subject re-forms itself. By "re-formation" here I mean the process of forming again in material as well as semiotic terms. As feminist, postcolonial, and critical race theorists have argued, the subject has been traditionally defined not only by what it is, but perhaps even more importantly by what it is not.[2] That is, the normative subject has been established through categories of existence constituted as other to its (masculine, white, able-bodied, "Western," rational) normativity. This normativity passes as the generic form against which all other characteristics or qualities become specific, idiosyncratic, and identifiable as other. It might be argued that the subject's refiguration in oppositional theories has been effected largely as a response to this order of things. What, indeed, is an oppositional politics that does not work against the marginalization of a particular group or constituency, whether this group is defined in religious, racial, sexual, or economic terms? And what is an oppositional politics that does not work against a dominant form of power and in relation to the worlds that it variously privileges, denigrates, or denies?

With regard to the subject in particular, oppositional theoretical strategies have ranged from claiming full subject status for previously marginalized groups to refiguring the terms on which the status of the subject has itself been founded. With regard to the child in particular, it is important to note that researchers explicitly concerned with childhood have found ways of redressing the historical absence of children's self-representations in the world of academic knowledge making. This has been accomplished most consistently through various methodologies that offer evidence of particular children's experience of the world (e.g., participant observation), combined with analyses of children's social, political, economic, and cultural location and activity (see Steedman 1995; Stephens 1995b; Walkerdine 1997; James, Jenkins, and Prout 1998).

However, while important attempts have been made to reconcile the discrepancies between the child and the normative subject (of rights, the law, citizenship, and so on), the child remains an anomalous figure in the field of subject theory itself. More specifically, as Jo-Anne Wallace has noted, the child is repeatedly figured even in oppositional theories as "the subject out of time . . . the subject yet to come—not yet literate, not yet capable of reason, not yet fully agential" (Wallace 1994: 298). Indeed, a close look at the child's figuration in theories of the subject suggests the absence of any significant difference between so-called traditional and oppositional theoretical positionings insofar as the child is concerned. Because the normative subject has been constituted so fundamentally through its others, the failure to address the child's simultaneous importance to and absence from oppositional theory limits any attempt to interrupt the subject's normativity. It therefore also limits attempts to re-theorize the subject in terms of differences that make a difference. That is, it limits any attempt to thoroughly re-imagine the subject in ways that account for the varieties of experience that obtain across time and space within (and beyond?) the life span.

Rather than simply criticize oppositional theories for their inadequacy with regard to the child, my aim is to respond to the theoretical requirements out of which figurations of the child might be said to arise, but to do so without recapitulating adult uses of the child. I therefore locate my own refiguration of the subject alongside other oppositional theories, in the hope of furthering our collective thinking beyond the restrictive and unequal bounds of the dominant subject. As such, this reading is both critical and collaborative; critical with regard to some theoretical uses of the child, and collaborative in the desire to imagine a more equitable account of existence across multiple axes of difference whose histories cannot be denied, and whose future may yet be determined.

The Child in Post-structuralist Theories

And it is at the center of the subject's disappearance that philosophical language proceeds . . . to the point where it becomes an absolute void—an opening which is communication: "at this point there is no need to elaborate; as my rapture escapes me, I immediately reenter the night of a lost child, anguished in his desire to prolong his ravishment, with no other end than exhaustion, no way of stopping short of fainting. It is such excruciating bliss. . . . Yes, night: the youth and the intoxication of thinking."—Michel Foucault, *Language, Countermemory, Practice: Selected Essays and Interviews*, quoting Maurice Blanchot

The girl and the child do not become; it is becoming itself that is . . . a child. The child does not become an adult . . . the child is the becoming-young of every age.—Giles Deleuze and Félix Guattari, *A Thousand Plateaus: Capitalism and Schizophrenia*

The monster child . . . is what, in the midst of man, throws him off course [son décours]; it is the possibility or risk of being adrift.—Jean-François Lyotard, *The Postmodern Explained: Correspondence, 1982–1985*

These three epigraphs are taken from the works of well-known French post-structuralist theorists, which have been exported to the English-based local-global world of transnational academic publishing through translation and other technologies. The first epigraph is taken from the work of Michel Foucault, whose commitment to understanding history in terms of the contingent making of the real (to suggest one way of reading that work) has been fundamental for my own thinking. Foucault's contributions to the field of theory include a consideration of the child as a body subjected through modern disciplinary regimes, particularly via discourses of sexuality and the rise of compulsory schooling (Foucault 1978). But as the epigraph written by Foucault suggests, when he turns to the subject and its disruption, or "disappearance," the child appears in an ahistorical guise. Foucault figures the "night of the lost child," as a site or space through which an alternative, implicitly adult subjectivity can be imagined.

To be a subject, according to Foucault, one must necessarily undergo a continual process of subjection. This process constitutes the subject as such, but it also imposes a necessary limit on the resulting form of existence. Subjection is both the condition of being a subject, and its limit. The limit that subjection imposes on the subject and so too on the subject's thinking is transgressed, however, by the transformation of the subject who thinks into an alternative form. More specifically, the subject under reformation here is the philosopher, whose transformation also instantiates the emergence of an alternative form of philosophical thinking, or theorizing. Conversely, to transform thinking requires the transformation—and indeed the transgression—of the subject who thinks (the philosopher).

The child-figure appears in Foucault's work at a point where he attempts to theorize subjectivity beyond the limits of the subject. Foucault figures the child as the alternative, inhabitable space that realizes the philosophical subject and its thinking in a transformative guise. The child takes the form of existence in which philosophical language fails, where it "proceeds to the limit" and an alternative form of existence "surges forth." This form of being is not a finite form of existence, but a kind of absence of form, "an absolute void." It is here, in this void, that what was once merely philosophical language becomes communication. It is only in this void, where being takes a nonsubjective form, that what used to be philosophical language becomes possible. In this place of existence, in this voided condition, the philosopher takes the form of a child, by inhabiting the child's time (the night) and space (the space of being lost). By occupying this time-space, the subject takes a form that is, precisely, no longer that of the subject. Instead, the child's time-space is the form that reforms the subject, that allows the subject to transgress its own prior limits. To inhabit this form "is such excruciating bliss" precisely because it enables the experience of possibility itself, an experience that the subject is by definition denied.

Just as the philosopher is reformed through this accounting of possible modes of experience, so too Foucault figures the child as the embodiment of experience free of any historical or social anchoring. As such, the child becomes a time-space made available for occupation by the (adult) subject. The void that the philosopher comes to occupy is, from this point of view, a void made by the erasure of the child as the bearer of experience. In order to be figured as an inhabitable space, the child is voided of experience equal to that of either the subject or the reformed philosopher.[3]

Whereas normative theories of the subject might figure the child as a negative or incomplete other that is "outside" (but also constitutive of) the normative subject, the subject in Foucault's formulation takes up the space of the child as a site of transgressive possibility. In either case, however, the child figured as this space remains necessary as a constitutive element for the subject, reformed or not. Just as the unlost child implicitly figured in Foucault's account remains constitutively other to the normative adult philosophical subject, so too the wandering child lost in the night remains constitutively other to Foucault's reformed philosopher-subject and its abundant possibility.

In the second epigraph, Deleuze and Guattari figure the female ("girl") child and the generic "child" not as persons with their own forms of embodiment, history, and location, but rather as the condition of becoming itself. Not only does the child not become the adult in this formulation, but the child is also once again figured as a form that can be inhabited by persons of every age. To "become young," in these terms, is to take the form of the child, which in turn is defined as a condition of becoming (rather than being).

To inhabit the child, then, is to inhabit the condition, once again, of possibility itself; and to inhabit the condition of possibility is to become a child. At the same time, though, this condition of possibility is not particular to the child itself: "The girl and the child do not become." Instead, the condition, or form, of childhood is generically available. As Sara Ahmed has argued with regard to Deleuze and Guattari's notion of becoming, their formulation relies on an economy of the Same, or "an image of the otherness of the other" (Ahmed 1998: 72). This relation of self (or subject) and other, in which the other is always other *to* the self such that both exist within a single economy, always establishes a hierarchical relation based on the absence of more significant differences. Here, the self defines the other in its own image; and so this formulation of the self retains and reproduces ontological privilege by refusing any otherness that it does not define or cannot contain. In the second epigraph, becoming defines the self in such a way that "the child" is figured only as a *form* of becoming. So too, no differences except those defined by the authors' notion of becoming are intelligible: there is no difference between children and adults, only differences of becoming young or not at every age.

Deleuze and Guattari's figuration of the child as a pure form to be inhabited is paralleled again in Jean-François Lyotard's work. The third epigraph is taken from *The Postmodern Explained*, a theoretical work published in the form of letters written to children. Each chapter begins with the name of a child-addressee printed along with a chapter title, and the date and place of writing. As one reviewer of the English version rather sarcastically put it, "If children can read these letters, there really is a postmodern condition, and it calls for urgent treatment" (Scruton 1992). A brief review of the book's title across all of its translations further indicates the child's problematic status in this work in its local-global circulation. Whereas the original title, *Le Postmoderne expliqué aux enfants* has been translated as *The Postmodern Explained to Children* in its Australian and British versions, the University of Minnesota Press (U.S.A.) translated the title simply as *The Postmodern Explained*, excising the child addressees. This confusion with regard to children as the subjects of Lyotard's address may have more to do with book sales than theoretical accuracy, but in any case, the problem of the child it suggests is more significantly apparent in the text itself.

For Lyotard, as for Foucault and Deleuze and Guattari, the child-figure disrupts the normative subject. The child is not only that which throws the subject "off course" but, in the original French term "son décours," this child figures a quality *of* the subject, so that the child is figured as a feature or potentiality internal *to* it. This figuration constitutes the child once again as a contentless form, which effects a transformative change in the subject, but does not itself constitute an entity in its own right. In this case, the child-figure that can be inhabited takes the form of the experience of becoming, once again, where becoming is both a longed for and desired "bliss." The bliss of becoming, in other words, becomes attainable by taking on the form that is the child. To become a child is to inhabit becoming itself.

In Foucault's, Deleuze and Guattari's, and Lyotard's reformulations of the subject, the child figures as that which reforms the subject, and so works in the service of the subject's disruption. As such, child-figures in the above theoretical formulations are not figures at all, but pure form. This use of the child to realize an alternative form of the subject clearly conforms to Jo-Ann Wallace's charge that oppositional theory tends to divest the child of any "specific materiality" (Wallace 1994: 288). In her attempt to address this problem, Wallace looks to children's self-representation as a possible resource, only to discover a further obstacle. "It is difficult at this stage to imagine how a theory of the child-subject might proceed," she suggests, not just because the child is inadequately represented in theory, but also because the child is "everywhere in representation (on Benetton's billboards, on television shows, in the news) but almost nowhere in public self-representation" (294). Wallace's investigation of oppositional theory in relation to the child ends at the juncture where the child as an aporia in subject-theory collides with the absence of adequate self-representations to redress that absence.

Wallace does not attempt to offer an alternative theory of the child-subject. Instead, she concludes with the following remarks: "Are there significant points of coincidence between discourses of 'the child' and the lives of children? . . . If nothing else, we need to begin with an interrogation of the ways in which our practices and our theory either invoke and position the child-subject or altogether elide the figure of 'the child' " (Wallace 1994: 298). Wallace's attention to the absence of "material specificity" in theoretical figurations of the child, and to the issues raised by the problem of representation offers some points of departure for such a project. First, the absence of material specificity speaks to the normative subject's privileged disembodiment, against which the (racialized, feminized, classed, disabled) bodies of others have traditionally been posed. This familiar feminist point extends as well to the child, insofar as the child becomes the form that the normative subject takes, in the above examples, to reform itself. The erasure of the child is effected, then, through its parallel disembodiment, which in turn provides a newly disembodied form for the reformed subject. Specificity, in contrast, is constituted through materiality, or embodiment. So the question that a reformed theory of the subject must ask if it is to account for the child as a specific kind of entity is: What kind of body?

In her dilemma concerning self-representation and the child, Wallace makes a claim not just to representation as politics, but also to the agency that makes self-representation possible. She argues that existing figurations of the child as a not-yet subject trouble many of the assumptions of what she calls the "agential subject" (Wallace 1994: 295). However, the problem for a theory of the subject that accounts for the child cannot be adequately addressed, I would argue, through the notion of self-representation insofar as the latter is bound up with assumptions about the agential subject. Must a subject be able to represent itself in order to be a subject? Must agency take the form of self-representation? To the problem of the subject's reformed embodiment, I add the question of agency: What kind of agency?

The problem with the post-structuralist formulations I have discussed above—Foucault's, Deleuze and Guattari's, and Lyotard's—can be described as the failure to account for the difference between the child and the adult as agentic bodies that are also capable of transformative change. Instead of accounting for this difference, they use the figure of the child as a site of possibility from which the (adult) subject gains the capacity for transformative change, while the child as an embodied entity that might itself be realized disappears altogether. I will return to the issue of the child's value for adult theories in this regard, but for now I want to focus on the problem of the child's figuration in adult theories as it relates to "actual" children themselves.

As I have already mentioned, Wallace identifies the absence of children's self-representations as an obstacle to imaging an alternative theory of the child-subject. A familiar, and often useful strategy in oppositional politics, self-representation here becomes the apparent condition of possibility for accounting for the child in oppositional theory; it becomes the condition, or ground, of political agency. However, Wallace does not suggest that it is important to give children a voice (to represent themselves), nor does she make a case for childhood as an identity from which a politics should be generated. Instead, she leaves open the question of how the problematic uses of the child in theories of the subject might be addressed. In any case, the specific problem posed by childhood in relation to theories of the subject is not contained in the absence of children's self-representations. Nor is the problem that oppositional theory has somehow failed to address the limits of voice or identity as the basis of political agency; self-representation is not problematic in itself as a political strategy, insofar as it does not necessarily presume that such representations are "true" in an absolute sense. How, then, to address the problematic figuration and use of the child in theories of the subject?

Feminist theory, with its history of challenges to the normative subject, together with challenges posed by various constituencies of women to feminism's own exclusions, provides a more useful point of departure for this project in some important ways. However, even the more self-reflexive approaches used in feminist theorizing make recourse to problematic figurations of the child. Before making use of feminist theories to reformulate the subject in my terms, it is necessary to examine their own uses of the child. What I wish to suggest is not the failure of feminist theories to figure the child in a way that speaks to my own concerns, but rather the particular value accorded to the child in some of its feminist figurations. Here again, I suggest that the very effectiveness of these theoretical contributions in articulating an alternative, oppositional theory of the subject depends in part on problematic claims about—and so to—the child. Because I want to use theories of the subject rather than refuse them as "other" to my own project, my question concerning uses of adult ontological privilege in feminist figurations of the child is the following: What is it that the child does, as a figure, for these theoretical formulations, and how might this value be addressed in ways that account more effectively for children's existence?

Feminist Childhood?

In *Daddy's Girl* (1997), Valerie Walkerdine interprets media representations of little girls in terms of how they speak to adult fantasies of childhood. She also considers them in terms of how little girls themselves negotiate these representations—how these representations function for little girls in the making of their own subjectivity. Using a simultaneously psychological/psychoanalytic and sociohistorical model of subjectivity, Walkerdine analyzes data on working-class girls and their families gathered through her own participant observation. Her interpretation of little girls' talk and behavior while watching popular images of little girls such as those in the film *Annie* is directed primarily at the working-class and gendered aspects of these little girls' experience as it informs the classing of adult femininity. Thus, while Walkerdine's research subjects are little girls and their families, the little girls are not the only subject of her theorizing. At times, they are subsumed under the categories of the working class and of working-class femininity. In this sense, the little girls are one among other cases through which working-class subjects and subjectivities might be understood. Indeed, Walkerdine describes her work in precisely these terms: "The working class that we will meet in the fictional narratives and the narratives that I construct of the lives of the little girls is about a working class that is coping, struggling to get by, to keep on, to make good, often against what seem like impossible odds" (43). Walkerdine's point about working-class subjectivity is an important one. She argues for a "psychology of survival" that describes working-class people's defenses as a negotiation of oppression, rather than as the maladaptive, pathological responses that traditional psychology would have them be. Nevertheless, little girls are figured in her description of this work as the stuff from which Walkerdine constructs a theory about a working class in general.

My point about Walkerdine's theorization is not that it fails to account for little girls' subjectivity. On the contrary, Walkerdine's work focuses on the making of little girls' subjectivity through their interactions with the world. Important arguments come out of this analysis, namely that adult male desires, themselves drawing on culturally available fantasies such as those provided in popular culture, are imposed on girl children and so are also involved in the making of their subjectivity. Her larger argument is that working-class girls incorporate culturally available fantasies of middle-class femininity as a way of imagining themselves outside of the limits imposed on them by class, such that adult male fantasies are constitutive of their subjectivity, but in no way exclusively so.

In a second description of *Daddy's Girl*, Walkerdine writes that it is about "the place of the popular in the making of feminine subjectivity, in this case the subjectivity of little girls" (Walkerdine 1997: 3). This way of articulating her project enacts a slippage that is evident as well in the book as a whole, between feminine subjectivity as a general concept, and little girls as specific cases of it. What slips out of Walkerdine's account, furthermore, is not little girls' feminine subjectivity per se, but Walkerdine's own existence as an adult woman and researcher in relation to the little girls she studies. Despite her clear commitment to articulating working-class girls' subjectivity in its own right, Walkerdine also makes use of the child in a much more problematic way, one that undercuts her attempt to put this commitment into theoretical practice.

Specifically, I would argue that Walkerdine herself occupies the space of little girls' subjectivity, filling that space with memories of her own working-class girlhood. I locate the problem not in Walkerdine's commitment or intent, but rather in the way her methodological-theoretical approach enacts adult privilege so as to occlude the existence of differences between the adult and the child. More specifically, she does not make a clear distinction between her memories of herself as a child and the experience of her research subjects.

A key section of the book establishes the ways in which little girls' fantasies are "already marked by phantasies inherent in the presence and the absence of the Other" (Walkerdine 1997: 181). In this section, Walkerdine turns to memories of her relationship with her father, interweaving them with a story about one of her research subjects, Joanne, and Joanne's father. "In order to explore this a bit further," she writes, "I want to go back to my fantasies as they related to my father's nickname for me, Tinky, short for Tinkerbell and my relating of Mr. Cole's special nickname for Joanne, Dodo, a childish mispronunciation of JoJo" (181). Comparing the two men's use of childish nicknames for their daughters, Walkerdine goes on to describe how the nickname signified her father's fantasies about her, but also her own fantasies in relation to him: "In the case of my own father's fantasy, Tinky signified for me the most potent aspect of my specialness for him. I associated it with a photograph of myself aged three winning a local fancy dress competition, dressed as a bluebell fairy. This is where I won and 'won him over': my fairy charms reciprocated his fantasy of me, designating me 'his girl,' and fuelling my Oedipal fantasies" (181).

As Walkerdine points out, this description of her own childhood fantasies does not stand alone, but only in relation to the fact that children's fantasies "are not one-sided, neither on the side of the parent, nor of the little girl" (Walkerdine 1997: 181). Furthermore, her use of childhood memories constitutes an explicitly self-reflexive methodological and theoretical strategy. As Walkerdine puts it, she is committed to accounting for the subjectivity inherent in all research, and to the subjective nature of any claim to knowledge, including her own. But what I wish to suggest is that working from one's own (adult) subjectivity to make claims about the child is fundamentally compromised by the fact that the child has been so consistently constituted as the adult's pre-subjective other. Moving from her own fantasies to those of working-class little girls, Walkerdine concludes that "the issue of fantasy and the eroticization of little girls within popular culture becomes a complex phenomenon in which cultural fantasies, fantasies of the parents and little girls' Oedipal fantasies mix and are given a cultural form which shapes them" (183). Walkerdine does not use her subjectivity as an adult to think through the problem of children's subjectivity. Instead, she uses memories of herself as a child and, more specifically, memories of her fantasies as a child.

In claiming knowledge of little girls' fantasies as a key part of their subjectivity, Walkerdine also contains children's fantasies within adult (Freudian) knowledge of the child's fantasy as Oedipal, which also clearly conditions her (adult) memory of her own fantasies (in the quote above). Again, Walkerdine is too careful a theorist to let this problem go unnoticed, remarking instead on the fact that psychoanalytic accounts generate universal and normalizing descriptions of feminine subjectivity that do not acknowledge the historically and culturally specific dimensions of lived reality. She also mentions her failure to identify with the adult women (mothers) in her study instead of or along with the little girls. But rather than questioning her own depiction of the child's subjectivity by way of psychoanalysis's ready-made fantasies to account for this failure, she turns instead to the possibility of little girls' pre-Oedipal fantasies, which concern little girls' relationships to their mothers. Unlike little girls, she suggests, working-class mothers "have no romance or glamour in their lives and very little leisure and all have dreams that decidedly did not come true" (Walkerdine 1997: 186). It is not that Walkerdine blames working-class women for their condition, but rather that "somehow, just as I wanted for my mother, I want more for them and these stories are nowhere to be found" (186). Walkerdine describes her selective attention to the little girls in terms of her identification with them, as she herself was once a working-class little girl: "It was my fantasy of myself as a child that wanted to place myself in the fantasy setting of these working-class homes" (186). And so Walkerdine finds stories of possibility in the lives of working-class girls, however compromised by working-class oppression, rather than in the lives of their (adult) mothers. In so doing she also figures little girls as a site of possibility against which their adult counterparts are found sadly wanting.

Walkerdine's account of her research subjects and her theorization of working-class little girls' subjectivity reworks dominant, generic theories of the subject in critical ways. But I think it is also fair to say that Walkerdine makes claims to her child research subjects by occupying their position with memories of herself as a child, rather than occupying her own position as an adult woman. It is not that her memories are somehow wrong or invalid for this process, but rather that the condition of possibility for Walkerdine's theorizing of the child's subjectivity, and of feminine working-class subjectivity more generally, is this occupation. What is left out is precisely the adult woman's relationship of privilege and power with regard to the child, and more specifically Walkerdine's own position of privilege as an adult, academic, and no longer working-class feminist researcher, in relation to the working-class girls with whom she worked.

Rather than discuss this problem in terms of Walkerdine's own psychosocial dynamics (as she does), I want to read in her struggle to articulate a methodologically and theoretically "subjective" or self-reflexive position the absence of an adequate language to express this position in terms of its privilege. It is not so much that Walkerdine's theory of working-class subjectivity, her "psychology of survival," is inadequate in itself, but rather that the means by which she arrives at it entails an exercise of privilege that is not accounted for: the privilege of occupying children's position by way of what are necessarily adult memories—or fantasies—about our own childhoods. Potentially erased or covered over through this process are working-class girls in their own present subjectivity and sociality, and their experience as children that may be quite different from how adults remember or fantasize about their own childhoods.

Walkerdine's description of her own fantasies as "Oedipal" signals the fact that adult memories of childhood are also located in wider local-global discursive frames, in this case psychoanalysis. I understand psychoanalysis as a technology of childhood that enables Walkerdine's occupation of childhood. Of course, this reliance on psychoanalysis can hardly be associated with Walkerdine alone. In oppositional theory, in particular, psychoanalysis has been brought together with Foucauldian understandings of subjection in order to describe more effectively how power works in and through subjects. Walkerdine's work with Julian Henriques, Wendy Hollway, and Cathy Urwin in Changing the Subject (Henriques et al. 1998) was among the first attempts to integrate psychological (including psychoanalytic) approaches to the subject with Foucauldian ones. This work brought questions of history and the social into what were then largely individualistic and ahistorical psychological theories of the subject. More recently, and in different interdisciplinary domains within an academic local-global, feminist theorists have attempted to bring psychic dimensions of social existence to the (Foucauldian) subject by way of psychoanalysis. It is to feminist theory's use of psychoanalysis as a technology of childhood that I now turn.

Feminism and Psychoanalysis: Technologies of Childhood?

Two works stand out for me in this field, namely Judith Butler's (1997) *The Psychic Life of Power* and Teresa de Lauretis's (1994a) "Habit Changes," a synopsis and further elaboration of *The Practice of Love* (de Lauretis 1994b). I read these texts here not simply as examples of psychoanalysis understood as a technology of childhood, but also for the possibilities they offer for theorizing outside or beyond that use.[4] I am interested in where and how the child appears, when it does, in oppositional feminist theories of the subject, and how problematic aspects of these appearances might be addressed through a re-theorization of the adult (privileged) subject as a site from which political change can be imagined—and realized.

Foucauldian theories of the subject work through a notion of subject positions that come before the formation of subjects themselves. From a Foucauldian point of view, subjects are generated in and through multiple discursive technologies, as demonstrated in Foucault's (1978) theory of sexuality as a technology of sex. The Foucauldian theorization of subject formation does not address the question of (intrapsychic) subjectivity in detail; it more consistently presumes the existence of subjectivity than accounts for it. Theorists interested in this question have combined Foucauldian theory with psychoanalysis, which provides a detailed articulation of subjectivity as both constitutive of and excessive to the subject per se. From the resulting point of view, the subject is formed through its subjection to power, but also through the psychic negotiation of a located, historical, and social reality that is itself constituted in and through particular forms of power (Walkerdine 1984; de Lauretis 1987b; Butler 1997). The subject is theorized as the effect of multiple discursive technologies that are involved in both subjectivation and in the making of subjectivity. As Walkerdine puts it in *Changing the Subject*, "Practices of disciplining and regulation ... are ... practices for the formation of subjects" that do not, nevertheless, "have the entire measure of the subject" Walkerdine 1984). So too, for Teresa de Lauretis (1994a, 1994b) the subject's "outside" lies in subjective experience (de Lauretis 1987a), which is, more precisely, both "inside" and "outside" the discursive apparatus of subject formation. For Judith Butler it lies in the subjectively enacted "unconscious of power" as it resists the normalizing effects of subjectivation (Butler 1997: 104).

I have suggested that psychoanalysis, itself a quintessential technology of the child, enables the child's occupation by the adult theorist in Walkerdine's *Daddy's Girl*. The psychoanalytic notion of subject formation also enables the child's figuration as the adult's pre-subjective other in Judith Butler's oppositional theorizations of the subject. Although the subject's formation through subjection is continual throughout the life span for Butler (in keeping with a Foucauldian account of subject formation), she suggests that a "founding" subordination initiates this process in childhood (Butler 1997: 7). In Butler's account, the formation of the subject through power "assumes a psychoanalytic valence" at the point where the child—as that which comes before the subject—develops a "passionate attachment" to its caretakers. "No subject," she writes, "emerges without a passionate attachment to those on whom he or she is fundamentally dependent (even if that passion is 'negative' in a psychoanalytic sense)" (7). The primary passion born of total dependence makes the child vulnerable to subordination and exploitation, Butler argues. It lays the ground for the subject's future ongoing subjection to power. The child's physical dependence on its caretakers is fundamental to this future subject's continued subjection because its relation to power takes the form of a passionate attachment for those who ensure its existence. That is, physical dependence is transformed into the child's desire—a desire for the caretaker as keeper of the child's continued existence.

Figured as a physically dependent body and being, the child becomes the origin of the subject's future relation to power, that is, to the shaping of existence in the form of the subject. Subjection is the form that human existence takes (or has taken to date), according to Butler's theory, and this subjection is founded not only on the child's originary dependence, but also even more importantly on the "passionate attachment" that this dependence engenders. Conversely, the child is also figured as the embodiment of originary dependence, a body whose subjectivity is constituted in and through this passionate attachment. As Butler puts it, the originary dependency of the child is quite specifically "not *political*" subordination, but rather the condition of future political subordination both for the child and the adult it will become (Butler 1997: 7).

In theorizing the subject's origin in this way, Butler makes a claim to knowledge about the child by way of a rearticulated psychoanalytic framework. This claim works by translating the child's (infant's) physical dependence into a subjective condition of passionate attachment that in turn becomes the ground of (adult) subjectivity. It is the first instance of subjectivity: "founding" because it is itself founded in an original, physical dependence that is by definition fundamental to human existence. This figuration of the child constitutes a claim to both the child's body and its subjectivity as the ground of the adult subject. The value of this claim, in Butler's formulation, is that it provides an account of the human as both a body and a subjectivity in the making that explains, in turn, why subjects are so often willing to be subjects, despite the fact that this always entails subjection.

The insistence that a subject is passionately attached to his or her own subordination has been invoked cynically by those who seek to debunk the claims of the subordinated. . . . Over and against this view, I would maintain that the attachment to subjection is produced through the workings of power, and that part of the operation of power is made clear in this psychic effect, one of the most insidious of its productions. . . . The subject is the modality of power that turns on itself; the subject is the effect of power in recoil. (Butler 1997: 6)

Like Walkerdine (who criticizes what she sees as the Left's over-investment in the working classes as resistant subjects), Butler wishes to account for the existence of subordination in a way that does not locate responsibility for their own subjection in these groups, but also does not assume that members of such groups automatically resist, or even desire resistance.

In theorizing the child's subjection as a foundational process for the subject, Butler does not fail to consider children altogether. Indeed, she reconsiders the problem of child sexual abuse in terms of this theoretical position. As she puts it, the question of sexual abuse of children is not simply a matter of either adult imposition of a sexuality on the child, or of the child's own fantasies of sexuality. Instead, the problem is that "the child's love, a love that is necessary for its existence, is exploited and a passionate attachment abused" (Butler 1997: 8). This is, no doubt, one possible way of accounting for the violence that is done to (disproportionately girl) children, and an effective one at that. But it is also precisely an imagined experience, offered not simply on behalf of the child, but in the service of accounting for an adult subject's susceptibility to exploitation. As a subject whose existence is violated by sexual abuse perpetrated by an adult, the child is indeed a more specific and precise entity, a kind of body with its own subjectivity rather than a space that can be occupied by the adult. And yet, how is it that the adult (theorist) can know, in this generalized way, the subjective effects of the child's physical dependence on the adult for its survival? On what grounds do we make such claims to knowledge?

Butler's explicit reliance on Freudian psychoanalysis in *The Psychic Life of Power* suggests that this knowledge is more or less implicitly based in psychoanalysis. It is, of course, a reworked version of psychoanalysis, one that does not rely on an adult "fantasy of origin" that grounds subjectivity in the pre-subjective child. But it seems equally clear—and here is where I find a way out of the dilemma that Butler's formulation produces for me—that Butler identifies an origin that precedes even the child and its passionate attachment. This origin is not a figure, but rather what Butler calls the "desire to survive," or "the desire for existence" itself (Butler 1997: 7). Ultimately, the child in Butler's psychoanalytic theory figures—gives body, and so realizes—this desire for existence. The desire for existence becomes the ground of the child's figuration; and this desire is realized in and through the child-body. Butler's figuration of the child also gives desire the form of a passionate attachment. And it is this passionate attachment, this refiguration of desire accomplished through the child, that secures the ongoing process of subjection in Butler's theory of the subject.

In my discussion of post-structuralist theories, I suggested that the figurations of the child in those theories were used to embody the (adult theorists') desire for the possibility of transformative change. I will return again to Butler's notion of the desire for existence in conjunction with the desire for transformative change in my attempt to account differently for the child in a reformed theory of the subject. But first I want to consider Teresa de Lauretis's reworking of Freudian psychoanalysis, which provides yet another example of the child's figuration as well as additional resources for theorizing. De Lauretis (1994a and 1994b) uses psychoanalysis with and against itself to theorize the (adult) lesbian subject. In so doing, she addresses the privileged status of the normative heterosexual psychoanalytic matrix within which the lesbian has been constituted as pathological. Like Walkerdine and Butler, de Lauretis thinks with but also past Freud and Foucault. Her reworking of theory, like Butler's, figures the child in a prob-

lematic but also suggestive way. In de Lauretis's reformulation of the subject, the child appears not in terms of its early bodily dependence, but in
terms of that which comes before sexuality itself, namely the "drives." Her
account of subjectivity goes something like this: all subjectivity is constituted in and through culture, or the social, but also always by way of consciousness, or rather the unconscious together with the conscious. Subjectivity always works through a subject, which is also always embodied.

Writing about sexuality as a constitutive feature of the subject's formation, de Lauretis argues that the subject is "permanently under construction," such that both the subject and the body are themselves constituted through a process, and so come after this process, as its effects.
More precisely, de Lauretis describes the subject as "the place in which, the
body in whom, the significant effects of signs take hold and are con-
tingently and continuously real-ized" (de Lauretis 1994b: 182–83, cited in
1994a: 304). That is, the subject undergoes a process of continual revision
in and through its body as that body is located in a wider field of social and
cultural processes (fantasies, practices, myths, and so on). These processes
are also necessarily semiotic, such that the subject and its body are always
mediated in and through the social, though they are not coterminous with
it. De Lauretis reads in Freud's *Three Essays on the Theory of Sexuality* a doubled theory of sexuality, one part of which is implicit and speaks to what is
otherwise named as sexual "perversion" in a different set of terms. In this
theory, sexuality of any kind is the effect of the subject's negotiation of
internal drives and external (social, cultural) pressures, which de Lauretis
names a process of sexual structuring, or "sexuation." This process takes
place in "original fantasies" that are also "fantasies of origin," or "cultural
myths that have a powerful hold on subjectivity" (de Lauretis 1994b: xv).
According to de Lauretis, original fantasies take hold of subjectivity as
follows: If sexual structuring, sexuation, or subjectivation, is an accumula-
tion of effects that does not accrue to a pre-existing subject or to a primal,
original materiality of the body, nevertheless the process takes place in and
for a bodily ego; and moreover, a body-ego that is constituted, literally
comes into being, through what Freud calls *Urphantasien*, primal or original
fantasies, which are also fantasies of origin" (de Lauretis 1994a: 303). The
body and subjectivity are thus brought into being as one; neither precedes
or exists apart from the other.

As de Lauretis clearly argues, her project aims to make use of psychoanalysis not for its own sake, but as *the* cultural technology through which

sexuality has and can be theorized and, indeed, lived. I will return to the question of where in the world this is or has been the case, but for the moment I want to focus on de Lauretis's invocation of original fantasies. Original fantasies are the locus through which the (always constructed) body as subject (body-ego) is not simply reconstructed, but actually comes into being. De Lauretis turns to one of these fantasies, the fantasy of castration, to offer an account of lesbian sexuation (in which the fantasy works through the fetish rather than the phallus per se).

I find this to be an extraordinarily effective and indeed seductive use of psychoanalysis to account for lesbian sexuality in its own right, but my interest here in de Lauretis's approach lies in her claims about the originary fantasies insofar as they come to life, so to speak, in the child. That is, I am concerned with the way that claims to the child authorized by psycho-analysis constitute the child once again only as the ground of adult subjec-tivity. As I have already mentioned, the child appears in de Lauretis's ac-count not as a body, but as the site of the subject's embodiment, its coming into being, its realization. For de Lauretis, the castration complex applies to female as well as male sexuation, and in particular ways to lesbian sexuation. She argues that while the castration complex has been articu-lated in terms of the boy's fear of loss of the penis, or its symbolic equiva-lent, the phallus, the castration complex can also be understood in terms of the fetish. The fetish, in this case, is that which is substituted for a lost body—not necessarily the penis, or the phallus, but *some* body (de Lauretis 1994a: 301).

By redefining this early loss as the loss of some body rather than of a generic (male) one that belongs to all subjects, de Lauretis is able to theo-rize not only lesbian sexuation, but the process of sexuation more generally as one that generates plural kinds of equally legitimate (nonpathological) sexualities. As de Lauretis puts it, "If homosexuality is merely another path taken by the drive in its cathexis or choice of object, rather than a pathology . . . then Freud's theory contains or implies, if by negation and ambiguity, a notion of perverse desire, where perverse means not patholog-ical but rather non-heterosexual or non-normatively heterosexual" (1994a: xiii). Consequently, the drive is originary in the human being, as a part of its very nature, or ontology.

The child is figured in this picture as the bodily site in which the sub-ject and its subjectivity originate in and through the drive. Turning to Laplanche and Pontalis's rearticulation of Freudian psychoanalysis, de

Lauretis suggests that the subject comes into being through the interaction between the child's drives, and external—parental or cultural—fantasies, or accounts of the world. Quoting Freud, de Lauretis identifies "an instinctual stimulus" that "does not arise from the external world but from within the organism itself" (de Lauretis 1994a: xv). This instinct originates in the body, or rather the organism, but it is only recognized by way of its "psychical representative" (xv), which is the content of fantasy. Instincts, then, are transformed or translated into fantasies, and so into the psychosocial domain of human existence. It is through the transformation of the instincts into fantasies, in other words, that the child as organism—that is, as human nature before or beside culture—is subjectivized, made subjective and a subject at one and the same time.

In de Lauretis's account, the child figured as the site of subjectivity's initiation is necessarily also the "subject" of original fantasies (1994a: xv). That is, it real-izes the subject, not only bringing it into being as an idea, but also making it real in simultaneously material and semiotic form. Once again quoting Freud, de Lauretis describes fantasies as similar to myths, in that they "provide a representation of, and solution to, the major enigmas which confront the child" (xv). In articulating a theory of perverse desire, de Lauretis reinvokes the child figured in Freud's work as the embodiment of human nature before culture. It is well known that Freud himself began his investigations as a scientist, and that psychoanalysis formed a turn, in his knowledge making, from the biological to the psychic that never completely left behind biology as the ground of human existence. In other words, Freudian psychoanalysis makes a claim to human culture by way of a claim to the originary nature of the human. And the precise moment of the human's transformation from nature to culture in Freudian psychoanalysis occurs in and through the body of the child, figured as a body wavering on the cusp between the two.

De Lauretis (1998) addresses the question of origin more directly in her discussion of Freud's Trieb. She notes that Freud himself made a distinction between two forms of Trieb, a somatic form and a psychic form, which have been translated into English as two different terms, "instinct" and "drive" respectively. This said, the difference between the two terms is ambiguous, according to de Lauretis, because while it is possible to name two different forms, they can actually only be recognized in their psychic guise. Thus Trieb signifies a "constitutive ambiguity" between the somatic and the psychic. De Lauretis offers Freud's own definition(s), finally, to establish the meaning of Trieb: considering mental life from a biological point of view, an " 'instinct' appears to us as a concept on the frontier between the mental and the somatic, as the psychic representative of the stimuli originating from within the organism and reaching the mind, as a measure of the demand made upon the mind for work in consequence of its connection with the body" (862; emphasis mine). Leaving aside the Cartesian dualism of mind and body on which this definition appears to rest, it is clear that the term "drive," in de Lauretis's reading, refers to that which originates from within the organism, which is to say that which is in the organism's nature. The "organism," here, is the human as nature and before culture. The body in which this original stimulus occurs, the body that takes form through the psychic representation of stimuli, is the infantile body.

The infantile body is not exactly the same thing as the body of the child in this formulation. Instead the child comes into being as a social category through the translation from the organic to the psychic. And yet the ambivalence between the psychic and the somatic that de Lauretis identifies in Freud's definition of the Trieb must also translate into an ambivalence lodged in the body of the child as it comes into being. That is, the child is implicitly figured as the embodied site of this ambivalence. As such, it is also figured as the originary site of the subject, the body in and through which the subject comes into being, where the body itself comes into being as the body of the subject by way of the drives.

This is not directly apparent in de Lauretis's account of subjectivation, but becomes so in her discussion of the drives. "The drives," she writes of Freud's theory, "are part of the human living organism—a concept broader than that of the body (or ego-body)—but the drives, even the sexual drive, are not identical with sexuality" (de Lauretis 1998: 864–65). Sexuality, instead, "is constituted through the intervention of fantasy, that is to say, as an effect of signs" (865). This means that the drives, once again, are translated into a psychic body, the "body-ego," through fantasy, which is the process that inaugurates subjectivity. According to de Lauretis, this formulation implies that "because the ego is, in part, a body-ego . . . it provides the material ground of subject formation" (863).

But it is clear, as well, that it is the human organism, as the material ground of the body-ego, that also provides the material ground of subject formation in de Lauretis's account. This is the case even though this organism, like the drives, cannot be apprehended by the subject as such. And this human organism is repeatedly referred to—figured—in Freud, and therefore in de Lauretis as well, as "the child." The human organism in this originary sense takes the form of the child, in other words, where the child is that human organism as it comes into being simultaneously as a body and a subject.

This embodiment of an originary process of subjectivation in the infant-child becomes more distinct when de Lauretis turns to fantasy as the process by which innate drives structure subjectivity (1998: 865). The origin of this process occurs through an initial loss, in childhood. Subjectivity, which necessarily entails a process of embodiment, is "prompted by the loss of the *first* object of satisfaction" (865, emphasis mine). This loss is one among the "enigmas" that the child must negotiate. What is prompted here, more specifically, is the translation of a drive (a property of the human living organism) into a fantasy, which in turn structures subjectivity by way of embodiment (the body-ego). As de Lauretis puts it, working once again between Foucault and Freud: "Only insofar as we are bodies can we become subjects, and conversely, only insofar as we are subjects do we acquire a sexed body" (863). Since this process is figured in and through the child, positioned between the human living organism and the body-ego, this child also figures, and grounds "us" as (adult) subjects.

De Lauretis's project aims to redress the assessment of putatively non-normative sexualities as pathological. She argues, more specifically, for a theory of lesbian subjectivity that is quite specifically noninfantile (not based in pre-Oedipal fantasies). At the same time, her account of subjectivity makes use of the child as the material ground of mature, adult subjectivity with specific regard to sexuality. My reading of de Lauretis insists on the problematic use of the child in this oppositional theory of the lesbian subject, or rather of lesbian subjectivity. What is problematic, for me, is not the equation of the child with the border between nature and culture, so much as it is the claim, via psychoanalysis, that we can know the form that children's fantasies take. De Lauretis has been careful to suggest that contemporary fantasies of origin, whether pre-Oedipal, Oedipal, or the fantasy of castration to which she turns, are historically and culturally located, and that as such, these fantasies can change, and so change what it is to be a subject (1994b). But in claiming fantasies in and for children themselves, psychoanalytic theory more likely imposes an *adult* fantasy of childhood on children. Again, de Lauretis makes plain that parental fantasies are constitutive of the child's own, and furthermore that her reworking of Freudian theory, like that theory itself, is a "passionate fiction."

But is it not possible that we simply do not and *cannot* know fully what children's fantasies are or may be? Is it necessary to make such a claim to knowledge of children (even in "fictional" form) in order to secure our own conditions of transformative possibility? Within Butler's theorization of the subject at the intersection of power and subjectivity, the child literally embodies a form of dependence that is not shared by the adult it will become. This embodied dependence is left behind, in the adult subject's past, but its legacy remains by way of the infant's originary "passionate attachment." In articulating this theory of the subject, Butler identifies the conditions in relation to which the possibility of change must be articulated. Specifically, she repeatedly argues that the major obstacle to reforming the subject is not simply the workings of power on the subject, but the subject's own investment in subjection. To refuse the subjection inherent in the relationship to power would be to risk that relationship, and one's very existence as a subject.

The only option, it appears, is to submit to one's own formation in and through regulatory power, and in so doing to be subjected. When Butler turns to the political possibility of opposition to power, the matter of available options becomes central. She asks: "If existence cannot be undone without falling into some kind of death, can existence nevertheless be risked, death courted or pursued, in order to expose and open to transformation the hold of social power on the conditions of life's persistence? . . . Is there a way to affirm complicity as a basis of political agency, yet insist that political agency may do more than reiterate the conditions of subordination?" (Butler 1997: 28–30, order reversed). In response to these questions, Butler argues that agency—as a property of the subject, which is also therefore contingent on subjection—cannot be a condition of oppositional politics. Instead, a resistant project must consider the necessity of refusing subject-ness for another kind of agency, and existence, one that does not presuppose or require the subject.

De Lauretis's solution to the problem of subjection is to suggest that fantasies, or the culturally available materials that "we" subjects draw upon in the continual reforming of our subjectivity, can be changed, thereby also changing the subjectivities that are constituted through them. Indeed, her re-theorization of the lesbian subject in terms of the castration complex constitutes one such rearticulation of psychoanalysis as an enduringly powerful cultural resource through which "we" (adults) know and live our sexuality.

The problem that I identify in both de Lauretis and Butler is the psychoanalytically authorized use of the child as the ground of the adult subject. I have deliberately limited my reading, so far, to this use of the child in their accounts, in order to emphasize the way in which psychoanalytic approaches authorize this use, and constitute the child as the adult's other. From this point of view, the oppositional use of psychoanalysis to retheorize the subject constitutes an exercise of adult privilege insofar as it makes use of the child as an other, either as a space that can be occupied by the adult (as in Walkerdine), or as a pre-subjective other that is the ground of adult subjectivity (as in Butler and de Lauretis). This said, it is also possible to read across Butler's and de Lauretis's Freudian/Foucauldian accounts of the subject in a way that enables an alternative story. Such an alternative story must account for both the child and the adult, as well as other categories of difference that constitute subjects and subjectivity, while also providing the possibility of transformative change in the subject, or subjects.

Theorizing Bodies and Agencies

The pivot point for this second reading is the subject's origin as designated in Butler's and de Lauretis's theories. In both theorizations of the subject, there is a point where human "nature" acts in the process of human subject making, and where this action, or agency, takes the form of the (embodied) child. In Butler's theory, the subject comes into being where the desire for existence takes form in the body of the child, as a "passionate attachment." So too, for de Lauretis, the subject comes into being where the innate drives take form in and as the child-body.

I have suggested that two of the key questions that must be addressed by a theory of the subject that is accountable to the child are the question of agency and the question of the body. With regard to the body and its agency, it becomes imaginable, reading with and against Butler and de Lauretis, to figure the child as the embodiment of what might be called not the agency of the id, ego, or superego (as in Freud, cf. de Lauretis 1998: 862); or the agency of (socially constituted) power (as in Foucault); but the *agency of nature*. This agency exists beyond the domain of the human and human knowledge, and as such cannot belong to either the adult or the child. I take the concept of agentic nature from the field of science studies, where considerations of inanimate and nonhuman entities have raised questions about both agency and nature (see especially Haraway 1991c; Latour 1987).

Whereas scientific claims to knowledge of nature have been made on the basis of nature figured as a passive object that can, precisely, be known, Haraway has argued that nature, or "the world's active agency" (1991c: 199), plays a role in the making of worlds. To view the world as itself agentic in this way refigures the grounds on which technoscience can make ontological claims. It insists that the world must be included as an active participant both in its own making, and in our knowledge of the world. This, in turn, means that while the world, or nature, is formative of our knowledge, we do not know the world and its agency in full. Instead, the world is knowable to us only in and through our interactions with it. Our knowledge of the world—and our figurations of the real—are therefore always necessarily mediated, contingent, and contestable. The world's agency makes us, and is with us, but we cannot possess it as an object, or simply use it as a resource without consequence: "We are not in charge of the world" (Haraway 1991a: 199).

Haraway's notion of the world's agency, or the agency of nature, arises out of her critique of available modes of knowledge making. Both traditional scientific objectivity and social constructionism are inadequate to the task of knowing the world effectively, Haraway argues, because science constitutes nature as a passive object that can therefore be fully known and used, while social constructionism fails to account for any agency outside of the social. In Haraway's words, the acceptance of the world's agency requires that we "give up mastery but keep searching for fidelity, knowing all the while we will be hoodwinked" (Haraway 1991a: 199). An understanding of nature as agentic requires a stance, therefore, in which we simultaneously make claims to nature and understand these claims to be partial and contingent.

Returning, now, to the question of the subject, I want to suggest that Butler's notion of the desire for existence and de Lauretis's use of Trieb, or drive, as that which operates in the human organism, can be thought of as ways of naming the agency of nature in the making of the subject. Perhaps the most important feature of this agency with regard to the child is that it acts both within and outside of the social, and so in a sense also before or beyond any social category or entity. This means that the agency of nature comes before the child. From this point of view, the child is a thoroughly social category and form of embodiment, constituted through the interaction of the agency of nature and a continually regenerating social world. The child's subjectivity, like the adult's, emerges out of and contributes to this agentic process, but differently so.

Reading this reformulation of the subject through the agency of nature back on the child's appearance in oppositional theories of the subject undermines the child's figuration as a space or form of being that comes before the subject. Given that some of the theories I considered above "oppose" the subjection that is entailed in the making of the subject, it is hardly surprising that they return to the child as a space that is, in a sense, free, or at least more free, from this subjection. Thus, the child is figured as the embodiment of becoming rather than being (in Deleuze and Guattari), as the site where thinking becomes possible (Foucault), as the condition that throws "man" off course (Lyotard). Within feminist theorizations of the subject via psychoanalysis, the (girl) child is figured as the ground of subject making, that which comes before "us" as subjects. Consequently, the child is also the figure to which theorists return in order to understand how (adult) subjects are made. In other words, despite alternative accounts of the child as a socially constituted category that children negotiate in various ways, the child remains a theoretical resource, insofar as it is continually figured as *the site of the subject's origin,* whether the origin in question is natural or cultural. It is precisely as a figuration of a body on its way to becoming a subject that the child becomes an object of adult knowledge and realization. As such, it also becomes a resource for both realizing the subject and transforming or contesting that realization. It is through figurations of the child, through a reclaiming of the child and its originary status that oppositional theory "works." So the child-figure's value for oppositional theories is its value as an originary site for the subject.

Consequently, oppositional theories' claims to the child enact what might be called an adult desire for the child. I want to recognize this desire as one that belongs to privileged adult subjects, but also to refuse the ontological privilege in relation to children that its claim on the child enacts. How, then, to imagine the subject's making in a way that does not make this claim? Turning back to my prior discussion of the child's value in and for adult theories, I want to suggest that the desire for possibility, or transformative change evident in the work of Foucault, Deleuze and Guattari, and Lyotard, is not problematic in itself. The problem lies in the embodiment of possibility as an other through the exercise of ontological privilege. To identify with and think through one's own childhood, as Walkerdine does, is also not a problem in itself. Indeed, our history of experience is part of what makes adult subjectivities what they are. But here again, to claim knowledge of children by way of adults' memories or fantasies of childhood is once again to realize adult worlds while erasing the existence and experience of "actual" children.

Thinking back to de Lauretis's and Butler's use of psychoanalysis to reform the subject, it seems possible to rearticulate the desire for the child and its possibility, evident in post-structuralist theories, as a desire for existence itself. In both de Lauretis's and Butler's formulations, the desire for existence can belong to both children and adults'. In its form as existence rather than passionate attachment, furthermore, this desire does not constitute adults as subjects but rather as embodied subjectivities that are consequently not entirely subjected.

Following Haraway (1991c), I think of existence, or the agency of nature, as a kind of wild card, an erratic, chaotic, and always potentially surprising form of activity that animates us, and our worlds.[5] Defined in this way, the agency of nature cannot be contained in the child-figure, or any other figure for that matter. Instead, this agency is active in and through the body, where the body may be realized as "human," "child," "adult," or perhaps even some other kind of body. The possibilities are constituted through the continual, located realization of what a body is, and how it is lived.

The subject in my refiguration is not materially grounded in the child, but instead in the agency of nature that realizes bodies and embodiment. Even a newborn infant, from this point of view, is necessarily a natural-cultural body, always already formed through the semiotically and materially specific processes of conception, growth, and birthing that are constitutive of its particular making. The newborn's existence cannot be known fully by adults because that existence is the effect of an agency that is excessive to adult knowledge (though perhaps not to our experience). It is also partly the condition of adults' existence, and so too of adult knowing. Finally, to re-theorize the subject in terms that do not make use of the child as the adult's pre-subjective other means establishing an un-knowing—the impossibility of total knowledge and of a total claim on the real (in Haraway's terms, the condition of being hoodwinked)—that is the condition of knowledge itself.

The Subject of Theory

I have argued that to use the child as a pre-subjective other that we can inhabit or know as theorists constitutes an exercise of adult privilege. The child's figuration in the theories I have explored does not work to realize children themselves as entities that are distinct from adults. Instead, the child is figured as a site of possibility and potential. The value of the child for these theories is not its value as a child, but rather as the embodiment of possibility in a form that can be known and, especially, experienced. The problem with the theoretical formulations I have discussed here is not that they make a claim to this possibility, but rather that they locate it in the child, through their figurations of the child as its embodiment.

I have attempted to counter this use by refiguring the site of subjective possibility not as a child, or a figure at all, but as the agency of existence. But if an oppositional theory of the subject is to account for the differences between entities realized according to potentially different ontic groundings, then it must be able to account for entities that are not constituted on the grounds of the subject. That is, to theorize existence in terms of (that is, either with or against) the subject itself enacts the privileging of the subject over other forms of existence; it refuses the alterity of existence as it may be lived by others. As Gayatri Spivak has argued with regard to women, a transnationally located theorization of "subjects" cannot be limited to the subject, but instead accounts for different historically and culturally located processes of formation (Spivak 1990). A theory of the subject must, in other words, account for alterity, for the heterogeneity of situated processes at work in the realization of differentiated bodies.

In a discussion of psychoanalysis as one among other theoretical tools privileged in various feminist approaches, Spivak offers the concept of "regulative psycho-biographies of the heterogeneously sexed subject" to account for forms of women's existence "elsewhere," that is, in a transnational frame (9). With this category, she suggests, "you begin to see how *completely* heterogeneous the field of women elsewhere is, because there you have to focus on regulative psycho-biographies which are *very* situation/culture specific indeed" (9). This notion of plural, but always specific and located forms of women's existence identifies the local-global limits of psychoanalytic approaches, offering in their place a way of accounting for the means by which power constitutes, but does not completely determine, the differential realization of experiences. Distinct, located forms of subjective existence—of "subalterns," "adults," "women," and "girls"—become intelligible in this alternative formulation; they are real-ized.

Just as scientific knowledge of nature can never be total, but always partial, so too a theory of the subject will fail to be effective if it claims to account explicitly for the differences between entities always and everywhere. And yet, it seems necessary to be accountable to the existence of adults as well as children elsewhere and otherwise. My own attempt to do this relies on postcolonial feminist articulations of the subject in power. This subject is constituted in relation to multiple discursive matrices in a transnational frame by which subjects are variously positioned, and privileged (Spivak 1990, Mohanty 1991). The embodied subject of postcolonial feminism is constituted through plural vectors of power working in and through the body. In order to account for a subject, it is necessary to at least acknowledge both the plurality and the specificity of the particular matrix that constitutes this subject as one kind rather than another.

I am reaching for a theory of the subject that can account for both actual and possible differences between children and adults not just "here," but also "elsewhere," and so in worlds that I (we?) variously know and do not know. A notion of the subject as a body that is always constituted both through the agency of nature and through particular discursive matrices begins to provide the ontic grounding for a theory that makes a claim to knowledge about a natural-cultural world and its workings, while remaining open to contestation. The theory I am imagining suggests that subjects cannot be known in advance. Instead, knowing requires coming to apprehend the singularity of all subjects, the complexity of their histories, and the modes of their subjection as these change over time and place. What I am reaching for is an account of subjects as subjectivities that are precisely singular, and so also never entirely knowable. To "theorize" this subject is to inhabit a different mode of knowing, necessarily partial and situated, that works always in and through the fact of not knowing, of not being able to know fully. This not knowing does not entail a refusal to make claims in and to the world. Instead, it establishes the existence of plural "real" worlds, and also of ontic politics as the form of politics through which these pluralities become intelligible, and can be more effectively negotiated.

Although I have offered a preliminary theoretical approach to the subject that is by definition a general claim, my intention is to imagine the subject in terms that preclude describing persons (bodies or entities) in general. My aim, then, is to think the subject in terms that can account for the particularity of children's existence, as well as adults'. This also means accounting for the singularity of histories and changes in the life of any singular subject, which may also include an account of that subject's childhood. From this point of view, even an infant is not simply the raw natural material of the future adult subject it will become but rather an entity that is the effect of the agency of nature and the discursive matrix through which it is formed and reformed. The infant "is" a subject and has subjectivity that is particular to this interaction, such that everything from culturally specific birthing practices to particular modes of embodiment, including racialization, gendering, sexualization, and so on, are constitutive of this entity *as* an infant. What might be called the absence of language here, or rather the presence of particular modes of embodied communication that do not include language per se, does not constitute this entity as presubjective in this formulation, and as such it cannot be occupied by adult fantasies or desires. Instead, this entity's existence, and its embodiment are the ground of its subjectivity, where "subjectivity" signifies embodied experience.

NOTES

Introduction

1 See, for example, Burman 1994a, 1994b; Steedman 1986; Walkerdine 1993; Stainton Rogers and Stainton Rogers 1992. Berlant's *The Queen of America Goes to Washington* (1997) speaks indirectly to this critique in her analysis of how contemporary U.S. citizenship has come to be imagined as "infantile." Berlant's compelling arguments about citizenship are not directly concerned with the distinction between the child (or children) and infantilized adults, or the reinscription of adult power through the use of childhood. She does, however, highlight a relationship between childhood, mutability, and the use of the child in claiming "the iconicity of the current model citizen, the child or youth on whose behalf national struggles are being waged" (1997: 21), which has strengthened my own sense of the value of this approach.

2 For exceptions, see Rose 1992 and Steedman 1995. In her analysis of the story of Peter Pan, Jacqueline Rose suggests that "*Peter Pan* gives us the child—for ever. It gives us the child, but it does not speak to the child" (1992: 1).

3 There has been an extended discussion within feminist and postcolonial theory concerning the relative stability or instability of identity categories. Within feminist theory, in particular, this debate has been articulated as the problem of essentialism. For discussions of these debates, see for example Fuss 1989; Riley 1988; Spelman 1990; Spivak 1988.

4 My own conceptualization and use of the material-semiotic in relation to figuration draws heavily on the work of Donna Haraway, and can be seen as a variation of her work on this subject. For Haraway, figuration entails "universes of knowledge, practice and power" and describes the effects of "all material-semiotic practices" (1997: 11). For an extended discussion of figures and figuration in relation to the material-semiotic, see Haraway's *Modest_Witness* (1997).

5 For cultural analyses of "the child within" see Ivy 1993; Shattuc 1997. For self-help and psychotherapeutic uses of this concept, see for example Abrams 1990; Bishop and Grunte 1992; Dickinson and Page 1989; Potter 1994.

6 My consideration of the child in terms of its cultural force as a figure draws on Carolyn Steedman's, which mobilizes these terms in a somewhat different way. For Steedman, the child's cultural force works through the modality of personification, or what in other places she names interiority. That is, the personification in the child of loss as a feature of internal experience generates "the ideational and figural force with which 'the child' has been invested by and for adults" (Steedman 1995: 5).

7 Historical assessments of childhood include Ariès 1962; Boswell 1988; Crawford 1999; Cunningham 1991, 1995; Hendrick 1997; Kincaid 1992; Morss 1990; Rose 1991; Steedman 1990. Sociological investigations of childhood include Best 1990; Hoyles and Evans 1989; Jackson 1982; James, Jenks, and Prout 1998; Postman 1994; Rose 1991; Scraton 1997; Steedman 1986; Stainton Rogers and Stainton Rogers 1992; Walkerdine 1993, 1997; Woodhead, Faulkner, and Littleton 1998; Willis 1977, 1990; Zelizer 1985. See also Corsaro 1997 for an overview of the sociology of childhood. Studies addressing childhood and culture include Blanc 1994; Berlant 1997; McRobbie 2000; Stephens 1995b.

8 Teresa de Lauretis (1987a) makes this point about language in relation to gender.

9 Some of the earlier feminist works that have most influenced my own include Bulkin, Pratt, and Smith 1988; Davis 1987; de Lauretis 1987b; hooks 1984; Lorde 1982; Mohanty 1991; Moraga 1983; Spillers 1987; Spivak 1988. Science and technology studies, for my purposes, includes work in the history of science (Gallagher and Laqueur 1987; Jordanova 1989; Scheibinger 1989; Tuana 1993; see also Laqueur 1990); cultural studies and anthropology (see Ainley 1998; Cartwright 1995; Hartouni 1997; Jacobus, Keller, and Shuttleworth 1990; Terry and Calvert 1997; Terry and Urla 1995); sociology of medicine (see Berg and Mol 1998; Clarke 1998; Stanworth 1987), and anthropology (see Edwards et al. 1993; Franklin 1996; Martin 1987, 1995; Rapp 1999). Research specifically relating technology and embodiment includes Balsamo 1996; Butler 1993; Cartwright 1995; Franklin 1996; Franklin and Ragoné 1998; Haraway 1989, 1991a, 1991b, 1997; Stabile 1992; Stafford 1991; Stanworth 1987; Strathern 1992a, 1992b.

1 *Developmentalism and the Child in Nineteenth-Century Science*

1 Fabian makes numerous references to the child in his discussion of Lévi-Strauss's failure to criticize anthropology's use and abuse of time. I do not pursue these references here because I am primarily concerned with the nineteenth century, but my arguments draw on Fabian's incisive critique.

2 A number of works other than those I write about in this chapter consider the child-figure in relation to either the colonizer or the colonized. For example, Gail Ching-Liang Low reads boyhood adventure stories as narratives that underwrote a male imperial imagination (1996: 36–65). For other discussions of the child and colonial orders, see the work of Ann Laura Stoler (1995: 137–64).

3 See also Bhabha 1985 (cited in Wallace 1994); Levy 1984; Low 1996; Stoler 1995.

4 The fields of science studies I have mentioned here are diverse in their theoretical and methodological approaches. No description, including the brief reference to the textual and nontextual, can approach even the many ways that science studies has itself been defined. (For overviews of science studies, see Rouse 1992; Traweek 1993; Escobar 1994; Haraway 1994; Hess 1997.)

5 I take this way of describing science from James Clifford, who suggests that "in the West . . . collecting has long been a strategy for the deployment of a possessive self, culture, and authenticity" (1988: 218). While Clifford is describing collecting as a practice of an "art-culture system," his treatment of it, as he suggests, also moves between art and science (228). In any case, what I take from Clifford is his definition of collection as a practice, in which the ordering of collections constitutes a system of value.

6 In *The Order of Things*, Michel Foucault (1970) describes a shift in the way nature was known, from what he calls the "living being" to "life." "Life," Foucault suggests, was the object of the emerging discipline of biology, as opposed to the "living being," which was the object of natural history. The difference between the two lies in the fact that "life" was organized in discontinuous time, while the living being was organized in temporally static terms of taxonomy. In other words, "life" was the "living being" set on a current of time that effected a change in that being: "life" is historical, while the "living being" is not.

7 In arguing that the French anatomist Georges Cuvier exhibits the nineteenth century's scientific, empirical attitude toward the body, as opposed to natural history's purely descriptive one, George Stocking Jr. shows how intimately this attitude was linked to the practice of collection, and its scientific uses. According to Stocking, Cuvier tried to extend the available collection of skulls for "scientific," detailed comparison. However, "Unfortunately, skulls were not easy to procure. Cuvier suggested therefore that when the voyage witnessed or took part in a battle involving savages, they must not fail to 'visit the places where the dead are deposited.' When they were able—'in any manner whatever'—to obtain a body, they should 'carefully note all that relates to the individual from whom the cadaver came.' . . . His attitude toward the savage was that of a grave-robber rather than the philanthropist" (Stocking 1968: 30–31).

8 Only when Gregor Mendel's experiments in genetics were resurrected early in the twentieth century did Darwinian evolution become widely accepted (Bowler 1988).

9 Sander Gilman (1985) notes how images of naked black girls portrayed as servants work to attach both positive and negative sexuality to the images of white women in nineteenth-century painting. However, aside from describing two representations as "unself-conscious innocence" and "hypersexuality" respectively, he does not consider the portrayal of children per se, but sees them as representations of female sexuality more generally. Gilman also notes nineteenth-century representations of lower-class girls as prone to prostitution owing to their exposure to immorality in their own homes, including parental seduction. The fact of child prostitution was also attributed to the lower-class female child's own nature, or the "vice of women" (42–55). Gilman's work on the intersections between sexuality, race, and madness from the Middle Ages to the present has been an important influence on my own, especially his attention to the way that various categories of difference are embedded in bodies at once.

10 There is a long tradition within the United States (as well as Europe) that pits the hypersexuality of the black female slave and the justification of rape by white men, on the one hand, against the purity of the white woman and her reproductive success in maintaining the purity of the race, on the other. (For a brilliant critique of this tradition, see Spillers 1987: 65–81.) Haller also notes that "to preserve the wholesomeness of the American stock from the folly of hybridization, [the American anthropologist Daniel G.]

Brinton looked to the American woman. 'It is the woman alone of the highest race that we must look to preserve the purity of the type, and with it the claims of the race to be the highest' " (Haller 1971: 118–19). Haller adds that while this was a common notion in the antebellum south, "Science . . . helped raise the cult of white womanhood to the scientific idolatry of race" (119).

2   Flexible Child-Bodies

1   This was ordered by the U.S. Congress in 1989 and signed by President George Bush. See *Decade of the Brain: Answers through Scientific Research* (National Advisory Neurological and Communicative Disorders and Stroke Council, 1989), cited in Dumit 1997.

2   Joseph Dumit (1997) argues that PET scans are used to make authoritative claims about the person and human nature as objective entities—that is, what they are in an ontological sense—which are also variously incorporated into how people see themselves subjectively.

3   An overview of Chugani's work can be found on the PET Faculty Home Page, on the Wayne State University web pages, at http://pet.wayne.edu/faculty.html.

4   Huttenlocher uses a similar set of research findings to make his own case about developmental synaptogenesis. From this research, Huttenlocher extracts the overall "principle [that] [t]here appears to be elimination of redundant connections, and electrical activity [generated via use] in the developing system appears to be important for the execution of this developmental program" (Huttenlocher 1994: 140).

5   Begley uses the metaphor of a computer's manufacture as a counter-example, as follows: "One ideal holds that the brain wires itself as the fetus develops, in a manner analogous to the way a computer is manufactured: that is, the chips and components are assembled and connected according to a preset circuit diagram. According to this analogy, a flip of a biological switch at some point in prenatal life turns on the computer . . . [but] the biology of brain development follows very different rules." The two authors have the same view of the developing brain, but different understandings of the computer. For Shatz, the computer is prewired and so predetermined, like a genetic body. For Begley, the computer at the time of manufacture does not have a preset circuitry, but is constituted as the circuitry is connected. (So much for the fixity of computer analogies.)

3   Available Childhood

1   The term "intercountry adoption" is used in the discourse of adoption transnationally. I use the term interchangeably with "transnational adoption."

2   For writings on kinship in the context of adoption see Kirk 1989; Modell 1994, 2000; and Wegar 1997.

3   See Petchesky 1987; Taylor 1992; Hartouni 1992; Franklin 1991, 1993b; Martin 1994; Stabile 1992; Casper 1995; Cartwright 1995; and Rapp 1997.

4   The number of children adopted transnationally by U.S. citizens in 1981 from all countries was 4,868; in 1987, 10,097 children were adopted, and in 1991, 9,008. These children are evenly divided by sex. Most were adopted at less than four years of age. Statistics on transnational adoption can be found on the National Adoption Information

Clearinghouse (NAIC) website—http://www.calib.com/naic, or from the National Adoption Reports, National Committee for Adoption, 1930 Seventh Street, N.W., Washington, DC, USA, 20009–6207.

5 These statistics are posted on the U.S. government website http://www.travel.state.gov; and by the NAIC (see note above).

6 President Clinton signed the *Child Citizenship Act of 2000* (Public Law No. 106–395, 106th congress, second session) into law on 30 October 2000, to take effect on 27 February 2001. This law applies to children of U.S. citizens, when those children are born abroad, and whether they are biological or adoptive children. For a listing of recent U.S. laws passed to facilitate adoption, see the NAIC website (listed above).

7 The promise of IVF far exceeds its actual results. Bartholet's frustration with the amount of money spent on this and other reproductive technologies relative to that spent on encouraging adoption as a valid way of making a family is an important part of her argument, but not one that I consider here. For a wide-ranging discussion regarding women's experience of the failure of IVF in contrast to its representation and implementation as a valid treatment for infertility, see *Embodied Progress* (Franklin 1997).

8 Commenting on this phenomenon, Haraway focuses on the gendered aspects of the scenario, or what feminists have called "masculinist birthing." She writes, "The curious erotics of single-parent masculine, technophilic reproduction cannot be missed. SimEve is like Zeus's Athena, child only of the seminal mind—of a man and of a computer program" (Haraway 1997: 39).

9 So-called "mixed race" children have been particularly ill served by strict racial matching systems because they cannot be "matched" to a distinct racial group, according to the logic of matching. With the decrease in available healthy white infants, writes Lansberry, adoption agencies began to place these "mixed" children in white families if the children were "half-white." It is important to note, furthermore, that the debate on transracial adoption in this chapter is organized around the binary of black and white, a binary through which so many debates about race tend to revolve in U.S. public arenas. Among the other racialized groups that have emerged in the debates on transracial adoption are Native Americans. The *Indian Child Welfare Act of 1978*, established because of pressure from Native American groups out of concern for tribal survival, requires that Indian children be placed in Indian homes. (See U.S. Administration for Native Americans 1979. See also U.S. Government hearings [Senate and House of Representatives Select Committees on Indian Affairs] on the *Indian Child Welfare Act*, held subsequent to its passage in 1978 through 1988.)

It should be noted, furthermore, that the transracial adoption of Native American children is also transnational adoption, given the status of Indian tribes in relation to the U.S. government (Joanne Barker, personal communication).

10 See also *Incorporations* (Crary and Kwinter 1992).

4 Rumored Realities

1 Child-organ stealing rumors, and organ-stealing rumors more generally, raise many important issues that I do not address directly here. For an in-depth analysis of organ procurement on a global scale, see the work of Organs Watch, an interdisciplinary team

of researchers, which can be found at http://sunsite.berkeley.edu/biotech/organswatch. The medical anthropologist Nancy Scheper-Hughes is a member of this team, and of the Bellagio Task Force, which was convened in 1997 to examine ethical, social, and medical implications of organ donation and transplantation. The Bellagio Task Force Report and the writings of Scheper-Hughes can also be found at the above website. (See also Scheper-Hughes 1998a, 1998b, 2000.)

2 Comaroff also extends the double work done by the category of child abuse, specifically, to its expression of "more profound crises" lying behind the "sense of loss . . . of a moral home in the world," and even further, to "the terms of Western modernism itself, among them, the secure contrasts of male and female, gifts and commodities, public and private, white and black, West and other, local and global" (Comaroff, n.d.: 26). This description concerns U.S.-based definitions of child abuse. While Comaroff's categorization of the United States as "modern" is useful in some respects, I am attempting to work across and against the assumptions imposed by a premodern/modern/postmodern mapping of the world.

3 I discuss transformations of the child-body in transnational adoption discourses in chapter 4. (See also Castañeda 1993.)

4 Reporting on the story and related issues in the Guatemalan press that lend credence to its truth, ranging from complete certainty to considerable doubt include Medinas Salas 1994; García 1994; "Norteamericana June Weinstock sigue grave," Prensa Libre, 31 March 1994; "MP denuncia desaparición de 75 niños," Prensa Libre, 6 April 1994; "Procurador pone en duda denuncias sobre tráfico de órganos," Siglo Veintiuno, 27 March 1994; Revolorio 1994a, 1994b, 1994c, 1994d, 1994e; and Colindres Morales 1994.

   Earlier reports about child-organ trafficking appeared in the Guatemalan press, for example, "¡¡Exportan bebés para 'destace'!!," El Gráfico, 24 January 1988; "Traficantes de niños operan en Guatemala," La República, 20 November 1993. Transnational news agencies operating in Latin America also put out reports on the story (see, for example, Brown 1994).

5 For news and news magazine reports printed outside Guatemala in addition to those cited in this chapter, see Morello 1994; Gleick 1994; Frankel and Orlebar 1994; T. Johnson 1994; López 1994; Fraser 1994; Pinero 1987; Scotto 1993; Mauro 1988; Ognyov 1987; Defence for Children International (DCI) 1987. For additional listings of all mainstream media reports, including films and news magazine television shows, see Leventhal 1994.

6 This term is particular to Guatemala, and refers to the nonindigenous descendants of Spanish colonialists.

7 Also cited as signs of the military's intent to destabilize the civilian government at this time were 1) the fact that in the months prior to the Weinstock incident, then Guatemalan President Ramiro de Leon Carpio appeared to have succumbed to military pressure by replacing two high-level officials sympathetic to human rights efforts with supporters of the army's bid for immunity from all prosecution for human rights abuses; and 2) the assassination on 1 April 1994 of Guatemala's constitutional court president, who had prevented the previous "civilian" president, Jorge Serrano Elias, from installing yet another dictatorship, and was considered to be friendly to human rights efforts (Orlebar 1994; Perera 1994; White 1994).

8   "Indígena," literally "indigenous," is the term used by indigenous peoples in Guatemala to refer to themselves, partly in contrast to the pejorative "indio" or (worse) its diminutive, "inditos." I use the term here in place of the term "indigenous" to refer specifically to Guatemalan indigenous groups.

9   In light of the repeated invocations of indígenas as passive respondents to military incitement, it is important to emphasize as well the extent and range of political forms of resistance carried out by various groups and groupings of indígenas who do not share a single indígena language, much less a homogenous "culture" or political affiliation, but who have forged political alliances in response to decades of genocidal military-governmental campaigns waged against them. The most recent of these began in the 1970s. (For an account of this recent history, see especially Manz 1988; Jonas 1991)

10 Kidnapping has become a familiar experience for wealthier Guatemalans, whose family members are returned for various amounts of ransom, and sometimes in exchange for political favors or actions along with a monetary sum.

11 The author, Véronique Campion-Vincent, cites Leventhal in this work, so that the two cite one another as experts on the rumor.

12 I first encountered Leventhal's connection to the child-organ stealing rumor through a search on the Internet using the phrase "organ stealing." His USIA report on the subject included an e-mail address, through which I arranged an interview with Leventhal at USIA in Washington, D.C., which took place in November of 1994. Some of what Leventhal said in the interview recapitulated his articles on the subject. In reporting on the program officer's views and strategies, I refer to both sources.

13 Counter-stories published in 1988 bearing Leventhal's mark identify the rumor as the product of both disinformation and misinformation. For example, in the *Washington Post*'s 1988 report titled "Nailing Disinformation: The Slum-Child Tale," "USIA officials" cite the Soviet Union's "disinformation propaganda apparatus" as a key actor in the rumor's global dissemination (John M. Goshko, 1988). Disinformation is not mentioned as an important factor in more recent circulations of the rumor either in Leventhal's reports or in news reports. The rumor is defined only as misinformation.

14 UNOS is discussed in more detail below.

15 The 1997 Bellagio Task Force, convened to investigate issues related to organ transplantation, came to a similar conclusion. See Rothman et al. 1997.

16 The report also states that Paraguay has suspended transnational adoptions in the wake of publicity.

17 The history of repression and genocide in Guatemala has, of course, taken much more complex turns than I am able to account for here. However, confidence in the power of various peace accords and other agreements and in the democratic commitments of successive governments remains low among many Guatemalans.

18 Amnesty International describes street children in Guatemala as follows: "5,000 such children, aged 5 to 18 (including children from other Central American countries, as well as Guatemalans), living on the streets of Guatemala City. Many are orphaned, abandoned, or handicapped; they search for food amongst the garbage and sleep under parked cars or on sidewalks. Some of the Guatemalan street children were displaced by army counter-insurgency campaigns of the early 1980s which led to the extrajudicial execution and "disappearance" of many thousands of people in the Guatemalan coun-

tryside, and the displacement of countless others to other departments within the country or Guatemala City. Some amongst the Salvadoran and Nicaraguan street children living in Guatemala were also made homeless, and sometimes orphaned, by political violence in their own countries. Other street children have been orphaned, abandoned or made homeless for other, principally family, reasons. Most reportedly survive through stealing, begging and prostitution" (Amnesty International 1990). According to Amnesty International, furthermore, more than 70 percent of all street children are indígena. While the Amnesty reports do include one case of an eighteen-year-old girl in its list of violence perpetrated against street children, the great majority of cases refer to male children, despite the fact that at least one-third of all street children are girls. While there is some attention to the issues that might obtain given these differences in the literature, it is particularly sparse regarding girls. This is a common omission in work on street children, which is only beginning to be addressed by child advocates.

The term "street children" has a contentious history. (For a discussion of the issue, an approach to "urban children in distress" as an aspect of globalization, and a review of effective assistance programs for these children, see Blanc et al. 1994.)

19 At this writing, the Guatemala News and Information Bureau (GNIB), along with other sources such as the Network in Solidarity with the People of Guatemala (NISGUA), report continued violence, some of it in new forms, in Guatemala. See, for example, the NISGUA archives at http://www.nisgua.org/. For a more conservative view of the current climate, see reports by the Washington Office on Latin America at http://www.wola.org/.

5   The Child, in Theory

1 This book is published by Duke University Press, which is itself located in Durham, North Carolina, U.S.A.; and London, England. A significant contributor to transnational academic traffic, the University of Minnesota Press has been instrumental, beginning in the 1980s, in translating and publishing French theory for an English-speaking readership. It has published works by such well-known theorists as Paul de Man, Georges Bataille, and Michel de Certeau, and is responsible for translating Giles Deleuze and Félix Guattari's (1987) A Thousand Plateaus, along with a number of works by Jean-François Lyotard. With branches in London, England, and Minneapolis, Minnesota (U.S.A.), the press is itself a transnational enterprise.

2 The issue of the subject's normativity, or the constitution of a normative subject in and through multiple others, has been variously addressed in queer, black, postcolonial, lesbian, and feminist theory (among others). The logic of my own argument regarding the child as one among other others owes its logic to this work. I include some of this work in the following pages where possible, omitting a much greater field of reference only for the sake of clarity and brevity.

3 There are clear resonances between my discussion of the Foucault-Blanchot use of the child and Teresa de Lauretis's account of woman as space in film, which in turn works as an analogy for gender more generally. (See de Lauretis 1987a, 1987b.)

4 My criticism of psychoanalytic approaches can be located in a longer history of feminist and other critiques of psychoanalysis on a number of grounds, a history that includes

Brennan 1989; Feldstein and Roof 1989; Gallop 1982; and Flax 1990, among the others cited directly in this article.

5 Wlad Godzich's discussion of "agentic givenness" as "the very condition of experience, experientiality itself" (Godzich 1994: 282–83) has also been formative for me in thinking through the concept of agency as it relates to the child-figure and the problem of privilege. I do not cite Godzich more directly here simply to avoid overloading the page with theoretical references. I thank Carla Scott for bringing Godzich's work to my attention.

REFERENCE LIST

Abrams, Jeremiah, ed. 1990. *Reclaiming the Inner Child.* Los Angeles: Tarcher.

Abu-Lughod, Janet L. 1989. *Before European Hegemony: The World System 1230–1350.* New York: Oxford University Press.

Adamec, Christine, and William L. Pierce. 1991. *The Encyclopedia of Adoption.* New York: Facts on File.

Ahmed, Sara. 1998. *Differences That Matter: Feminist Theory and Postmodernism.* Cambridge: Cambridge University Press.

——. 1999. "Fantasies of Becoming (the Other)." *European Journal of Cultural Studies* 2, no. 1:47–63.

Ainley, Rosa, ed. 1998. *New Frontiers of Space, Bodies, and Gender.* New York and London: Routledge.

Allen, Anita. 1988. *Uneasy Access: Privacy for Women in a Free Society.* Totowa, N.J.: Rowan and Littlefield.

——. 1992. "Responses to 'Where Do Black Children Belong?' " *Reconstruction* 1, no. 4:46–48.

Alstein, Rita J., and Howard Simon. 1991. *Intercountry Adoption: A Multinational Perspective.* New York: Praeger.

——. 2000. *Adoption Across Borders: Serving the Child in Transracial and Intercountry Adoptions.* Oxford: Rowman and Littlefield Publishers, Inc.

Amnesty International. 1990. *Guatemala, Extrajudicial Executions and Human Rights Abuses Against Street Children.* New York: Amnesty International, U.S.A.

——. 1992. *Guatemala, Children in Fear.* New York: Amnesty International, U.S.A.

Anzaldúa, Gloria, and Cherríe Moraga, eds. 1983. *This Bridge Called My Back: Writings by Radical Women of Color.* 2d ed. New York: Kitchen Table Press.

Appadurai, Arjun. 1990. "Disjuncture and Difference in the Global Cultural Economy." *Public Culture* 2, no. 2 (spring): 1–24.

Appiah, Anthony. 1992. *In My Father's House: Africa in the Philosophy of Culture.* New York and Oxford: Oxford University Press.

Ariès, Philippe. 1962. *Centuries of Childhood: A Social History of Family Life.* Translated by Robert Baldick. New York: Vintage Books.

Aslin, Richard. 1998. "The Developing Brain Comes of Age." *Early Development and Parenting* 7:125–28.

Bakhtin, Mikhail. 1981. *The Dialogic Imagination*. Translated by Caryl Emerson and Michael Holquist. Austin: University of Texas Press.

Balsamo, Anne. 1996. *Technologies of the Gendered Body: Reading Cyborg Women*. Durham, N.C., and London: Duke University Press.

Bartholet, Elizabeth. 1991. "Where Do Black Children Belong? The Politics of Race Matching in Adoption." *Pennsylvania Law Review* 139:1163, 1198–99.

———. 1992a. *"International Adoption,"* No. 5. Los Angeles: Center for the Future of Children. Pamphlet.

———. 1992b. "International Adoption: Overview." In *Adoption Law and Practice*. New York: Times Mirror Books.

———. 1992c. "Where Do Black Children Belong? The Politics of Race Matching in Adoption." *Reconstruction* 1, no. 4:22–43.

———. 1993. *Family Bonds: Adoption and the Politics of Parenting*. Boston: Houghton Mifflin.

Beer, Gillian. 1983. *Darwin's Plots: Evolutionary Narrative in Darwin, George Eliot, and Nineteenth-Century Fiction*. London, Boston, Melbourne, and Henley: Routledge and Kegan Paul.

Begley, Sharon. 1996. "Your Child's Brain." *Newsweek*, 19 February, 55–62.

Bell, David, and Barbara M. Kennedy, eds. 2000. *The Cybercultures Reader*. New York and London: Routledge.

Benes, Francis M. 1994. "Development of the Corticolimbic System." In *Human Behavior and the Developing Brain*, edited by Geraldine Dawson and Kurt W. Fischer. New York and London: Guilford Press, 176–206.

Berg, Marc, and Annemarie Mol, eds. 1998. *Differences in Medicine: Unraveling Practices, Techniques, and Bodies*. Durham, N.C.: Duke University Press.

Berlant, Lauren. 1997. *The Queen of America Goes to Washington City: Essays on Sex and Citizenship*. Durham, N.C.: Duke University Press.

Best, Joel. 1990. *Threatened Children: Rhetoric and Concern about Child-Victims*. Chicago: University of Chicago Press.

Bhabha, Homi. 1985. "Signs Taken for Wonders: Questions of Ambivalence and Authority under a Tree outside Delhi, May 1817." *Critical Inquiry* 12, no. 1:144–65.

———. 1994. *The Location of Culture*. London and New York: Routledge.

Biddick, Kathleen. 1993. "Stranded Histories: Feminist Allegories of Artificial Life." In *Research in Philosophy and Technology: Technology and Feminism*, edited by Joan Rothschild and Frederick Ferre. Greenwich, Conn.: Jai Press, 165–82.

Bishop, Jacqui, and Mary Grunte. 1992. *How to Love Yourself When You Don't Know How: Healing All Your Inner Children*. Barrytown, N.Y.: Station Hill Press.

Blanc, Cristina Szanton, et al. 1994. *Urban Children in Distress: Global Predicaments and Innovative Strategies*. Switzerland, Australia, Belgium, France, Germany, Great Britain, India, Japan, Malaysia, Netherlands, Russia, Singapore: Gordon and Breach; USA/UNICEF, International Child Development Centre, Florence, Italy.

Bleier, Ruth. 1984. *Science and Gender: A Critique of Biology and Its Theories on Women*. Athene Series. New York, Oxford, Sydney, Frankfurt: Pergamon Press.

——, ed. 1986. *Feminist Approaches to Science.* Athene Series. New York, Oxford, Sydney, Frankfurt: Pergamon Press.

Booth, W. 1994. "Witch Hunt." *The Washington Post,* 17 May, C1.

Boswell, John. 1988. *The Kindness of Strangers: The Abandonment of Children in Western Europe from Late Antiquity to the Renaissance.* New York: Pantheon Books.

Bové, Paul. 1992. *Mastering Discourse: The Politics of Intellectual Culture.* Durham, N.C.: Duke University Press.

Bowler, Peter J. 1988. *The Non-Darwinian Revolution: Interpreting a Historical Myth.* Baltimore: Johns Hopkins University Press.

Boyden, Jo. 1990. "Childhood and the Policy-Makers: A Comparative Perspective on the Globalization of Childhood." In *Constructing and Reconstructing Childhood: Contemporary Issues in the Sociological Study of Childhood,* edited by Alison James and Alan Prout. London: Falmer Press, 184–216.

Brah, Avtar. 1996. *Cartographies of Diaspora: Contesting Identities.* London and New York: Routledge.

Brennan, Teresa, ed. 1989. *Between Feminism and Psychoanalysis.* London and New York: Routledge.

Brighton Women and Science Group (Lynda Birke, Wendy Faulkner, Sandy Best, Deirdre Janson-Smith, Kathy Overfield), eds. 1980. *Alice Through the Microscope: The Power of Science over Women's Lives.* London: Virago.

Brown, Jennifer C. 1994. "Guatemala: Tráfico de órganos: ámito or realidad?" Interpress Services, 11 June.

Brunvand, J. H. 1993. *The Baby Train and Other Lusty Urban Legends.* New York and London: W. W. Norton and Co.

Bulkin, Elly, Minnie Bruce Pratt, and Barbara Smith. 1988. *Yours in Struggle: Three Feminist Perspectives on Anti-Semitism and Racism.* Ithaca, N.Y.: Firebrand Books.

Burman, Erica. 1994a. "Innocents Abroad: Western Fantasies of Childhood and the Iconography of Emergencies." *Disasters* 18, no. 3:238–53.

——. 1994b. *Deconstructing Developmental Psychology.* London and New York: Routledge.

Butler, Judith. 1993. *Bodies That Matter: On the Discursive Limits of "Sex."* London and New York: Routledge.

——. 1997. *The Psychic Life of Power: Theories in Subjection.* Stanford, Calif.: Stanford University Press.

Campion-Vincent, Véronique. 1990. "The 'Baby Parts' Story: A New Latin American Legend." *Western Folklore* 49 (January): 9–25.

Canguilhem, Georges. 1978. *On the Normal and the Pathological.* Translated by Carolyn R. Fawcett. Dordrecht and Boston: D. Reidel Publishing Co.

——. 1991. *The Normal and the Pathological.* Translated by Carolyn R. Fawcett and Robert S. Cohen. New York: Zone Books.

Cartwright, Lisa. 1995. *Screening the Body: Tracing Medical Visual Culture.* Minneapolis: University of Minnesota Press.

Casper, Monica. 1995. "Fetal Cyborgs and Technomoms on the Reproductive Frontier." In *The Cyborg Handbook,* edited by Chris Hables Gray with the assistance of Heidi J. Figueroa-Sarriera and Steven Mentor. New York: Routledge.

Castañeda, Claudia. 1993. "The 'Subject' of Trans-national Adoption." Qualifying Essay, History of Consciousness Department, University of California at Santa Cruz.

Chambers, Iain, and Lidia Curti, eds. 1996. *The Post-colonial Question: Common Skies, Divided Horizons.* London and New York: Routledge.

Chow, Rey. 1993. *Writing Diaspora: Tactics of Intervention in Contemporary Cultural Studies.* Bloomington and Indianapolis: Indiana University Press.

Chugani, Harry T. 1994. "Development of Regional Brain Glucose Metabolism in Relation to Behavior and Plasticity." In *Human Behavior and the Developing Brain,* edited by Geraldine Dawson and Kurt W. Fischer. New York and London: Guilford Press, 153–75.

Clarke, Adele. 1995. "Modernity, Postmodernity, and Reproductive Processes, c. 1890–1990." In *The Cyborg Handbook,* edited by Heidi J. Figueroa-Sarriera, Chris Hables Gray, and Steven Mentor. New York: Routledge.

——. 1998. *Disciplining Reproduction: Modernity, American Life Sciences, and the Problem of Sex.* Berkeley and London: University of California Press.

Clifford, James. 1988. *The Predicament of Culture: Twentieth-Century Ethnography, Literature, and Art.* Cambridge, Mass., and London: Harvard University Press.

——. 1994. "Diasporas." *Cultural Anthropology* 9, no. 3:302–38.

Clifford, James, and Vivek Dhareshwar, eds. 1989. "Traveling Theories and Traveling Theorists." *Inscriptions* 5. Santa Cruz, Calif.: Group for the Critical Study of Colonial Discourse and the Center for Cultural Studies at the University of California, Santa Cruz.

Coleman, William. 1971. *Biology in the Nineteenth Century: Problems of Form, Function, and Transformation.* New York: Wiley Publishers.

Colindres, F., and C. Morales. 1994. "Tráfico de órganos." *Crónica,* no. 5 (8 April). Reprinted as "Guatemala: Babies for Sale." *World Press Review* 41, no. 5 (May 1994): 45.

Colors. 1993. Issue on Race. Spring/summer, no. 4.

Comaroff, Jean. N.d. "Consuming Passions: Child Abuse, Fetishism, and the 'New World Order.'" Unpublished manuscript.

Coombe, Rosemary J. 1991. "Objects of Property and Subjects of Politics: Intellectual Property Laws and Democratic Dialogue." *Texas Law Review* 69, no. 7:1853–80.

Cordier, Jean-Michel. 1988. "La Baby Connection." *L'Humanité,* 21 October, 22.

Corsaro, William A. 1997. *The Sociology of Childhood.* Thousand Oaks, Calif.: Pine Forge Press.

Crary, Jonathan, and Sanford Kwinter, eds. 1992. *Incorporations.* Cambridge, Mass.: MIT Press.

Crawford, Sally. 1999. *Childhood in Anglo-Saxon England.* Stroud, U.K.: Sutton Publishers.

Crawfurd, John. 1866. "On the Physical and Mental Characteristics of the European Asiatic Races of Man." *Transactions of the Ethnological Society of London* 5:58–81.

Cunningham, Hugh. 1991. *The Children of the Poor: Representations of the Child Since the Seventeenth Century.* Oxford: Blackwell Books.

——. 1995. *Children and Childhood in Western Society Since 1500.* London and New York: Longman Press.

Darwin, Charles. 1965. "A Biographical Sketch of an Infant." In *The Child,* edited by William Kessen. New York: John Wiley and Sons, Inc. Originally published in *Mind,* 2, no. 7 (July 1877): 285–94.

Das, Veena. 1996. *The Practice of Organ Transplants: Gift, Sale, or Theft?* Unpublished manuscript.

Davis, Angela. 1983. *Women, Race, and Class.* New York: Vintage Books.

Dawson, Geraldine, and Kurt W. Fischer, eds. 1994. *Human Behavior and the Developing Brain.* New York and London: Guilford Press.

de Certeau, Michel. 1986. *Heterologies: Discourse on the Other.* Minneapolis: University of Minnesota Press.

Defence for Children International (DCI). 1987. "Adoption for Organ Transplants: In Search of the Truth." *International Children's Rights Monitor* 4, no. 1:16.

de Lauretis, Teresa. 1987a. "The Technology of Gender." In *Technologies of Gender.* Bloomington and Indianapolis: Indiana University Press.

———. 1987b. *Technologies of Gender.* Bloomington and Indianapolis: Indiana University Press.

———. 1994a. "Habit Changes." *Differences* 6.2, no. 3:296–313.

———. 1994b. *The Practice of Love: Perverse Desire.* Bloomington: Indiana University Press.

———. 1998. "The Stubborn Drive." *Critical Inquiry* 24 (summer): 851–77.

Deleuze, Giles, and Félix Guattari. 1987. *A Thousand Plateaus: Capitalism and Schizophrenia.* Translated by Brian Massumi. Minneapolis and London: University of Minnesota Press.

Dickinson, Richard W., and Carole Gift Page. 1989. *The Child in Each of Us.* Wheaton, Illinois: Victor Books.

Dominguez, Virginia. 1994. "A Taste for 'The Other': Intellectual Complicity in Racializing Practices." *Current Anthropology* 35, no. 4:333–48.

Downey, Gary Lee, and Joseph Dumit, eds. 1997. *Cyborgs and Citadels: Anthropological Interventions in Emerging Sciences and Technologies.* Santa Fe: School of American Research.

Dumit, Joseph. 1997. "A Digital Image of the Category of the Person: PET Scanning and Objective Self-fashioning." In *Cyborgs and Citadels,* edited by Joseph Dumit and Gary Downey. Santa Fe: School of American Research Press, 83–102.

Dunn, Robert. 1864. "Civilisation and Cerebral Development: Some Observations on the Influence of Civilisation upon the Development of the Brain in the Different Races of Man." *Transactions of the Ethnological Society of London* 4:13–33.

Edwards, Jeannette, Sarah Franklin, Eric Hirsch, Frances Price, and Marilyn Strathern, eds. 1993. *Technologies of Procreation: Kinship in the Age of Assisted Conception.* Manchester: Manchester University Press.

Edwards, Paul. 1996. *The Closed World: Computers and the Politics of Discourse in Cold War America.* Cambridge, Mass.: MIT Press.

Eekelaar, John, and Peter Sarcevic, eds. 1993. *Parenthood in Modern Society.* Dordrecht, Boston, London: Martinus Nijhoff Publishers.

Escobar, Arturo. 1994. "Welcome to Cyberia: Notes on the Anthropology of Cyberculture." *Current Anthropology* 35, no. 3 (June): 211–30.

Fabian, Johannes. 1983. *Time and the Other: How Anthropology Makes Its Object.* New York: Columbia University Press.

Fausto-Sterling, Anne. 1985. *Myths of Gender: Biological Theories about Women and Men.* New York: Basic Books.

Featherstone, Mike, ed. 1990. *Global Culture: Nationalization, Globalization, and Modernity.* London, Newbury Park, Calif., and New Delhi: Sage Publications.

Featherstone, Mike, Scott Lash, and Roland Robertson, eds. 1995. *Global Modernities.* London, Newbury Park, Calif., and New Delhi: Sage Publications.

Feldstein, Richard, and Judith Roof, eds. 1989. *Feminism and Psychoanalysis*. Ithaca, N.Y.: Cornell University Press.

Fernando, Sonali. 1992. "Blackened Images." *Ten-8* 2, no. 3:140–7.

Fischer, Kurt W., and Samuel P. Rose. 1994. "Dynamic Development of Coordination of Components in Brain and Behavior: A Framework for Theory and Research." In *Human Behavior and the Developing Brain*, edited by Geraldine Dawson and Kurt W. Fischer. New York and London: Guilford Press, 3–66.

Flax, Jane. 1990. *Thinking Fragments: Psychoanalysis, Feminism, and Postmodernism in the Contemporary West*. Berkeley: University of California Press.

"Foreigners Attacked in Guatemala." 1994. Special to the *New York Times*, 5 April: A5.

Foucault, Michel. 1970. *The Order of Things*. New York: Random House, Inc. Reprint, New York: Vintage Books, 1973.

———. 1977. *Language, Countermemory, Practice: Selected Essays and Interviews*. Translated by Donald F. Bouchard and Sherry Simon. Ithaca, N.Y.: Cornell University Press.

———. 1978. *History of Sexuality. Vol. 1, An Introduction*. New York: Pantheon.

Frankel, Marc, and Edward Orlebar. 1994. "Child Stealers Go Home. Guatemala: An Attempt to Destabilize the Regime?" *Newsweek*, 18 April, 24.

Frankel, Marc. 1995. "Too Good to Be True." *Newsweek*, 26 June, 20–22.

Franklin, Sarah. 1991. "Fetal Fascinations: New Medical Constructions of Fetal Personhood." In *Off-Centre: Feminism and Cultural Studies*, edited by Celia Lury, Sarah Franklin, and Jackie Stacey. London: HarperCollins.

———. 1993a. "Life Itself." Paper presented at Center for Cultural Change, Lancaster University, Lancaster, U.K., 15 January.

———. 1993b. "Postmodern Procreation: Representing Reproductive Practice." *Procreation Stories* (special issue of *Science as Culture*) 3, no. 17:522–62.

———. 1997. *Embodied Progress: A Cultural Account of Assisted Conception*. New York and London: Routledge.

Franklin, Sarah, Celia Lury, and Jackie Stacey. 2000. *Global Nature/Global Culture*. London, Newbury Park, Calif., and New Delhi: Sage Publications.

Franklin, Sarah, and Helena Ragoné. 1998. *Reproducing Reproduction: Kinship, Power, and Technological Innovation*. Philadelphia: University of Pennsylvania Press.

Fraser, Stephen. 1994. "What's Happening to the Children?" *Guatemala Weekly*, 18–24 June.

Fujimura, Joan. 1996. *Crafting Science: A Sociology of the Quest for the Genetics of Cancer*. Cambridge, Mass.: Harvard University Press.

Fusco, Coco. 1995. *English Is Broken Here: Notes on Cultural Fusion in the Americas*. New York: New Press.

Fuss, Diana. 1989. *Essentially Speaking: Feminism, Nature, and Difference*. London and New York: Routledge.

Galison, Peter. 1997. *Image and Logic: A Material Culture of Microphysics*. Chicago: University of Chicago Press.

Gallagher, Catherine, and Thomas Laqueur, eds. 1987. *The Making of the Modern Body*. Berkeley and Los Angeles: University of California Press.

Gallop, Jane. 1982. *Feminism and Psychoanalysis: The Daughter's Seduction*. London: Macmillan.

Gamble, Clive. 1992. "Uttermost Ends of the Earth." *Antiquity* 66, no. 252:710–11.

García, Mario David. 1994. "Se ha hecho frecuente la compra de niños para mutilarlos." *Prensa Libre*, 13 March.

Gergen, Kenneth. 1993. *Refiguring Self and Psychology*. Dartmouth, N.H.: Aldershot.

Gilbert, Scott F. 1995. "Resurrecting the Body: Has Postmodernism Had Any Effect on Biology?" *Science in Context* 8, no. 4:563–77.

Gilbert, Scott F., John M. Opitz, and Rudolf A. Raff. 1996. "Resynthesizing Evolutionary and Developmental Biology." *Developmental Biology* 173, no. 2:357–72.

Gilman, Sander L. 1985. *Difference and Pathology*. Ithaca, N.Y.: Cornell University Press.

Gilroy, Paul. 1987. *There Ain't No Black in the Union Jack*. Cambridge: Polity Press.

——. 1993. *The Black Atlantic: Modernity and Double Consciousness*. London: Verso.

Ginsburg, Faye, and Anna Tsing, eds. 1990. *Uncertain Terms: Negotiating Gender in American Culture*. Boston: Beacon Press.

Gleick, E. 1994. "Rumor and Rage: Stories that Foreigners are Stealing Babies Lead to an American Woman's Brutal Beating in Guatemala." *People Magazine*, 25 April, 78–80.

Godzich, Wlad. 1994. *The Culture of Literacy*. Cambridge, Mass., and London: Harvard University Press.

Goldberg, Theo, ed. 1990. *Anatomy of Racism*. Minneapolis: University of Minnesota Press.

Goonathilake, Susantha. 1998. *Toward a Global Science: Mining Civilizational Knowledge*. Bloomington: Indiana University Press.

Goshko, John M. 1988. "Nailing Disinformation: The Slum-Child Tale." *The Washington Post*, 26 August, A19.

Gould, Stephen Jay. 1977. *Ontogeny and Phylogeny*. Cambridge, Mass., and London: Harvard University Press, Belknap Press.

Gray, Chris Hables, Heidi J. Figueroa-Sarriera, and Steven Mentor, eds. 1995. *The Cyborg Handbook*. New York and London: Routledge.

Greenfield, Susan. 1997. *The Human Brain: A Guided Tour*. London: Phoenix.

Greenough, W. T., James E. Black, and Christopher Wallace. 1993. "Experience and Brain Development." In *Brain Development and Cognition: A Reader*, edited by Mark H. Johnson. London and Cambridge, Mass.: Blackwell Publishers.

Griffiths, Ezra E. H. 1992. "Responses to 'Where Do Black Children Belong?'" *Reconstruction* 1, no. 4:48–49.

Gupta, Akhil. 1998. *Postcolonial Developments: Agriculture in the Making of Modern India*. Durham, N.C.: Duke University Press; and Oxford: Oxford University Press.

Gupta, Akhil, and James Ferguson. 1992. "Beyond 'Culture': Space, Identity, and the Politics of Difference." *Cultural Anthropology* 7, no. 1:6–23.

Gusterson, Hugh. 1996. *Nuclear Rites: A Weapons Laboratory at the End of the Cold War*. Berkeley: University of California Press.

Hague convention on the Protection of Children and Co-operation in Respect of Inter-Country Adoption. 1993. Hague Convention on Private International Law, #33. http://www.hcch.net/e/conventions/index.html.

Haines, Valerie. 1991. "Spencer, Darwin, and the Question of Reciprocal Influence." *Journal of the History of Biology* 24 (fall), no. 3:409–31.

Haley, Bruce. 1978. *The Healthy Body and Victorian Culture*. Cambridge, Mass.: Harvard University Press.

Hall, Stuart. 1988. *The Hard Road to Renewal: Thatcherism and the Crisis of the Left*. London: Verso.

———. 1991. "The Local and the Global: Globalization and Ethnicity." In *Culture, Globalization, and the World System*, edited by Anthony D. King. London: Macmillan, 41–86.

———. 1992. "What Is This 'Black' in Black Popular Culture?" In *Black Popular Culture*, edited by Gina Dent. Seattle: Bay Press, 21–37.

Haller, John M. 1971. *Outcasts from Evolution: Scientific Attitudes of Racial Inferiority, 1859–1900*. Urbana: University of Illinois Press.

Haraway, Donna. 1989. *Primate Visions: Gender, Race, and Nature in the World of Modern Science*. New York and London: Routledge.

———. 1991a. *Simians, Cyborgs, and Women: The Reinvention of Nature*. New York: Routledge.

———. 1991b. "Biopolitics of Postmodern Bodies: Constitutions of Self in Immune System Discourse." In *Simians, Cyborgs, and Women: The Reinvention of Nature*. New York: Routledge, 203–30.

———. 1991c. "Situated Knowledges: The Science Question in Feminism and the Privilege of Partial Perspective." In *Simians, Cyborgs, and Women: The Reinvention of Nature*. New York: Routledge, 183–201.

———. 1992. "The Promises of Monsters: A Regenerative Politics for Inappropriate/d Others." In *Cultural Studies*, edited by Cary Nelson, Lawrence Grossberg, and Paula Treichler. London: Routledge.

———. 1994. "A Game of Cat's Cradle: Science Studies, Feminist Theory, Cultural Studies." *Configurations: A Journal of Literature and Science* 2, no. 1 (winter): 59–71.

———. 1995. "Universal Donors in a Vampire Culture: It's All in the Family. Biological Kinship Categories in the Twentieth-Century United States." In *Uncommon Ground: Toward Reinventing Nature*, edited by William Cronin. New York: Norton, 321–66.

———. 1997. *Modest_Witness@second_Millennium.FemaleMan_Meets_Oncomouse*. New York and London: Routledge.

Harding, Sandra. 1991. *Whose Science? Whose Knowledge? Thinking From Women's Lives*. Ithaca, N.Y.: Cornell University Press.

Harding, Sandra, and Jean O'Barr, eds. 1987. *Sex and Scientific Inquiry*. Chicago and London: University of Chicago Press.

Hartouni, Valerie. 1992. "Reproductive Technologies and the Negotiation of Public Meanings: The Case of Baby M." In *Provoking Agents: Theorizing Gender and Agency*, edited by Kegan Gardiner. Urbana: University of Illinois Press.

———. 1997. *Cultural Conceptions: On Reproductive Technologies and the Making of Life*. Minneapolis and London: University of Minnesota Press.

Harvey, David. 1989. *The Condition of Postmodernity*. Cambridge, Mass., and Oxford: Basil Blackwell.

Hassell, Katayoun. 1999. "Difference, Generalisation, and Responsible Critique: Papua New Guinea's Village Courts." Ph.D. diss., University of Melbourne, Melbourne, Australia.

Hayles, N. Katherine. 1992. "The Materiality of Informatics." *Configurations* 1, no. 1:147–70.

Held, Richard. 1993. "Binocular Vision: Behavioral and Neuronal Development." In *Brain Development and Cognition: A Reader*, edited by Mark H. Johnson. London and Cambridge, Mass.: Blackwell Publishers.

Helmreich, Stefan. 1998. *Silicon Second Nature: Culturing Artificial Life in a Digital World*. Berkeley, Los Angeles, and London: University of California Press.

Hendrick, Harry. 1990. "Constructions and Reconstructions of Childhood: An Interpretive Survey, 1800 to the Present." In *Constructing and Reconstructing Childhood: Contemporary Issues in the Sociological Study of Childhood*, edited by Alison James and Alan Prout. London: Falmer Press, 35–59.

——. 1997. *Children, Childhood, and English Society, 1880–1990*. Cambridge: Cambridge University Press.

Henriques, Julian, Wendy Hollway, Cathy Urwin, and Valerie Walkerdine. 1998. Reprint. *Changing the Subject*. London and New York: Routledge. Original edition, London: Methuen and Co. Ltd., 1984.

Hess, David J. 1995. *Science and Technology in a Multicultural World*. New York: Columbia University Press.

——. 1997. "If You're Thinking of Living in STS . . . A Guide for the Perplexed." In *Cyborgs and Citadels: Anthropological Interventions in Emerging Sciences and Technologies*, edited by Gary Lee Downey and Joseph Dumit. Santa Fe: School of American Research Press, 143–64.

Holland, Patricia. 1992. *What Is A Child? Popular Images of Childhood*. London: Virago.

Hollinger, Joan Heifetz. 1988. *Adoption Law and Practice*. New York: M. Bender.

——. 1992. "Responses to 'Where Do Black Children Belong?' " *Reconstruction* 1, no. 4:49–51.

hooks, bell. 1984. *Feminist Theory from Margin to Center*. Boston: South End Press.

——. 1992. *Black Looks: Race and Representation*. Boston: South End Press.

——. 1994. *Outlaw Culture*. New York and London: Routledge.

Hoyles, Martin, and Phil Evans. 1989. *The Politics of Childhood*. London: Journeyman Press.

Huttenlocher, Peter R. 1994. "Synaptogenesis in Human Cerebral Cortex." In *Human Behavior and the Developing Brain*, edited by Geraldine Dawson and Kurt W. Fischer. New York and London: Guilford Press, 137–52.

Ivy, Marilyn. 1993. "Have You Seen Me? Recovering the Inner Child in Late Twentieth-Century America." *Social Text* 11 (winter), no. 37:227–52.

Jackson, Mark. 1995. "Images of Deviance: Visual Representations of Mental Defectives in Early Twentieth-Century Medical Texts." *British Journal for the History of Science* 28, no. 98 (September): 319–37.

Jackson, Stevi. 1982. *Childhood and Sexuality*. London: Blackwell Publishers.

Jacob, François. 1974. *The Logic of Living Systems: A History of Heredity*. Translated by Betty E. Spillman. London: Allen Lane.

Jacobus, Mary, Evelyn Fox Keller, and Sally Shuttleworth, eds. 1990. *Body/Politics: Women and the Discourses of Science*. London and New York: Routledge.

James, Alison, Chris Jenks, and Alan Prout. 1998. *Theorizing Childhood*. Cambridge: Polity Press.

James, Alison, and Alan Prout. 1990. "A New Paradigm for the Sociology of Childhood? Provenance, Promise, and Problems." In *Constructing and Reconstructing Childhood: Contemporary Issues in the Sociological Study of Childhood*, edited by Alison James and Alan Prout. London: Falmer Press.

Jameson, Fredric. 1984. "Postmodernism, Or the Cultural Logic of Late Capitalism." *New Left Review* 146:53–92.

Johnson, Mark H., ed. 1993. *Brain Development and Cognition: A Reader*. London and Cambridge, Mass.: Blackwell Publishers.

Johnson, Tim. 1994. "Rumors, Rage, Xenophobia in Guatemala: Baby-Snatching Tales Stir Scary Backlash." *Miami Herald*, 27 March, A1.

Jonas, Suzanne. 1991. *The Battle for Guatemala*. Boulder, San Francisco, and Oxford: Westview Press.

Jordanova, Ludmilla. 1989. *Sexual Visions: Images of Gender in Science and Medicine between the Eighteenth and Twentieth Centuries*. Madison: University of Wisconsin.

——, ed. 1986. *Languages of Nature*. London: Free Association Books.

Joseph, May. 1999. *Nomadic Identities: The Performance of Citizenship*. Minneapolis and London: University of Minnesota Press.

Kadetsky, Elizabeth. 1994. "Guatemala Inflamed." *The Village Voice*, 31 May, 25–29.

Kaplan, Cora. 1996. "A 'Heterogeneous Thing': Female Childhood and the Rise of Racial Thinking in Victorian Britain." In *Human, All Too Human*, edited by Diana Fuss. New York and London: Routledge.

Kessen, William. 1965. *The Child*. New York: John Wiley and Sons, Inc.

Kincaid, James R. 1992. *Child-Loving: The Erotic Child and Victorian Culture*. New York and London: Routledge.

——. 2000. *Erotic Innocence: The Culture of Child Molesting*. Durham, N.C.: Duke University Press.

Kirk, H. David. 1989. *Adoptive Kinship: A Modern Institution in Need of Reform*. Vancouver Island, British Columbia: Ben-Simon Publications.

Kolb, Bryan. 1993. "Brain Development, Plasticity, and Behavior." In *Brain Development and Cognition: A Reader*, edited by Mark H. Johnson. London and Cambridge, Mass.: Blackwell Publishers, 338–56.

Lankester, E. Ray. 1885. "Recent Progress in Biology." *The Popular Science Monthly* 28 (August).

Lansberry, Lorraine. 1992. "Responses to 'Where Do Black Children Belong?' " *Reconstruction* 1, no. 4:52–53.

Laqueur, Thomas. 1990. *Making Sex: Body and Gender from the Greeks to Freud*. Cambridge, Mass.: Harvard University Press.

Latour, Bruno. 1987. *Science in Action: How to Follow Scientists and Engineers through Society*. Cambridge, Mass.: Harvard University Press.

Lee, Nick. 1998. "Towards an Immature Sociology." *The Sociological Review*, 46, no. 3: 458–83.

Leventhal, Todd. 1994. *The Child Organ Trafficking Rumor: A Modern "Urban Legend."* Report submitted by the United States Information Agency (USIA) to the United Nations Special Rapporteur on the Sale of Children, Child Prostitution, and Child Pornography.

——. 1995a. Interview by author. United States Information Agency, Washington, D.C., November 17.

——. 1995b. "The Illegal Transportation and Sale of Human Organs: Reality or Myth?" Paper presented at European Police Executive Conference, Ghent, Belgium.

Levy, Anita. 1984. *Other Women*. Princeton, N.J.: Princeton University Press.

Light, Paul, Sue Sheldon, and Martin Woodhead, eds. 1991. *Learning to Think*. Child Development in Social Context Series, vol. 2. New York and London: Routledge, in association with The Open University.

Lock, Margaret, and Deborah R. Gordon, eds. 1988. *Biomedicine Examined*. Dordrecht: Kluwer Academic Publishers.

López, Laura. 1994. "Dangerous Rumors: Suspicions Rise Over the Origin of Antiforeigner Hostility that Provoked Assaults on American Women." *Time*, 18 April, 48.

Lorde, Audre. 1982. *Zami: A New Spelling of My Name*. Trumansburg, N.Y.: Crossing Press.

———. 1984. *Sister Outsider: Essays and Speeches by Audre Lorde.* Trumansburg, N.Y.: Crossing Press.

Low, Gail Ching-Liang. 1996. *White Skin, Black Masks: Representation and Colonialism.* London and New York: Routledge.

Lury, Celia. 2000. "United Colors of Diversity: Benetton's Advertising Campaign and the New Universalisms of Global Culture. A Feminist Analysis." In *Global Nature/Global Culture,* edited by Sarah Franklin, Celia Lury, and Jackie Stacey. London, Newbury Park, and Delhi: Sage Publications.

Lykke, Nina, and Rosi Braidotti. 1996. *Between Monsters, Goddesses, and Cyborgs: Feminist Confrontations with Science, Medicine, and Cyberspace.* London: Zed Books.

Lyotard, Jean-François. 1988. *Le Postmoderne Expliqué aux Enfants.* Paris: Éditions Galilee.

———. 1992. *The Postmodern Explained: Correspondence, 1982–1985.* Edited by Julian Pefanis and Morgan Thomas. Translated by Don Barry, Bernadette Maher, Julian Pefanis, Virginia Spate, and Morgan Thomas. Minneapolis and London: University of Minnesota Press.

Manz, Beatriz. 1988. *Refugees of a Hidden War.* Albany: State University of New York Press.

Martin, Emily. 1987. *The Woman in the Body: A Cultural Account of Reproduction.* Boston: Beacon Press.

———. 1994. *Flexible Bodies: Tracking Immunity in American Culture from the Days of Polio to the Age of AIDS.* Boston: Beacon Press.

Mauro, Luis. 1988. "Babies 'Kidnapped' for US Organ Banks." *Daily Telegraph* (London), 8 September, 3.

McGrath, Roberta. 1988. "Medical Police." *Ten-8*, 14:13–18.

McRobbie, Angela. 2000. *Feminism and Youth Culture.* 2d ed. London: Macmillan.

Medinas Salas, Juan Carlos. 1994. "Santa María Cotz (editorial)." *Prensa Libre*, 11 March.

Mills, Debra L., Sharon A. Coffey-Corina, and Helen J. Neville. 1993. "Neurobiology of Cognitive and Language Processing: Effects of Early Experience." In *Brain Development and Cognition: A Reader,* edited by Mark H. Johnson. London and Cambridge, Mass.: Blackwell Publishers.

Modell, Judith. 1994. *Kinship with Strangers: Adoption in American Culture.* Berkeley: University of California Press.

———. 2001. *A Sealed and Secret Kinship: Policies and Practices in American Adoption.* New York: Berghahn Books.

Mohanty, Chandra Talpade. 1991. "Under Western Eyes: Feminist Scholarship and Colonial Discourses." In *Third World Women and the Politics of Feminism,* edited by Ann Russo, Chandra Talpade Mohanty, and Lourdes Torres. Bloomington and Indianapolis: Indiana University Press.

Mol, Annemarie. 1999. "Ontological Politics: A Word and Some Questions." In *Actor Network Theory and After,* edited by John Law. London: Blackwell, 1999.

Moraga, Cherríe. 1983. *Loving in the War Years: Lo Que Nunca Pasó por Sus Labios.* Boston: South End Press.

Morello, Carol. 1994. "A Nation in the Grip of Panic: In Guatemala a Deathly Fear of Baby-Snatching." *Philadelphia Inquirer*, 10 April.

Morris, Meaghan. 1988. "At Henry Parkes Motel." *Cultural Studies* 2, no. 1 (January): 1–47.

Morrison, Toni, ed. 1992. *Race-ing Justice, En-gendering Power: Essays on Anita Hill, Clarence Thomas, and the Construction of Social Reality.* New York: Pantheon Books.

Morss, John R. 1990. *The Biologising of Childhood: Developmental Psychology and the Darwinian Myth.* Have, East Sussex, U.K.: L. Erlbaum.

Mudimbe, V. Y. 1988. *The Invention of Africa: Gnosis, Philosophy and the Order of Knowledge.* London: James Currey.

——. 1995. *The Idea of Africa.* Bloomington and Indianapolis: Indiana University Press; London: James Currey.

Nader, Laura, ed. 1996. *Naked Science: Anthropological Inquiry into Boundaries, Power, Knowledge.* New York and London: Routledge.

National Committee for Adoption. 1992. "National Adoption Reports." Washington, D.C.

National Organ Transplant Act. U.S. Public Law. 98th Cong., 2d sess., 19 October 1984.

Nsamenang, A. B. 1992. *Human Development in Cultural Context: A Third World Perspective.* London, Newbury Park, Calif., New Delhi: Sage Publications.

Ognyov, N. 1987. "What Lay Behind 'Boundless Humaneness.'" *Pravda,* 5 April.

Omi, Richard, and Howard Winant. 1986. *Racial Formation in the United States, from the 1960s to the 1980s.* New York: Routledge and Kegan Paul.

Oppenheimer, Jane M. 1967. "Embryology and Evolution: Nineteenth-Century Hopes and Twentieth-Century Realities." In *Essays in the History of Embryology and Biology,* edited by Jane M. Oppenheimer. Cambridge, Mass.: MIT Press.

——. 1982. "Ernst Heinrich Haeckel as an Intermediary in the Transmutation of an Idea." *Proceedings of the American Philosophical Society* 126, no. 5:347–55.

Orlebar, Edward. 1994. "Child Kidnaping Rumors Fuel Attacks on Americans." *Los Angeles Times,* 2 April, A1, A22.

Perera, Victor. 1986. *Rites: A Guatemalan Boyhood.* San Diego: Harcourt, Brace, Jovanovich.

——. 1993. *Unfinished Conquest: The Guatemalan Tragedy.* Berkeley: University of California Press.

——. 1994. "Behind the Kidnapping of Children for their Organs." *Los Angeles Times,* 1 May, M1, M6.

Pérez-Torres, Rafael. 1994. "Nomads and Migrants: Negotiating a Multicultural Postmodernism." *Cultural Critique* 26 (winter): 161–89.

Petchesky, Rosalind. 1987. "Fetal Images: The Power of Visual Culture in the Politics of Reproduction." In *Reproductive Technologies: Gender, Motherhood, and Medicine,* edited by Michelle Stanworth. Cambridge, UK: Polity Press.

Piaget, Jean. [1947] 1966. *The Psychology of Intelligence.* Totowa, N.J.: Littlefield, Adams and Co.

Pierce, William L. 1992. "Responses to 'Where Do Black Children Belong?'" *Reconstruction* 1, no. 4:53–54.

Pinero, Maïté. 1987. "A vendre coeurs d'enfants." *L'Humanité,* 14 April, 18.

——. 1992. "Enlèvements d'enfants et trafic d'organes." *Le Monde Diplomatique* (August): 16–17.

Postman, Neil. 1994. *The Disappearance of Childhood.* 2d ed. New York: Vintage Books.

Potter, Ann E. 1994. *Inside Out: Rebuilding Self and Personality through Inner Child Therapy.* Rev. ed. Muncie, Ind.: Accelerated Development, Inc.

Prakash, Gyan. 1992. "Science Gone Native in Colonial India." *Representations* 40 (fall): 153–78.

——. 1999. *Another Reason.* Princeton, N.J.: Princeton University Press.

Pukas, Anna. 1995. "The Global Lie That Cannot Be Silenced." *Sunday Times* (London), 19 July, sec. 3, p. 4.

Rabinow, Paul. 1996. *Making PCR: A Story of Biotechnology*. Chicago: University of Chicago Press.

Ramachandran, V. S. 1993. "Behavioral and Magnetoencephalographic Correlates of Plasticity in the Adult Human Brain." *Proceedings of the National Academy of Sciences* 90:10413–420.

Rapp, Rayna. 1997. "Real Time Fetus: The Role of the Sonogram in the Age of Monitored Reproduction." In *Cyborgs and Citadels: Anthropological Interventions in Emerging Sciences and Technologies*, edited by Gary Lee Downey and Joseph Dumit. Santa Fe: School of American Research Press.

———. 1999. *Testing Women, Testing the Fetus: The Social Impact of Amniocentesis in America*. New York and London: Routledge.

Reed, Evelyn. 1978. *Sexism and Science*. New York and Toronto: Pathfinder Press.

Ressler, Everett M., Neil Boothby, and Daniel J. Steinbeck. 1988. *Unaccompanied Children: Care and Protection in Wars, Natural Disasters, and Refugee Movements*. New York: Oxford University Press.

Revolorio, Julio. 1994a. "Calma en San Cristóbal Verapaz, tras el intento de linchamiento." *Siglo Veintiuno*, 31 March.

———. 1994b. "Departamento de Estado inquiere sobre la turista." *Siglo Veintiuno*, 31 March.

———. 1994c. "MP insiste en implantar el Estado de Excepción." *Siglo Veintiuno*, 31 March.

———. 1994d. "Carranza: Pretenden enfrentar a gobierno guatemalteco con EUA." *Siglo Veintiuno*, 31 March.

———. 1994e. "Obispo Flores: Imperan espantosa descomposición social y anarquía." *Siglo Veintiuno*, 31 March.

Riley, Denise. 1988. *Am I That Name?: Feminism and the Category of 'Women' in History*. London: Macmillan.

Rogoff, Barbara, Mary Guavain, and Shari Ellis. 1991. "Development Viewed in Its Cultural Context." In *Learning to Think*, edited by Paul Light, Sue Sheldon, and Martin Woodhead. Child Development in Social Context Series, vol. 2. New York and London: Routledge, in association with The Open University.

Rony, Fatimah. 1992. "Those Who Squat and Those Who Sit: The Iconography of Race in the 1895 Films of Regnault, Felix, Louis." *Camera Obscura* 28 (January): 263–89.

Rose, Jacqueline. 1992. *The Case of Peter Pan, or The Impossibility of Children's Fiction*. Rev. ed. London: Macmillan.

Rose, Lionel. 1991. *The Erosion of Childhood: Child Oppression in Britain, 1860–1918*. London and New York: Routledge.

Rosin, I. 1996. *Traces of Guilt*. Documentary film. London and Boston: BBC/A&E Productions.

Ross, Andrew. 1991. *Strange Weather: Culture, Science and Technology in the Age of Limits*. London: Verso.

Rothman, D. J., E. Rose, T. Awaya, B. Cohen, A. Daar, S. L. Dzemeshkevich, C. J. Lee, R. Munro, H. Reyes, S. M. Rothman, K. F. Schoen, N. Scheper-Hughes, Z. Shapira, and H. Smit. 1997. "The Bellagio Task Force Report on Transplantation, Bodily Integrity, and the International Traffic in Organs." *Transplantation Proceedings* 29, no. 6:2739–45.

Rouse, Joseph. 1992. "What Are Cultural Studies of Scientific Knowledges?" *Configurations* 1, no. 1:57–94.

Rudwick, Martin. 1992. *Scenes From Deep Time*. Chicago and London: University of Chicago Press.

Said, Edward W. 1978. *Orientalism*. London: Routledge and Kegan Paul.

———. 1993. *Culture and Imperialism*. London: Chatto and Windus.

Scheibinger, Londa. 1993. *Nature's Body: Gender in the Making of Modern Science*. Boston: Beacon Press.

Schemo, Diana Jean. 1996. "Courts Condone Illegal Baby Trade." *The Manchester Guardian*, 22 March, 14.

Scheper-Hughes, Nancy. 1990. "Theft of Life." *Society* 27, no. 6 (September/October): 57–62.

———. 1992. *Death Without Weeping: The Violence of Everyday Life in Brazil*. Berkeley, Los Angeles, Oxford: University of California Press.

———. 1998a. "Bodies of Apartheid: Witchcraft, Rumor, and Racism Confound South Africa's Organ Transplant Program." *Worldview* 11, no. 4 (October): 47–57.

———. 1998b. "Truth and Rumor on the Organ Trail." *Natural History Magazine* (October): 48–57.

———. 2000. "The Global Traffic in Organs." *Current Anthropology* 41, no. 2:191–224.

Scotto, Marcel. 1993. "Un rapport de Léon Schwartzenberg sur les transplantations: Le Parlement européen condamne la comerce des organes." *Le Monde*, 16 September, A12.

Scraton, Philip, ed. 1997. *Childhood in Crisis?* London: UCL Press.

Scruton, Roger. 1992. "In Inverted Commas, The Faint Sarcastic Smile on the Face of the Postmodernist." *Times Literary Supplement*, 18 December, 3–4.

Segalowitz, Sidney J. 1994. "Developmental Psychology and Brain Development: A Historical Perspective." In *Human Behavior and the Developing Brain*, edited by Geraldine Dawson and Kurt W. Fischer. New York and London: Guilford Press.

Segalowitz, Sidney J., and Linda Rose-Krasnor. 1992. "The Construct of Brain Maturation in Theories of Child Development." *Brain and Cognition* 20, no. 1 (September): 1–7.

Shapiro, Michael. 1994. "Moral Geographies and the Ethics of Post-Sovereignty." *Public Culture* 6, no. 3:479–502.

Shattuc, Jane M. 1997. *The Talking Cure: TV Talk Shows and Women*. New York and London: Routledge.

Shatz, Carla. 1992. "The Developing Brain." *Scientific American* 267, no. 3:61–67.

Simms, Joseph. 1887. "Human Brain-Weights." *The Popular Science Monthly* 31 (July): 355–59.

Simon, Rita J. 1992. "Responses to 'Where Do Black Children Belong?'" *Reconstruction* 1, no. 4: 54–55.

Simon, Rita J., and Howard Altstein. 1977. *Transracial Adoption*. New York: Wiley.

———. 1987. *Transracial Adoptees and their Families: A Study of Identity and Commitment*. New York: Praeger.

Simon, Rita J., Howard Altstein, and Marygold S. Melli. 1994. *Case for Transracial Adoption*. Washington, D.C.: American University Press.

Sofia, Zöe. 1984. "Exterminating Fetuses: Abortion, Semiotics, and the Sexo-Semiotics of Extraterrestrialism." *Diacritics* 14, no. 2:47–59.

Spelman, Elizabeth. 1990. *Inessential Woman: Problems of Exclusion in Feminist Thought*. London: Women's Press.

Spencer, Herbert. 1876. "The Comparative Psychology of Man." *The Popular Science Monthly* 8 (January): 257–69.

———. 1889. *Illustrations of Universal Progress*. New York: D. Appleton and Co.

———. [1860] 1963. *Education: Moral, Intellectual, and Physical*. New York: D. Appleton and Co.

Spillers, Hortense. 1987. "Mama's Baby, Papa's Maybe: An American Grammar Book." *Diacritics* 17, no. 2:65–81.

Spivak, Gayatri. 1988. "Can the Subaltern Speak?" In *Marxist Interpretations of Literature and Culture: Limits, Frontiers, Boundaries*, edited by Larry Grossberg and Cary Nelson. Urbana: University of Illinois Press.

———. 1990. "Criticism, Feminism, and the Institution." In *The Post-Colonial Critic*, edited by Sarah Harasym. New York and London: Routledge.

———. 1999. *A Critique of Postcolonial Reason: Toward a History of the Vanishing Present*. Cambridge, Mass.: Harvard University Press.

Stabile, Carol. 1992. "Shooting the Mother: Fetal Photography and the Politics of Disappearance." *Camera Obscura* 28 (January): 179–205.

Stafford, Barbara Maria. 1991. *Body Criticism: Imaging the Unseen in Enlightenment Art and Medicine*. Cambridge, Mass.: MIT Press.

Stainton Rogers, Rex, and Wendy Stainton Rogers. 1992. *Stories of Childhood, Shifting Agendas of Child Concern*. New York, London, Toronto, Sydney, Tokyo, and Singapore: Harvester Wheatshaft.

Stanworth, Michelle, ed. 1987. *Reproductive Technologies: Gender, Motherhood, and Medicine*. London: Polity Press.

Steedman, Carolyn. 1982. *The Tidy House: Little Girls Writing*. London: Virago Press.

———. 1986. *Landscape for a Good Woman*. London: Virago.

———. 1990. *Childhood, Culture, and Class in Britain: Margaret McMillan, 1860–1931*. London: Virago.

———. 1992. "Bodies, Figures, and Physiology." In *In the Name of the Child: Health and Welfare 1880–1940*, edited by Roger Cooter. London: Routledge Press.

———. 1995. *Strange Dislocations: Childhood and the Idea of Human Interiority, 1780–1930*. London: Virago Press.

Stepan, Nancy Lays. 1982. *The Idea of Race in Science: Great Britain 1800–1960*. London: Macmillan.

Stephens, Sharon. 1995a. "Children and the Politics of Culture in 'Late Capitalism.'" In *Children and the Politics of Culture*, edited by Sharon Stephens. Princeton, N.J.: Princeton University Press.

———, ed. 1995b. *Children and the Politics of Culture*. Princeton, N.J.: Princeton University Press.

Stocking, George W. 1968. *Race, Culture, and Evolution: Essays in the History of Anthropology*. London: Free Press.

Stoler, Ann. 1995. *Race and the Education of Desire*. Durham, N.C., and London: Duke University Press.

Strathern, Marilyn. 1992a. *Reproducing the Future*. New York: Routledge.

———. 1992b. *After Nature: English Kinship in the Late-Twentieth Century*. Cambridge: Cambridge University Press.

Suleiman, Susan Rubin. 1991. "Feminism and Postmodernism: A Question of Politics." In *The Post-Modern Reader*, edited by Charles Jencks. New York: St. Martin's Press.

Tanner, J. M. 1981. *A History of the Study of Human Growth*. Cambridge: Cambridge University Press.

Taussig, Michael. 1992. *The Nervous System*. New York and London: Routledge.

Taylor, Janelle S. 1992. "The Public Fetus and the Family Car: From Abortion Politics to a Volvo Advertisement." *Public Culture* 4, no. 2:67–80.

Temple, Christine. 1997. *Developmental Cognitive Neuropsychology*. East Sussex, U.K.: Psychology Press.

Terry, Jennifer, and Melodie Calvert, eds. 1997. *Processed Lives: Gender and Technology in Everyday Life*. London and New York: Routledge.

Terry, Jennifer, and Jacqueline Urla, eds. 1995. *Deviant Bodies*. Bloomington and Indianapolis: Indiana University Press.

Thatcher, Robert W. 1994. "Cyclical Cortical Reorganization: Origins of Human Cognitive Development." In *Human Behavior and the Developing Brain*, edited by Geraldine Dawson and Kurt W. Fischer. New York and London: Guilford Press.

Thomas, David G., and C. Donel Crow. 1994. "Development of Evoked Electrical Brain Activity in Infancy." In *Human Behavior and the Developing Brain*, edited by Geraldine Dawson and Kurt W. Fischer. New York and London: Guilford Press.

Thompson, Larry. 1994. *Correcting the Code: Inventing the Genetic Cure for the Human Body*. New York: Simon and Schuster.

Thorne, Barrie. 1987. "Re-Visioning Women and Social Change: Where Are the Children?" *Gender and Society* 1, no. 1 (March): 85–109.

Time. 1993. "The New Face of America." Special issue (fall).

Tomlinson, John. 1999. *Globalisation and Culture*. Cambridge: Polity Press.

Traweek, Sharon. 1988. *Beamtimes and Lifetimes: The World of High-Energy Physicists*. Cambridge, Mass., and London: Harvard University Press.

———. 1993. "An Introduction to Cultural and Social Studies of Sciences and Technologies." *Culture, Medicine, and Psychiatry* 17, no. 1 (March): 3–25.

Trinh, T. Minh-ha. 1989. *Woman, Native, Other*. Bloomington and Indianapolis: Indiana University Press.

Tuana, Nancy. 1993. *The Less Noble Sex: Scientific, Religious and Philosophical Conceptions of Woman's Nature*. Bloomington and Indianapolis: Indiana University Press.

Turner, Patricia. 1992. "Ambivalent Patrons: The Role of Rumor and Contemporary Legends in African-American Decisions." *Journal of American Folklore* 105, no. 418:424–41.

United Nations Economic and Social Council, Commission of Human Rights. 1993. *Sale of Children*, no. E/Cn.4/1993/67. Report submitted by Vitit Muntabhorn, Special Rapporteur appointed in accordance with Commission on Human Rights resolution 1992/76.

———. 1994a. *Sale of Children*, no. E/Cn.4/1994/84. Report submitted by Vitit Muntabhorn, Special Rapporteur appointed in accordance with Commission on Human Rights resolution 1992/76.

———. 1994b. *Sale of Children, Child Prostitution, and Pornography*, no. E/Cn.4/1994/84/Add. 1. Visit by Special Rapporteur to Nepal.

United Network for Organ Sharing (UNOS). 1994. *Questions and Answers about U.S. Organ Allocation*. UNOS, P.O. Box 13770, 1100 Boulders Parkway, Suite 500, Richmond, Virginia, U.S.A. 23225-8770. Pamphlet. bondww@comm1.unos.org.

U.S. Administration for Native Americans. 1979. "The Indian Child Welfare Act of 1978: Questions and Answers." Washington, D.C.: Department of Health, Education, and Welfare, Office of Human Development Services.

van der Molen, Maurits W., and Peter C. M. Molenaar. 1994. "Cognitive Psychophysiology: A Window to Cognitive Development and Brain Maturation." In *Human Behavior and the*

Developing Brain, edited by Geraldine Dawson and Kurt W. Fischer. New York and London: Guilford Press.

Verran, Helen. 1998. "Re-imagining Land Ownership in Australia." *Postcolonial Studies* 1, no. 2:237–54.

Waldby, Catherine. 1996. *AIDS and the Body Politic: Biomedicine and Sexual Difference*. New York and London: Routledge.

Walkerdine, Valerie. 1984. "Developmental Psychology and Child-Centred Pedagogy: The Insertion of Piaget into Early Education." In *Changing the Subject*, edited by Julian Henriques, Wendy Hollway, Cathy Urwin, and Valerie Walkerdine. London: Methuen and Co. Ltd. Reissued in 1998 by Routledge, London and New York.

—. 1993. "Beyond Developmentalism." *Theory and Psychology* 3, no. 4:451–69.

—. 1997. *Daddy's Girl: Young Girls and Popular Culture*. London: Macmillan.

Wallace, Jo-Ann. 1994. "De-scribing *The Water Babies*: 'The Child' in Post-Colonial Theory." In *De-Scribing Empire*, edited by Chris Tiffin and Alan Lawson. London and New York: Routledge.

—. 1995. "Technologies of 'the Child': Towards a Theory of the Child Subject." *Textual Practice* 9 (summer): 285–302.

Wallerstein, Immanuel. 1991. *Geopolitics and Geoculture: Essays on the Changing World-System*. Cambridge: Cambridge University Press.

Watson-Verran, Helen, and David Turnbull. 1995. "Science and Other Indigenous Knowledge-Systems." In *Handbook of Science and Technology Studies*, edited by Gerald Markle, Sheila Jasanoff, James Petersen, and Trevor Pinch. London, Newbury Park, Calif., and New Delhi: Sage Publications.

Wegar, Katarina. 1997. *Adoption, Identity, and Kinship: The Debate Over Sealed Birth Records*. New Haven: Yale University Press.

West, Cornel. 1989. "Black Culture and Postmodernism." In *Remaking History*, edited by Barbara Kruger and Phil Mariani. Seattle: Bay Press.

White, Isobel. 1994. "Who Is Stealing Guatemala's Children? Behind the Attacks on U.S. Tourists." *Report on Guatemala* 15, no. 2 (spring): 2–5.

Williams, Patricia. 1991. *The Alchemy of Race and Rights*. Cambridge, Mass.: Harvard University Press.

Willis, Paul. 1977. *Learning to Labour: How Working Class Kids Get Working Class Jobs*. Aldershot, UK: Saxon House.

—. 1990. *Common Culture: Symbolic Work at Play in the Everyday Cultures of the Young*. Buckingham, UK: Open University Press.

Woodhead, Martin, Dorothy Faulkner, and Karen Littleton, eds. 1998. *Cultural Worlds of Early Childhood*. London and New York: Routledge.

Wright, Elizabeth, ed. 1992. *Feminism and Psychoanalysis: A Critical Dictionary*. Oxford: Blackwell.

Young, Robert. 1985. *Darwin's Metaphor: Nature's Place in Victorian Culture*. Cambridge: Cambridge University Press.

Young, Robert M. 1973. "The Role of Psychology in the Nineteenth-Century Evolutionary Debate." In *Historical Conceptions of Psychology*, edited by Julian James, Mary Henle, and John J. Sullivan. New York: Springer.

Zelizer, Viviane. 1985. *Pricing the Priceless Child: The Changing Social Value of Children*. New York: Basic Books.

INDEX

Claudia Castañeda is Lecturer at the Institute for Women's
Studies and the Centre for Science Studies, Lancaster
University, United Kingdom.

Library of Congress Cataloging-in-Publication Data
Castaneda, Claudia.
Figurations : child, bodies, worlds / by Claudia Castaneda.
p. cm. — (Next wave)
Includes bibliographical references and index.
ISBN 0-8223-2958-1 (cloth : alk. paper)
ISBN 0-8223-2969-7 (pbk. : alk. paper)
1. Children. 2. Feminism. 3. Science Studies.
I. Title. II. Series.
HQ781 .C37 2002   305.23—dc21   2002006951